CONTROL THEORY
IN THE PRACTICE OF
REALITY THERAPY

CONTROL THEORY
IN THE PRACTICE OF
REALITY THERAPY

Case Studies

Edited by
NAOMI GLASSER
Commentary by
WILLIAM GLASSER, M.D.

PERENNIAL LIBRARY

Harper & Row, Publishers, New York
Grand Rapids, Philadelphia, St. Louis, San Francisco
London, Singapore, Sydney, Tokyo, Toronto

CONTROL THEORY IN THE PRACTICE OF REALITY THERAPY. Copyright © 1989 by Naomi Glasser. All rights reserved. Printed in the United States of America. No part of this book may be used or reproduced in any manner whatsoever without written permission except in the case of brief quotations embodied in critical articles and reviews. For information address Harper & Row, Publishers, Inc., 10 East 53rd Street, New York, N.Y. 10022.

Designed by Alma Orenstein

Library of Congress Cataloging-in-Publication Data

Control theory in the practice of reality therapy:
  edited by Naomi Glasser: commentary by William Glasser.—1st ed.
  p.   cm.
  Includes index.
  ISBN 0-06-055174-7
  ISBN 0-06-096400-6 (pbk.)
  1. Reality therapy—Case studies. 2. Control theory—Case
studies. I. Glasser, Naomi. II. Glasser, William, 1925- .
  [DNLM: 1. Glasser, William, 1925- . 2. Psychotherapy—methods—
case studies. 3. Reality Therapy—case studies. WM 420 C7635]
RC489.R37C66   1989
616.89'14—dc19
DNLM/DLC   89-45092

89 90 91 92 93 HC/FG 10 9 8 7 6 5 4 3 2 1
    94 95 96 HC/FG 10 9 8   (pbk.)

For Bess Rosenfeld

Sometimes we cry, but mostly we laugh.
For over sixty years my life has been better
because you are my sister and my friend.

Contents

9 **Finding Her Own Way**   163

*Breaking Away from the Family Mold and Developing a
Strong, Comfortable Identity*

SHELLEY ANNE BRIERLEY

10 **Becoming a Certain Man**   188

*An Immature Young Man Sets Realistic Goals and
Learns to Value Himself*

SUZY HALLOCK

11 **So Good at Acting Bad**   205

*A Teenage Girl Who Just Wants to Make Trouble at
School Changes Her Image*

BARBARA HAMMEL

12 **Father and Son Learn Together**   224

*A Father Gives Up Depressing and Criticizing as a Son
Struggles to Develop Responsible Behaviors*

GEORGELLEN HOFHINE

13 **Pictures in Conflict**   239

*A Family Deals with the Unrealistic Wants of Elderly
Aunts*

ROBERT E. WUBBOLDING

Acknowledgments

The authors of the case studies in this book, with great skill and patience, did remarkable therapy with difficult cases. Having watched their clients start to take better control of their lives, they volunteered to share their experiences in writing so that others could use the concepts of control theory while practicing reality therapy. No one had done this before, and it was a difficult task that took many months. I thank them all for their hard work and for their acceptance of me as editor.

And we all thank Dr. William Glasser. Without his creativity and teaching, none of this could have been written.

Introduction

In the early 1960s Dr. William Glasser, dissatisfied with what he had been taught, especially the idea that people with psychological problems are not responsible for their behavior, created reality therapy. Dr. Glasser's ideas and, in 1965, his book *Reality Therapy,* gained widespread acceptance immediately, and this interest has continued to grow not only in the United States but throughout the world.

By the 1970s, counselors were using reality therapy effectively in a great diversity of settings. To explain exactly how people were helped by this method of counseling, we published a book of case studies, *What Are You Doing?*

In the 1980s, Dr. Glasser added control theory to his teaching and writing, bringing a new dimension to reality therapy. Control theory is an explanation of how and why we behave, and when introduced by a skillful therapist into the counseling interaction, it makes an already effective therapy even more powerful. It is useful for the therapist and usable for the client. As reality therapists began to use these new ideas and became enthusiastic about them, it became obvious to me that it was necessary to publish a new set of cases to show the use of control theory in the practice of reality therapy.

Each of the cases in this book is written by a counselor certified in reality therapy by the Institute for Reality Therapy;

many are on the teaching staff, which functions worldwide.[1] As you will see, the cases they describe were all difficult to counsel. Each presents a different problem and a different concept to teach; in fact, this was the basis for their selection. The therapists were not chosen because they had any special training or because they were more gifted than the thousands of others who have studied with Dr. Glasser and his faculty. Any capable counselor trained by the Institute for Reality Therapy would do therapy much as described in these cases.

Within the framework of their own personalities, using ingenuity and creativity, these counselors all incorporate the basic control theory concepts explained by Dr. Glasser in Chapter 1. Clients are able to learn that, good or bad, they are in control of their own lives, and if they want to make the effort, they can learn to be in much more effective control than they were before counseling.

Each case is meant to stand alone as an example of excellent reality therapy counseling, and a special effort has been made to show how each counselor has blended control theory into the therapeutic process. In addition, commentary by Dr. Glasser follows each case. After reading these cases and the commentary, any counselor should be able to understand enough about these ideas to begin to use them in therapy. It will also be clear to those not in counseling who wish to learn to choose more satisfying and responsible behaviors how they can use these control theory concepts in their own lives.

Naomi Glasser

As you read this book, I would like you to keep the following in mind. The core of reality therapy is the idea that, regardless of what has happened or what we are doing, we choose all that we do with our lives and are responsible for those choices. But reality therapy emphasizes that accepting responsibility for irresponsible behavior does not mean that there need be any risk of being punished or rejected by family or friends as long

---

[1]For a list of the chapter authors, including their locations and affiliations with the Institute for Reality Therapy, see pages 305–308.

there is an attempt to move toward more responsibility. In fact, our experience is that when clients understand this, instead of trying to avoid responsibility, they become more willing to make the effort to learn more responsible choices. While learning to do this, they appreciate the warm, supportive environment that characterizes our approach.

William Glasser, M.D.

Although all of the case studies in this book are real, the names and identifying details of the individuals mentioned have been changed in order to protect their privacy.

1

Control Theory

WILLIAM GLASSER, M.D.

ONTROL THEORY explains how all living organisms function. This book deals mostly with human psychology, but since control theory also provides a good explanation of physiology, the book includes several cases that explain how psychology and physiology blend in what is popularly called psychosomatic illness. Control theory is also practical. Reality therapists not only use this theory to identify what is wrong with their clients and in what direction to go to help them, but, as is shown over and over in this book, they also make an active effort to teach control theory to any client they believe may be receptive to these ideas. These clients are then able to use control theory to make more responsible choices in their lives, which both shortens therapy and extends its effectiveness.

Almost all clients come to counseling because they are not able to cope successfully with what is going on in their lives. In most cases, they believe that they are suffering because they are the victims of people or events over which they have no control. Control theory does not deny that many of us are treated badly and that we may, indeed, be victims of events that seem to us to be beyond our control. But what control theory teaches, and what is illustrated in this book, is that the only behavior we can control is our own. This means that the only way that we can control events around us is through what we can do. As you read these cases, you will see the therapists, using the patience and compassion that is the core of good reality therapy, teach clients, many of whom have suffered greatly, to begin to take effective control of their own lives despite what has happened to them.

Clients are able to do this because, through counseling, they have gained the strength to see that what they are doing to cope with the painful reality of their lives is not working, and to see that they can do better. Regardless of what is happening to them, most people are able to learn that they are rarely forced to do anything, good or bad. We choose all the important things we do with our lives which, as I will shortly explain, includes how we feel and, to a great extent, even our health. Almost all the people who come or are sent for counseling are not making the best possible choices regardless of the situations they are in.

This is what makes control theory hopeful. If people choose what they are doing and feeling, with the help of a good counselor they can learn to make better choices. The message of control theory is that once we understand its basic ideas, specifically the needs, the pictures in heads, and the concept of total behavior, no matter how bad things seem, we can choose to do better with our lives—providing we are willing to make the effort to do so.

Most people, however, do not believe they have a choice. They follow an age-old, common-sense idea of how we behave which is called the stimulus-response theory. For example, most people believe that they do not choose their behaviors, especially in the sense that they do not choose how they feel or how their body functions. They believe that what they feel and what goes on in their bodies are natural responses or reactions to things outside of them, the stimuli, over which they have little or no control. Most people believe, for example, that when they are disappointed, they have no choice but to feel bad, to get an upset stomach, or to be unable to sleep or work.

Control theory explains that the disappointment, for example, over an unhappy marriage, does not make us feel bad or get sick or, for that matter, do or think anything. All the disappointment is is information. In fact, all we ever get from the outside world is information. For example, if we find out that our child failed an important examination and will not graduate, it is up to us to choose how to act on that information. What we decide to do is our choice, and the goal of reality therapy is to help clients figure out and put into practice better choices than those they have been making.

Nowhere is this more clearly seen than in the case of Sarah, in the chapter "I'm Not Going to Let Them Affect Me." When this seventeen-year-old high school girl, who had been physically and sexually abused by her parents and her brothers since she was a small child, started counseling, she did not have any sense that she could do anything except "react" with suffering to the terrible situation (the stimuli), in which she thought she had to live. Her counselor was able to teach her that she had a whole series of choices that could lead her to a better life. It was also made clear that if she did nothing to change her life, this also was her choice. To make this choice clear, the counselor asked Sarah over and over, "Is this what is best for you?"

Reality therapy, augmented by the insights of control theory, teaches that we need not be victims of our past or our present unless we choose to be so. Whether we do well or badly, we have much more control over our lives than most of us believe, and the more effectively we exercise this control, the more fulfilled our lives will be.

As all the cases in this book bring out, control theory is based on the concept that we are all driven by basic needs and that all of our behavior is our best attempt to deal with the world so that we can best satisfy these needs. These needs—survival, love, power, fun, and freedom—are built into our genetic structure and are just as much a part of our genetic heritage as our arms and legs. This means that when we are born, driven by these genetically based needs, we must learn to live in the best way we can to satisfy them. We are not born a blank slate that must learn to adapt to the world: we are born driven by these needs, and they will drive us relentlessly to try to control the world around us all of our lives. To control, however, does not mean to dominate. It means control as when we steer (control, not dominate) our car.

At birth, we know neither what these needs are nor how to satisfy them. What we do know at birth, and will know for the rest of our lives, is how we feel. From this knowledge, most of us gain some idea of what our needs are. For example, a little baby does not know anything about food or eating or survival. But he does know that he hurts a lot, and when he is fed, he usually feels better. As this occurs over and over, the baby begins to learn about food and much later about eating for survival. But long before we know what our needs are, our desire to feel better leads all of us constantly to attempt to satisfy them. And even if we never find out what our needs are, we will still try to satisfy them through our efforts to feel good.

Starting at birth, we begin to behave in the world, and all we will do for the rest of our lives is behave. And while we are always clearly aware of how we feel when we behave, we are usually unaware that our feelings are not separate from the rest of our behavior. In fact, as I will explain shortly when I introduce the concept of total behavior, they are always an integral part of our behavior itself.

For example, JJ, in the chapter "Why Bother Going On?" came for counseling after one son was killed playing football and another was found to be using drugs. Her complaint that she was very depressed was an understatement. What she did not know, which she learned in counseling as the counselor introduced her to control theory, was that she was choosing a behavior that included the misery she complained about. She thought that she was going to be miserable forever because of what had happened. It is unlikely that she or anyone else in her situation could have chosen anything but misery at the time she was seen, but with skillful help, she gradually learned that there were other behaviors she could choose that would allow her to feel much better.

Keep in mind that control theory does not contend that

anyone chooses pain or misery because he or she wants to feel bad. JJ chose it because she had discovered, as almost all of us do, that she could deal with the tragic events of her life better through behaviors that included pain than with any other behavior. Pain, terrible as it is, gave her more control over her life, but until she learned some control theory, she had no idea that this was going on. She thought she had to continue this choice indefinitely.

I have now explained enough so that it makes sense to define the term _control theory_, because this definition will further clarify what I am trying to convey. Control theory contends that _our behavior is always our best attempt to control the world and ourselves as part of that world so that we can best satisfy our needs._

To cope with the events of her life, JJ chose the misery and pain in a desperate effort to see if the world had some compassion for how much she had suffered. She also chose the misery because it immobilized her and, in doing so, restrained the anger that she could barely keep under control. If, for example, she had not controlled the anger to the extent she did, she might have committed suicide.

The tragic events of her life were tremendously frustrating to her needs for love and power, and when a need is frustrated, we cannot be passive: we must do something. What we all learn to do, usually as very small children, is to choose some sort of misery to deal with frustration. We learn that when we are miserable, people reach out and try to help and also that we can better control the anger that could lead to destructive acts that make things even worse. As I explain this, I am in no way minimizing JJ's suffering, but only setting the stage for an understanding of how therapy helped her.

This brief explanation of control theory will become much more clear as you read the cases. Every client, at the time that therapy begins, is choosing some sort of painful, self-destructive behavior in a misguided or misunderstood attempt to regain control over a poorly controlled, need-frustrated life. What the counselor does in almost every case is teach the client that he or she has needs that must be satisfied and that there are better ways to satisfy them than what he or she is choosing to do now.

Another concept that will be covered throughout the cases is the idea of the pictures in the client's head. This is a vital control theory concept because these pictures, which together form a special world of pictures in the client's memory, are the most important part of the client's life or, for that matter, anyone's life. These pictures are stored in a special part of our memories and begin to be introduced into this special world shortly after birth. This starts a process that continues all our lives.

For example, driven by the needs for love and survival, a small baby may discover that whenever she hurts and chooses to cry in pain (we seem to be born with the ability to cry), something outside of her seems to take over, and soon her pain is replaced by pleasure and satisfaction. The baby, using her senses, soon learns who this outside something is and stores that knowledge in the special world in her memory.

This special world, also called the internal world or the all-we-want world, represents a world in which we would want to live. The image of ourselves in that special world is also the image of what we would like to be. This world of pictures could be likened to our personal Shangri-La or the ideal world that we would like to be a part of. Gloria, in the chapter "Starved for Affection," had severe eating and dieting problems, but she also had a picture of herself as a person who was attractive both physically and socially: unfortunately, she had no effective behaviors to attain this ideal picture in the real world. What she had was a group of physically and socially self-destructive behaviors that were completely ineffective for her. The therapist put her in touch with these pictures and helped her to understand that what she was choosing to do with her life would not get her close to what she wanted. Until we have a good idea of what it is we want, we are not able to understand how badly the behaviors we are choosing are working for us. It is not easy for most clients to tell even a caring counselor what they want, especially if they fear that they have little chance of getting it. The skill of the reality therapist is to counsel in such a noncriticizing, accepting way that clients will reveal what is in their special world.

As stated earlier, all we ever do is behave, but what initiates this behavior is not readily apparent. It all starts with the pictures in our heads, the pictures in the special world that I have just described. Whenever we want something, no matter what, we are then forced by the way we are built to sense (look, listen, touch, taste, or smell) the world to determine how close we are to getting what we want. If we want to be thin and attractive, for example, we must continually look into a mirror to see how thin we are. If we want to be rich, we must continually check how much money we have and what we are doing to make more.

Our behavior, then, is actually generated by the difference between what we want, the pictures in our heads, and what we have, which is what we sense is going on in the world that is related to what we want at the time. When there is a difference, we must behave to try to reduce this difference. Therefore, when I say we choose our behavior, what I am mean is that when this difference exists, we must make a choice to do something. What we do is our choice in almost all cases, but that we always must do something is not our choice; it is the biology of our existence. Whether we like it or not, we will behave in some way or other. Our behavior may be sensible or it may be crazy, it may be prosaic or creative, but whatever it is, it is always the best we can generate at the time.

When our behavior is generated by huge differences between what we want as compared to what we have, we may not even be aware of the fact that we are choosing it. Sometimes, as when we are depressed, anxious, phobic, or psychotic, it seems to be happening to us, but there is still a large element of choice even in these behaviors, as I will shortly explain. There are rare instances, however, when we may be totally unaware of what we are actually choosing to do. When we get to the case of Sarah in Chapter 5, I will explain the fascinating control theory that underlies these rare occurrences.

As I have been explaining control theory, I have used the word *behavior* as if the reader knew exactly what I meant and as if I accepted the dictionary definition of this word. The dictionary defines *behavior* as "conduct or action" or as "a response to stimulation." I have already explained that it is not a response to stimulation, but to be very accurate I must now explain that behavior is much more than conduct or action: it includes thinking, feeling, and physiology. Unless this expanded concept of behavior is completely understood, the idea of choosing our behavior when, for example, we are depressed or anxious, will not make sense. Control theory explains that our behavior is always made up of four individual components: acting, thinking, feeling, and the concurrent physiology, all of which always blend together to make a whole or a total behavior. This means that when a client says he is depressed, the pain or misery he is complaining that he feels is only one of the four components that make up the total behavior. This is the feeling component. The other three components, which are always present, are his actions, thoughts, and physiology. His actions may be that he is sitting around lethargically. The thoughts may be, "What's the use? There is nothing I can do." And his physiology may be that his stomach hurts or that he is having trouble sleeping.

When a client with this total behavior says that he is depressed (and most would), what he is really saying, although he is not aware that he is saying it, is that he is choosing to depress. This is because depressing is the best total behavior that he can figure out to satisfy his needs at this time. Notice that in the previous two sentences, I changed the word *depressed*, which is an adjective and should not be used to describe behavior, to either *depressing* or choosing *to depress*, which are both verb forms. Since control theory explains that we choose all of our behaviors, in this book you will see that we always use the more accurate verb form to designate a total behavior. And just as we do not use the adjective *depressed*, we do not use the noun *depression*. We always use the verb form to describe behavior.

When using the verb form, we usually describe the total behavior by the component that is most obvious. For example, we will use the feeling component to describe most miserable total behaviors because, when people are miserabling, the feeling component is much more obvious than the acting, thinking, or physiologic components. We would say that a person who is moving fast on his feet is running, because in this instance the acting is most obvious. If we see a statue of a seated man supporting his head with his hand, we would say that he is a thinker who is thinking, because this seems most obvious.

As we learn to do this, it begins to feel natural for us to take responsibility for what we are complaining about, and we usually complain a lot less and spend our time figuring out a better total behavior. For example, if I say I am depressing or I am choosing to depress, it is very hard for me to think that this is happening to me. I have to begin to think that I have a choice and that maybe I could do something better.

If a client were psychotic, then the most obvious part of his psychosis would be how he thinks and acts. We would say that he was choosing to hallucinate or delude or catatonic or, in an overall sense, to crazy. If the client suffered from a peptic ulcer as did Susan in the chapter "Finding Her Own Way," we would say, as did the therapist, that she was mostly involved in the physiologic component of her total behavior. She was choosing to ulcerate or, in an overall sense, to sick.

But most people do not understand the concept of total behavior and vehemently deny that they have any choice in the misery, sickness, or craziness about which they or others complain. Even people who commit crimes of action like murder often try to convince juries that they had no choice in what they did. They say that their crimes were a product of a mental illness that caused them to lose control. But control theory rejects this argument by claiming that any action that has a discernible purpose is always voluntary. If there is no discernible purpose, then it might, at least in theory, be involuntary, but this would eliminate crime. Crime always has a discernible purpose. If, for example, a man raped a tree and then claimed insanity, I would accept that defense.

From the standpoint of therapy, it is safe to say that of the four components of our total behavior, two of them, actions and thoughts, are always voluntarily chosen. If you picture your total behavior as a four-wheel drive car, each component would be one wheel of the car. The needs would be the engine, and the car would always be steered in the direction that you, the driver, thought would get you closest to the picture you wanted at that time from your special world. The following diagram should help you to understand this concept. It is taken from the larger diagram that we use to teach control theory in our intensive seminars.

As in a car, you have total and voluntary control over where you steer the front wheels of your "car" which in this analogy are your actions and thoughts. As you will see in the cases, this is what each therapist eventually teaches the client. No matter what the client is complaining of, if he wants to make the effort, he can choose to steer his life in a better direction than he is steering it now. We know from our own lives, and from the observation of many others, that we have nowhere near the quick or arbitrary control over our feelings and/or our physiology as we have over our actions and thoughts.

For example, Tim, in the chapter "Father and Son Learn Together," angered a great deal when his father would not let him live with him, but he did not think he could stop angering until he learned in therapy that it was getting him nowhere. When he began to choose more responsible actions and thoughts like going to school and getting a job, he stopped angering and got what he wanted.

All of us learn, usually early in life, how to add misery,

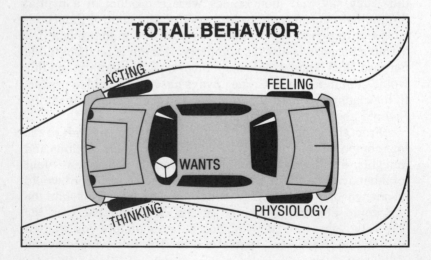

craziness, sickness, and aberrant actions like fighting to a wide variety of total behaviors. Do you know a small child who has not learned to pout and depress to control an adult, or to fight to try to control another child? These lessons are not forgotten, and we continue to improve this ability to add misery or anger to our lives in an attempt to control ourselves or others for the rest of our lives. The cases in this book run the gamut of the miserabling and the disabling that people who see counselors typically have learned as total behaviors in an unfortunate attempt to gain better control over their lives.

Exactly how each of us learns to do this is not clear, but the next time you are severely frustrated and choose to depress, stop and introspect for a moment. If you do, I think you will admit that you are more than a little aware that you are actually choosing the misery as well as the temporary inactivity and hopeless thoughts that usually accompany this choice. It is not important that you know exactly how this is done: my book *Control Theory*[1] provides a more in-depth explanation of most of what is described here. What is important to understand is that not only can misery be chosen, but it also can be relieved through better choices, a process clearly illustrated by every case in this book.

Keep in mind the axiom that total behavior, the whole, is always the sum of all its parts. Therefore, when we choose a symptomatic total behavior like depressing, there is more going on than just feeling. We are also acting and thinking, and our physiology is active and appropriate for the total behavior. But as we also know, the corollary to the axiom is that if you change any part, you necessarily change the whole. Therefore, reality therapy focuses on the parts of the total behavior that can be changed because, in doing so, the whole will also be changed. New and usually better total behaviors will then emerge. Nowhere is this better illustrated than in the case of Everett, in the chapter "Value Judgments Sometimes Don't Come Easily." When this seemingly incorrigible inmate of a maximum-security prison learned control theory, he chose physical fitness work-

[1]William Glasser, *Control Theory* (New York: Harper & Row, 1984).

outs and art and gradually was able to subdue the angering that threatened to keep him locked up forever.

In all the cases in this book, the clients changed their actions and thoughts to new actions and thoughts that were better able to satisfy their needs. In doing so, they all got much closer to the pictures in their special worlds. So it is the actions and thoughts (the front wheels), much more than the feelings and physiology (the rear wheels), that reality therapy focuses upon. As previously stated, it is not that we deny the existence or downgrade the importance of feelings or physiology, but since the goal of all counseling is change, there is no use focusing on what the client cannot change.

You will notice in most of the cases that the therapist stays as much as possible in the present when talking to the client. This is because all of our problems can be solved only in the here and now. This does not mean that all problems are new: to the contrary, most problems have their origin in the past, some in the far-distant past. But no matter how frustrating the past was, and in many of these cases the past was indeed very frustrating, there is no way that any therapist can undo the frustrations of the past. All that can be done is to help the client to make more need-satisfying choices now.

If clients are able to satisfy their needs now, then they will gain the ability to surmount what happened in the past. It is when the present is still filled with frustration that the past remains fresh and painful. It is unlikely that many clients will be able to forget their past; certainly Sarah, the abused seventeen-year-old girl previously mentioned, will never be able to forget her past no matter how well she is able to satisfy her needs in the present. But the better the choices she can make now, the less she will dwell in the past, wishing in vain that her family had been different.

Still, many people have a natural tendency to want to tell the counselor how bad things were and what should have been different in the past. The client wants the therapist to realize what she has suffered and to be compassionate for that suffering. But the client may also want the therapist to excuse her for what she does now on the basis of how much she has suffered in the past. And the client, recognizing that it is very hard to face the present because so much has to be done, may want to stay in the "safe" past to avoid the hard work of dealing with the present.

So the counselor is caught in a dilemma: she must be a compassionate person so that the client will gain the strength to work in the present while communicating to the client what the client may not want to hear, which is that her needs must be satisfied and her problems solved in the present. The case of June in the chapter "The Little Girl Grows Up" in particular illustrates this therapeutic dilemma and how it may take a while for the counselor to lead the client away from the past and into the present.

If this counselor had not eventually done this, it would not have been reality therapy. Although she does spend a great deal of time in the past, she still is able to get to the present, demonstrating that what we teach is flexible and that there are no hard and fast rules. What we ask is that our counselors have a clear control theory reason for doing what they do. If they seem to differ from the usual practice of reality therapy, dwelling a long time on the past or listening a long time to feelings, it will usually be to solidify the relationship between client and therapist, which in turn helps the client to gain the strength that he or she needs to move ahead.

Another aspect of reality therapy shown clearly in these cases is that we do not give up easily. Since we know that it is almost always possible to help clients to satisfy their needs now, we do not become discouraged by a long history of misery. We are not trying to do the impossible, which is to change their history. We also try to teach our clients that the only person's life they can control is their own, so we do not spend much time focusing on what others are doing. This might lead the client to believe that he or she could change other people, which is impossible. Others in the client's life may and usually do change as the clients change, but still it takes a long time for many clients to learn this difficult lesson and we must be patient with them as they do this.

What we continually try to transmit to the client when they

ask, as they frequently do, "Can you help me?" is that we can. But what we really do is to help them to help themselves. And since we believe that almost everyone can help himself, we do not include "giving up" as one of our options. Clients have depended on people in the past, and many of these people have given up. Clients need from us a clear message that we are not going to do the same. It is not so much that we talk about not giving up as that we just don't do it. The message is our actions, not our talk, because actions are what get the message across. The case of Rachel, in the chapter "A Priceless Gift," illustrates this action message clearly. Here is a five-year-old who eventually blossoms, but it took years, and no one involved in her treatment ever thought of giving up.

Over and over as you read these cases, you may ask, "How did the counselors remain so constant and so upbeat in the face of so much frustration?" The answer is that they did because they are strong. It takes a lot of strength to be a good counselor. They need this strength because they know that although it is almost always self-destructive, many clients try to frustrate the therapy in an effort to prove that the therapist is inadequate. These clients then can say to themselves, "See, it isn't my fault. The therapist is unable to help, so how could I possibly help myself?"

Reality therapists are familiar with this ploy, and they do not fall for it. Once the client discovers that he cannot control the therapist, he begins to get the idea that he really cannot control anyone else but himself. As soon as he gets this idea, therapy proceeds at a good pace, but it takes a lot of effort before some clients get this idea. It may also seem to take a lot of time, but some of these cases, difficult as they were, were handled in less than six months of counseling.

Finally, as you observe the process of therapy, so well illustrated in this book, you will see clearly that reality therapists counsel in the true sense of the word. That is, they help the clients make the better choices that need to be made; in many cases, they even suggest what might be a course of action for clients. The only caution is that they do not do this until the client has answered the basic reality therapy question, "Is what

you are doing (or choosing to do) getting you what you want?"
This question may be asked in a variety of ways, or it may be
implied so strongly that it is not actually asked, but it always
precedes the suggestion of what to do. If the client has not made
the judgment that what he or she is doing is not working, then
suggesting something else is premature.

Regardless of the presenting problem, most clients have
problems getting along as they would like with other people,
usually their families or loved ones. That they need to get along
better with or to move away from these people is usually obvious, so many of the therapists' suggestions are also obvious.
Nevertheless, therapists realize that people are sensitive about
being "told what to do," so they do not "tell." They "suggest,"
and usually say, "If this is not a good idea, then what do you
think might be better?" Sometimes they do not say this pre-
cisely, but the way they make the suggestion makes it clear to
the client that this is what is meant.

What therapists want to achieve in counseling is for their
clients to override their past and learn how to live effectively in
the present without them. The break need not be clean; the door
is always open. Some of the cases, especially "Finding Her Own
Way," illustrate this open door. But more and more the therapist
teaches the client, "It is your life, and you have to make the
many hard choices that it takes to live it in a satisfying way. I
cannot live your life for you or solve your problems, but I can,
and will, help." This message should be loud and clear as you
read this book.

All of us hear many people deride counseling and say that
it does not help: all it does is make people dependent. As control
theory clearly points out, nothing makes people anything: they
make themselves what they are. In my experience, when you
have a problem that has led you to make wrong choices and as
a result have led yourself into a miserable life, good counseling
is the best, quickest, and least expensive way to get the help you
need to turn your life around. It gets to the core of the problem
and leaves you better prepared either to avoid or to solve problems in the future. If these cases point out anything, they point
out the truth of this contention.

2

From Acting Out to Joining In

A Young Teenager Learns
Better Behaviors

ROGER D. ZEEMAN

IN THE SAME YEAR that *Control Theory* was published, I started seeing Patti. She was twelve years old and in the seventh grade. And, by the time she reached thirteen and one-half, this highly intelligent, very attractive young lady with very curly, dark brown hair and eyes almost as dark as her hair had provided my most challenging year as a counseling psychologist.

"Attractive" and "intelligent" did not describe Patti at our first meeting. She was morose, pale, and reticent. Her parents, struggling with their own marital relationship and difficulties of personal identity, described one nightmarish situation after another: threatening them with a knife, climbing on the roof and threatening to jump, expressing furor at them by using the most profane and violent vocabulary, and ingesting excessive quantities of Tylenol in another suicidal gesture.

I wondered initially how Patti had stayed away from hospi-

16

talization. However, she always managed to recover and behave more appropriately following each "spell" of acting out or
depressing behavior. Additionally, she paid monthly visits to a
major medical center psychiatrist who monitored trials of various antidepressant medications. The psychiatrist provided
some consultation to Patti and the family, but the primary treatment was psychopharmacological.

School was a problem as well. Patti was "unable" to wake
up in time to catch the school bus, so her mother or father drove
the twelve miles to school daily. This distance was also blamed
for the fact that Patti had no friends: there was no one her age
in the neighborhood. Her attendance at school was sporadic, as
she had more than the average share of colds and assorted
upper-respiratory infections.

As I usually do at the first interview, I asked her parents
about the positive or successful aspects of Patti's character.
After much thought, her parents did come up with some posi-
tives: she cared about her thirteen-year-old brother, loved her
family, and cleaned up her room.

Feeling overwhelmed by the problems presented, I was relieved (actually buoyed) to hear that Patti did have a number of
likes and interests. She described her enjoyment of shopping for
clothes, listening to popular music, talking on the phone to a girl
in her class (she did have a friend after all), roller skating,
horseback riding, and bike riding. I was pleased that Patti enjoyed talking on the phone because I use the telephone, as well
as mail, to check regularly on the plans I develop with children
or adolescents. Communication between formal sessions helps
to maintain a friendly atmosphere and provides a comfortable
counseling environment. I have even used computer electronic
mail to send reminders back and forth. In addition to facilitating
friendship, initiating a call or sending an electronic mail message gives a child a sense of increased control over his or her
own destiny and an enhanced feeling of self-worth.

Patti, apathetic and noncommittal, nevertheless agreed to
another meeting. I explained that I would typically spend about
thirty-five minutes with her and ten with either or both of her
parents. I offered no prediction about the number of sessions we

would spend together, but this seemed irrelevant since Patti had not really agreed that there were problems to solve, much less goals to pursue.

When Patti returned the following week, we chatted very briefly about what she had been doing and I began to teach her a card game called Rack-O. She enjoyed the game and managed a faint smile once or twice. We talked as we played, and I pressed hard to hear some things she had done or was planning to do. Patti mentioned two activities: a cousin's "slumber" birthday party that she had recently attended and enjoyed and a plan to roller skate on the coming weekend. I pointed out these two as examples of her ability to be in situations where she had chosen not to be depressed. I expressed confidence in her and urged her to "cheer up." This approach, taken directly from Dr. Glasser's early lectures on reality therapy, urges the client to take increasing responsibility for her behavior, emphasizing her powerful decision-making capabilities in the struggle to give up "depressing."

Patti's difficulty in getting to school was severe. I enlisted help from two outstanding people in the local school district, the attendance officer and the guidance counselor. Both were sensitive, experienced, and knowledgeable individuals with whom I had worked previously. We worked out a communication plan that would monitor Patti's attendance and tardiness. The attendance officer worked with her at home to discuss the laws and possible court involvement. The counselor provided the much-needed support in school—brief weekly meetings with Patti to discuss homework assignments, her relationships with peers, and her relationships with teachers. In addition, the counselor maintained ongoing communication with Patti's teachers, urging them to encourage her while avoiding unnecessary pressure.

Patti and I developed specific plans for her to talk to one or two girls in school with whom she wanted to be friends. We discussed what she had in common with these girls and rehearsed conversations in which she made small talk about after-school activities or what was happening in some of their classes. The plan included deciding on the best time and place to initiate a discussion—in homeroom, between classes, or at lunch. After agreeing to the plan, Patti actually talked to three girls, each more than one time. We both knew then, although it was unspoken, that she had the ability to change.

After only a few sessions, Patti had achieved an A– on a draft report and had reduced her name calling of her father to a comparatively mild "jerk."

We alternated between Rack-O and chess and kept working on friendships, parent relationships (mostly fighting and name calling), school work, and plans for activities such as skating. After our sixth session, I decided that Patti trusted me sufficiently to allow me to be supportive of her during conversations with both her parents. I scheduled time during the next several sessions for a twenty-minute family discussion. The rules were simple: stick to the facts as much as possible; treat one another decently and with some respect; avoid put-downs. My role was largely that of mediator to keep the discussion on track and to help each family member listen and "hear" what the others were saying. The level of hostility was kept fairly low. I was able to model rational disagreement and methods of compromise for parents and teenager. We focused on what each person really wanted and what each could do to help the other achieve his or her objective. There was no talk of "depression," except in our rare conversations of the medical regimen from the psychiatrist. Occasionally, I managed to interject some remark about loving traits among family members.

However, during session eleven, I spent time with Patti's parents before seeing her, only to learn of another series of major verbal battles. (At least Patti had stopped throwing things.) Her father reported extreme profanity directed at him and her mother. My growing optimism was put on hold—particularly when I asked Patti to join us and, showing no sign of remorse, she refused to elaborate on the fighting. In the absence of her response, I asked her father to describe, as objectively as he could, the circumstances leading up to the argument and to repeat specifically the words that Patti had used. I offered Patti the chance to comment, but she pouted and declined. The purpose of this interchange was to diffuse the future impact of the vocabulary and, more significantly, to make the behavior "public." I asked her parents to decide on the threshold of verbal abuse they were willing to tolerate and to advise Patti of the disciplinary action to be taken when she exceeded that threshold. I asked them to record in writing the next such occurrence, including a description of the "provocation," each person's behavior, and the outcome. Later, privately, I asked Patti to place a value judgment on this sort of behavior. She said that it did not accomplish anything beneficial for her, but her parents were so unreasonable that she "could not control" her temper. We brainstormed alternate ways to behave when she perceived parental unreasonableness: telling her parents either to stop or calm down, reminding them that she was capable of making more decisions herself, and even reminding them that she was seeing me to figure out better ways to handle these problems. I reemphasized the fact that she did have control over the response she chose.

On a more positive note, Patti's discussion of friends and extracurricular activities revealed that, at least in social areas, she *was* making better choices. She attended a school dance and participated in a charity jump-rope-a-thon. I spoke of these successes and complimented her while she beat me in Rack-O.

My experience applying reality therapy to preteens had led me to the conclusion that ten to twenty sessions with an occasional check-back is usually enough to secure the desired changes. However, I knew that even with the added power of control theory, my relationship with Patti was going to be a long one. We could not begin to talk about long-range goals (or "pictures") while we struggled together to get through one day at a time.

Gradually, I taught Patti's parents reality therapy and control theory by discussion. When all four of us talked, it was sometimes about literature, pamphlets, or books. But more often our discussions were like the following:

MOTHER: Patti is still not getting up in the morning and we have to drive her to school. She signs in late every day.

FATHER: And when I wake her up she is abusive.

ROGER: [to Patti] What do you say?

PATTI: I don't remember. I'm too sleepy. And I haven't done it for days.

ROGER: [to Father] What does she say?

FATHER: [repeats profanity]

ROGER: She's improved over the last few days?

MOTHER: True. She even made it to school on time once.

ROGER: How did you do it?

PATTI: I just woke up. And I needed to talk to a friend before school.

ROGER: Could you meet your friend more often?

PATTI: No, she usually doesn't get to school until second period.

ROGER: What could you all do to change this?

FATHER: We can't just let her sleep all day.

ROGER: Have you talked to the attendance officer lately? Remember, she is very competent and will take Patti to court if need be.

PATTI: I could get up by myself if I could hear my alarm.

ROGER: How many clocks do you have?

PATTI: One, and I reach out in my sleep and turn it off.

ROGER: Could you get more and put them out of reach? And do you really want to get up by yourself and get to school on time?

PATTI: You know I do. I have been doing much better. This was a bad week.

ROGER: You mean you chose to react to your disappointments by being abusive to your father and getting to school late. How did these choices help?

PATTI: They didn't help, but I've been in a bad mood.

ROGER: Are you doing anything to cheer yourself up?

MOTHER: She was chosen by the principal to lead a tour of elementary students visiting the school.

FATHER: It is lucky the tour wasn't in the morning or you never would have made it.

ROGER: [to Father] How does it help things to bring that up?

FATHER: I'm sorry. She just really gets me mad.

ROGER: When will you decide to be less mad at her?

MOTHER: You know, Herb, you do get carried away.

ROGER: Patti, you didn't tell me about being chosen as a tour leader. They couldn't have made a better choice. Those little kids will be lucky to have you. What did you have to do to get picked?

PATTI: He said he picked me because my grades went up.

ROGER: You're really getting recognition for all your success. I'm proud of you. So who's getting the clocks, and where will they be in the room?

MOTHER: We could all go to the five-and-ten and pick some up.

ROGER: [to Patti] Will you set them at night? What time for each? Let's figure out exactly where to put them. I'll write it all down. How will I know you've done it? Can I call you tomorrow night?

Whenever Patti started to change her behavior in a positive direction, I asked her: "How are you doing it? What happened? What did you yourself contribute to the success?" I started to make "house calls" to intervene when tempers at home flared. Whether sessions were in the office or at home, I followed up with calls and letters that reviewed material discussed during sessions and reminded Patti of plans or conclusions. Because the letters rarely contained any new material, they were not discussed during sessions, except for my occasional inquiries as to whether they had been received and read. Letters seemed particularly effective for Patti, a girl with excellent comprehension and reading ability who was enrolled in several honors courses. I wrote this letter during our third month together:

Dear Patti,

I would like you to think about what happened the other night so you can learn from the experience. Remember when you said, in anger, that you had a high IQ? Well, your intelligence can help you a lot in solving your problems. This is so because every time you choose to get angry or sad you can force yourself to use your brain to make a *different choice* and to do something better for yourself. This is difficult, but it is possible. Your high IQ will help you to have control over yourself because it helps you to think of other things you can do besides sitting around and getting mad.

If you choose to make real bad choices, you control all the adults in your life by "backing them into a corner." This means that you challenge them and limit *their* choices. You are a charming, delightful, pretty, smart girl when you choose to be. It is my job to help you make better choices more of the time. No matter what you do or say [she had gotten angry at me], I will still care about you, be your friend, and be there for you all the time. (You cannot get rid of me!)

Read this over a couple of times, Patti, because it is not so easy to understand.

I worked with Patti's parents, in her presence, to assure that intimidation by her *not* be accepted as a means of control or decision making. When Patti was not present, we talked about "giving her a reason to change"—being positive and praiseful about even the smallest accomplishments as well as talking about future plans and aspirations. The "one-day-at-a-time" strategy was working better and better. Patti was accomplishing day-long periods of good "moods," and her parents were genuinely pleased if they could experience an entire day without conflict. The family had dreaded, and therefore avoided, taking vacations together. As a result of their more favorable experiences with one another, they decided to take their first family vacation, which turned out to be enjoyable. Patti spent much positive time with her brother, swimming and sightseeing. One week after their return, things were still calm. In fact, there had been only one serious incident of disagreement all week. Patti started to look better, with a brighter face, a smile, and some light in her eyes. She actually expressed pride in self-control, making better choices, and keeping busy. She walked fourteen miles in a charity walk-a-thon. She even put the antidepressant medicine in perspective: "It keeps me from getting down in the dumps, but I need to control anger." I could not even beat her at Rack-O any more.

To keep our involvement strong and change the pace from an office setting, Patti and I had a breakfast session at a fast-food restaurant. She was depressing but only acknowledged

tiredness. Her summer plans included a work-study arrangement for horseback riding, and she had participated successfully in an Arbor Day program at school. Nevertheless, as is
usual with people who depress, she resisted accepting credit for
these accomplishments. It was often difficult to understand the
motivation behind Patti's mood choices. Things seemed to be
improving, but one would hardly realize that judging from this
breakfast meeting. Could Patti's present depressing be related
to our recent discussion of whether or not her medication was
necessary? Was she resisting the demands of her everyday
schedule after a unique vacation? Did she perceive a need to
prove that she still depended on me? Was she merely reverting
to a learned behavior from force of habit? Perhaps all of these
played some part.

Patti, who in the past had strongly resisted discussing anything to do with her future, now responded to my inquiries. She
pictured herself working with animals, perhaps in the veterinary
field. She related with some pride her enjoyment and success
with horseback riding and horse grooming. The acknowledg-
ment that she had received had enhanced her self-esteem and
reduced her defensiveness. Here was a sustained eight-week
activity that she had mastered, proving to herself her ability to
fulfill substantial personal responsibility and commitment. Her
improved self-concept was further demonstrated by the fact
that she became only a little mad when her brother ate some
special cake she had saved for herself. Months ago, she would
have literally tried to kill him or herself after such an incident.

Patti was now verbalizing control theory more and more.
She practically discounted her dependence on medication and
acknowledged her own decision-making ability. She viewed
any conflict with her brother in a more typical sibling rivalry
manner: "He never gets blamed for anything. . . ." At vacation
time, I wrote the following letter:

Dear Patti,

Since we are not meeting for a couple of weeks, I'd like to
review a few things. First, please remember your agreement to

prepare a list of things to do that are interesting or fun and that will keep you busy. Second, please remember to phone me if you need encouragement, suggestions, or just want to talk.

Be determined to enjoy your vacation time with the family. Keep control of the emotions which get you into trouble, relax, and have a good time.

Remember, Patti, you will *not* return to the poor behavior of the past unless you choose to do so. The last several weeks of success, your terrific work in school [she was, of late, achieving A's in several subjects], and the happiness in your family should prove to you how far you have come. Everyone changes moods, so don't let that discourage you.

I am very proud of what you have accomplished, and I hope you are too. You can control and choose what you do, think, and feel. Do not forget.

Don't practice Rack-O too much. I need a chance to catch up. Have fun.

At the end of the summer, the psychiatrist decided to reduce Patti's medication gradually until, after seven weeks, it was discontinued.

Interestingly, Patti's parents were now beginning to find fault with normal teenage decisions. No longer having a major crisis with which to deal, they had time to pay attention to small things—twenty minutes lateness or some responsibility left undone. Patti's behavior had entered the range of normality, but her parents still needed her as a focus—perhaps to avoid their own problems, which were now, in comparison, even more serious. In fact, I was not very successful at getting Patti's parents to recognize the relationship between their lifestyle and personal choices and those of their daughter. I stressed their roles as models in Patti's life and recommended on several occasions that they enter individual or marital counseling. Her father continually spoke of his long-term depression and dissatisfaction with work. Her mother hardly ever ventured from the house and never drove more than a few miles. I made small plans with them to have family discussions, go places, identify enjoyable things to do together, and increase their interest and involvement in each other's lives, but their commitments were feeble and their follow-through even less effective. Reluctantly, I was taking over as the primary model for Patti, helping her to develop meaningful goals, standards, and values. I also began spending a short amount of time in some sessions with her brother, Michael. I took an interest in his academic and artistic pursuits and listened to his perceptions of his sister and her psychological problems. I reinforced his uniqueness and praised his ability to carry on with the important things in his life despite Patti's bickering and her quest always to be on center stage in the family.

Ten months after our initial session, Patti's life included good friends, horseback riding, the school band, generally good grades, and regular on-time school attendance on the bus.

The family and I discussed reducing our sessions to every other week. I pointed out Patti's strengths and accomplishments, at the same time warning that an occasional incident did not mean regression but rather temporary return to former behavior choices. I also reminded everyone that normal teenager-parent relations had disagreements built-in. I worked hard to get Patti and her parents to understand that their disagreements could not be addressed with criticism. The more successful I was in getting them to reduce their criticism of one another, the more progress Patti seemed to achieve.

As before, I was becoming increasingly optimistic until a frantic call came from Patti's mother. In the background I could hear Patti screaming in anger. On the surface, the argument was over some chewing gum that her brother had taken, but we all knew that more was happening. I defused the situation over the telephone:

ROGER: Patti, what are you doing?
PATTI: My brother's being a jerk.
ROGER: What are *you* doing?
PATTI: I told my mother I didn't take anything. I just want them to leave me alone.
ROGER: It sounds like you're acting really angry and excited.
PATTI: Every time anything happens I get blamed.
ROGER: Are you willing to calm down and do something else?

PATTI: I am calm. I'm perfectly fine.

ROGER: Well, you didn't sound calm when I heard you screaming and cursing in the background! First of all, think about
our talks about your brother and getting jealous of him.
Second, tell me what you can do instead of acting crazy.

PATTI: I'm going to call [a friend] and meet her at the park.

ROGER: What will you do when you get back home?

PATTI: I'll just leave Michael alone.

ROGER: Can you figure out a different way to deal with your
anger next time?

PATTI: I could ignore the whole thing or talk to them.

ROGER: You could call me, too.

PATTI: Yes.

ROGER: Remember, you have been doing just great. You've
proved that you can control yourself and choose reasonable ways to settle these things. Think about all our discussions before you decide to blow up. We'll meet together
soon.

PATTI: Okay.

I then followed up with this letter:

Dear Patti,

I was concerned about your level of anger last night. You
have decided to give this up, remember? You are going to make me
look like a bad psychologist when you decide to lose control in the
same week that I recommend reducing your sessions to every
other week! Let me go over a few things. First, you need to review
in your head how to express your anger in ways that are more
acceptable. There is no sense in going back to your old way of
expressing your temper. We both know that it is a bad choice and
doesn't get anywhere. So, if you need to be angry, review in your
brain what else you can do—be by yourself, call a friend, call me,
take a walk, or whatever you decide.

The issue last night was avoidable. It wasn't really a disagreement over bubble gum. Remember, you talked to me about
the "popular kids" in your class and the election. Then as soon
as we opened the door, your mother praised your brother for

getting nominated. Would you be surprised if you experienced
some jealousy that you had trouble dealing with? Then, not expressing it, you waited for an opportunity to lose your cool and
get mad at him. We've talked about this together so I know you
understand it.

You, yourself, are intelligent, charming, express yourself
well, are a good friend to others, and have a lot of abilities. Remember these things about yourself. Your highest potential has
not been reached because of your poor control over some emotions. But, you know now that you can definitely change this. You
have had some great weeks and excellent results in school. You
are just beginning to see what your full potential might be.

In a few years you'll be a real star and hardly remember the
troubles your past has given you. Now is the time to keep turning
things around. It is with the work you are putting in. *You are in
control of your life* so make decisions which will help you.

Patti and I prepared for the end of our counseling relationship. Our sessions were devoted to discussions of power, control, goals, and happiness. I reviewed with Patti her unproduc-
tive uses of power in the family—threatening to be nasty or
acting crazy in order to get her parents or brother to do what she
wanted. She had learned that while this technique may work
temporarily, such a choice reduces the chances for being normal
and happy and breaks down any loving family relationships.
When she stopped to think things out rather than respond impul-
sively, Patti knew that she had control over her life and could
enjoy the positive outcomes of reasonable choices. Her goals
were clearer; she had expressed some career interests and was
motivated to achieve in school. She had also learned that involvement in interesting activities contributed to her feelings of
well-being and self-esteem and her enjoyment of appropriate
friendships. I reminded the family of my continuing availability
by telephone or in person, if necessary. And, finally, I encouraged them to avail themselves of the guidance and psychological support services of Patti's public school.

Epilogue

Two years after discharge from therapy, at age fifteen, Patti relapsed. The word *depression* had crept back into the family vocabulary. Her morning procrastination returned, and she was once more being chauffeured to school. Her parents asked me to see her again.

I quickly ascertained that, although Patti had chosen some self-destructive and acting-out behavior, it was not at all the same as before. Her appearance gave it away: she looked relaxed, calm, bright-eyed, alert, and energetic. She was part of an award-winning band that practiced constantly. There was one problem that concerned a course and a teacher at school. I removed Patti's parents from that conflict and took responsibility so that they could devote their energy to rekindling their relationship with Patti without nagging or criticism. I enlisted help from the counselor, school psychologist, and vice-principal, attended a meeting at school, and participated in changing her scheduling and teachers.

I spent a session with Patti's parents reviewing their approaches and followed up with this letter:

Dear Marilyn and Herb,

Let's recap last evening's discussion.

Remember the morning routine and review the arrangements a day before. Stop thinking of Patti as "angry," "depressed," "emotionally disturbed," "incapable," etc. She is a girl with lots of poor behavior choices and things to work out. No question about that. But she is capable of working hard to change her behavior if she agrees (as she seems to) that it is in her best interest.

Make sure she knows in advance what to expect, and secure her agreement (or compromise) whenever possible. If you decide that some of her behavior is absolutely unacceptable and intolerable, let her know in advance what the consequences will be. Choose reasonable consequences that she won't like but which will fit, not exceed, the "crime." Only deal this way with the few most serious and awful behaviors, ignore the rest.

Use every possible opportunity when things are somewhat calm to negotiate. Ask Patti what she really wants. Make a plan that is very specific, and stick to it.

Remember to keep analyzing what you each do and change your behavior, your feelings (yes, you can change your feelings), your responses, your choices. Focus on what you do and let Patti deal with her behavior and its natural consequences. If she is unsuccessful carrying out the most ordinary fifteen-year-old tasks, then call me or talk to other people you trust, but don't try to take over for her. Expect her to be successful. Let me repeat . . . act as if you expect her to be successful. Remind her of her ability to make good decisions when you have the opportunity. Tell her about past decisions she made which worked out well.

This is all difficult. I know. But your ability to change what you are thinking, expecting, and doing now will impact on the future. Have as much hope as you like, I do too . . . but don't try to rush things. Change will come, but it will take time. Patti proved it two years ago.

To Patti, I wrote this reminder of our talks:

This week you agreed to work on expressing your anger in different ways and getting rid of the angry feeling. Think of other things you can do to substitute for being angry. (Wrestle with your brother, chase the dog, read a novel, or whatever . . . be creative!)

Remind yourself that you are fifteen years old and want to be more independent from your parents. Let go of your demands and have your parents help you only when it is appropriate.

Do what is good for you without punishing anyone else. You are a super person. You have proven before in your life that you can work hard and put energy into changing what is going wrong. Work hard now . . . you'll be happier soon. Guaranteed!

Patti was even more insightful about her behavioral choices than she had been when we stopped our sessions two years before. She had a new symptom—"headaching"—which almost disappeared soon after counseling resumed.

Patti had learned well what was required to change. She worked hard to get to school on time in the morning by bus. She received a new alarm clock and made it to school on time four out of five days.

Then I learned a startling bit of information. During her rise to championship on the band, her parents had never attended a performance! With Patti's crying need for acceptance and recognition, what an opportunity they had missed! At my urging, her father attended a dress rehearsal within days. Shortly thereafter, Patti met a senior boy she really liked and enjoyed. This afforded me the opportunity to reinforce Patti for "all the traits he finds wonderful in you"—intelligence, lovableness, fun, caring, and so on.

The crisis passed. Patti did not quite return to the successful level of control she had achieved two years ago. She clung to her moments of anger at her parents. Although some of these were vaguely reminiscent of earlier scenes, they were not as scary or as intense. And the frequency remained quite low.

At this writing, Patti is a successful student, a teenager involved with peers of both sexes, active in a "positively addicting" competitive activity, and at least as happy as she has ever been. When I last saw her, I reminded her that she may well be the strongest person in her family because she knew exactly what needed to be said and done to improve each situation. She knew what words to choose and what action to take to get desired results. All she had to do was do it.

DR. GLASSER'S COMMENTS ON "FROM ACTING OUT TO JOINING IN"

With great ingenuity and a willingness to go beyond the confines of the office, Dr. Zeeman created the need-satisfying counseling environment that is essential to reality therapy. In this environment, Patti began to learn the new total behaviors she needed if she were to satisfy her needs. Through her interaction with Dr. Zeeman—the acceptance, the listening, the questioning, and the games they played—she began to learn how to make friends, achieve in school, and use good language. Gradually these new total behaviors began to replace the angering, depressing, and cursing, that she had learned to use so well before. What is instructive about this case, which will also be evident in most of the other cases in this book, is that people who learn new and more effective behaviors do not forget the behaviors they had used often in the past, even though these behaviors seem to almost everyone else so painful and ineffective.

Time after time, Patti reverted to what she knew, the old angering and depressing, especially when her obviously strong need for power was frustrated. When used as much as Patti used them, such behaviors become habitual, and because our lives are frequently visited by frustration, it takes much concentration, practice, patience, and usually outside support—like Patti got from Dr. Zeeman—to gain the strength to subdue bad habits.

This is why counseling takes so long, but it is also why it is so effective when other treatments, for example, medication alone, fail. Few people besides a counselor would have had the time or the patience to support Patti so consistently through the wide, unpredictable swings she chose in her attempt to satisfy her needs. Her parents, teachers, and psychiatrist certainly did not. This case demonstrates clearly how easy it is to revert to self-destructive behaviors even after two years of fairly consistently making better choices to deal with frustration.

The question that arises is, could Patti have achieved what she did on her own? To me, the answer is obvious: no. This was a girl with an above-average need for power. She could not accept the passive "good girl" role that her parents wanted her to so that they could control her and satisfy their needs. Patti fought this attempt at control with angering. When that did not work, she learned to slide quickly into depressing with all its attendant symptoms, such as sleeping, to avoid frustration. And, as I have stated, she learned these behaviors well. Without Dr. Zeeman's intervention, she had the capacity to become a seriously disturbed teenager who may well have required hospitalization for being uncontrollable. She would have been a danger to others and a candidate for self-mutilation or even suicide if she decided to turn so much anger against herself.

Patti had to deal with parents immersed in an ancient conflict: how to satisfy their own needs and still be good parents. This conflict is basic to almost any relationship but for parents it always surfaces. Perhaps because they had so many problems in their own relationship, they did not recognize Patti's needs. This was shown by the fact that even after she was doing better, her parents still did not attend her greatest success, playing in the band, until they were told to do so. Even then, only her father went. All parents try their best, but many do not do well enough and can benefit greatly from the guidance of a patient counselor like Dr. Zeeman.

Counselors should note that parents need this guidance for a long time. What they should be doing for their children is not obvious to them, even when it is clear to almost everyone else. If Dr. Zeeman had taken for granted that Patti's parents knew how to be supportive of her, he would never have achieved what he did with this child.

Patti's case illustrates how self-destructive both parents and children can be to gain what they wrongly but firmly believe they want. What was happening in this family before counseling was reminiscent of a classic Greek tragedy. All the characters believed they were doing what they should to satisfy their needs, even though it brought them to the point of destroying themselves or those they claimed to love. As this book will show, there is rarely one right way to satisfy our needs, especially where others are concerned.

There are responsible ways to satisfy our needs, which means not depriving another person of the chance to satisfy his or her needs. It is also responsible, especially in raising a child, to help the other person to satisfy his or her needs. There are also irresponsible ways and it is irresponsible either to harm yourself or another as you attempt to satisfy your needs. It was irresponsible for Patti to curse her parents but also irresponsible for them to fail to attend her band concerts. In how we deal with each other two wrongs never make a right; they increase the wrong.

While many people are able to learn this on their own, our clients often seem unable or unwilling to do so. Not until they insert the therapist into their special, all-we-want worlds do they seem able to give up their convictions that theirs is the "right" way and to find the better way that is almost always there. Watch for this tendency as you read the remaining cases, and you will better appreciate what counseling is and why it is so needed.

3

Symptoms: The Price We Pay to Control

Choosing Anxiety and Fear as a Way to Cope with Life's Problems

TOM ASHLEY STROHL

WHEN I ENTERED my waiting room and called "Jennifer," a tall, thin, casually dressed woman stood up. She appeared nervous. Leading her into my office, I offered her a chair and told her I wanted a little background information. Jennifer had been born in 1948, making her thirty-eight when we first met. She lived in a suburban townhouse development with her husband of seventeen years and their three children, ages fifteen, twelve, and ten. She had worked the night shift in a nursing home as a nurse's aide for three years, but had quit that job a couple of months ago.

"How did you come to hear of me?" I asked.

"My family doctor told me I had agoraphobia. He gave me some pills to take three times a day and told me to talk to you."

"What did he tell you about agoraphobia?" I asked.

"He really didn't say anything. He told me that was what

34

my problem was and that the medicine and counseling could help."

"Have you been feeling anxious?" Jennifer responded with an emphatic "Yes." I asked her to tell me about her anxiety, and I interspersed her story with some questions pertaining to the symptoms of agoraphobia, as they are described in the American Psychiatric Association's *Diagnostic and Statistical Manual,* Third Edition. Jennifer went on to paint a classic picture of an individual experiencing agoraphobia with panic attacks.

About six months ago, she had had her first panic attack. It was nighttime, and she was lying in bed next to her husband. When he wanted to become intimate, a feeling of fearfulness and a wave of panic seemed to come from out of the blue. Her breathing became erratic, her palms sweaty, her limbs weak. Then her heart began to pound and throb as though, she felt, it were going to burst out of her chest. Afraid she was having a heart attack, she contemplated going to the local hospital emergency room. Two more attacks followed in the next month. The last one, which she described as a "total collapse," occurred while she was driving to her mother's house. From then on, a general anxiousness developed and increased, leading to a constriction of her normal activities. She was afraid of driving a car or being in public places. She avoided food shopping, feeling unable to go even to the local shopping mall. She began calling in sick to work. Eventually her family doctor told her to quit her job, which she did willingly. To all intents and purposes, she imprisoned herself in her home. For the first time in her marriage, instead of playing her usual caretaker role, she was being cared for. While the medicine produced temporary relief, at this point she had decided to try counseling.

At the end of her story I said, "Do you know that you don't have an illness?"

"I don't?"

"No, you don't."

"Thank goodness. That's a relief. I was afraid something was wrong with me, or I was going crazy. But I don't understand. Isn't agoraphobia an illness? There are pills for it."

"All the things you told me about—the anxious feelings, the

worrying and fearful thoughts, the behavior of avoiding public places, as well as the physiology of sweaty palms and shaky legs—those are behaviors that so many people do, doctors have given that group of behaviors a label. They call it agoraphobia."

"You mean this is common, that I'm not strange or anything?"

"Many people have tried to cope with their lives in the same unhelpful way. You're not strange or sick. The label 'agoraphobia' is just a way of describing what you're doing. The medicine works somewhat because our physiology, thoughts, feelings, and behavior are all interconnected and work as a total system. The medicine chemically affects your physiology, which blocks your ability to feel anxious sensations. That gives you some relief, so you are able to think less anxious thoughts and act less anxious behavior. But the medicine doesn't solve the problem. It just blocks the anxious feeling. Your feelings won't hurt you, and you shouldn't be afraid of them. As a matter of fact, our feelings are the best indicator of how well we are living our lives and meeting our needs. Your feelings are very helpful signals that you need to learn to read: they're signaling that you are not meeting your needs effectively and that your life isn't heading in the direction you want it to. Continue your medicine for now if you think it helps, since it is designed to affect your physiology. In counseling we will focus on the other parts of your total behavior—your thoughts, feelings, and actions." That sounded reasonable to Jennifer.

I told her that we would meet for one hour a week to talk about her life and how she was meeting her needs. It would be her responsibility to pay me fifty dollars for each of our talks, and I would give her a billing statement. She would then have to deal with the insurance company regarding her mental-health benefits. I told her that in my opinion she had the ability to help herself through counseling and that I would be willing to meet with her for as long as it took.

I ended by giving her two homework assignments. First, she was to use her anxious feelings as helpful signals alerting her that she was feeling increasingly out of control and to record these signals in a journal describing both the situations occurring at that time and her corresponding thoughts and actions. (She was to bring the journal to the counseling sessions, and we would go over it together.) Second, she was to try to picture herself as a non-anxious, cool, calm, collected person and to develop a picture of her life the way she wanted it to be. We would discuss this in our talks. Jennifer agreed to do these two assignments. She looked visibly more relaxed than she had at the beginning of the session. We smiled. I extended my hand and said as we shook hands, "It was nice meeting you. I'll look forward to working with you."

This first session set the tone for the year and a half of work that would follow. I remained friendly, consistent, and not over-whelmed by Jennifer's problems, no matter how difficult and painful they became. I steadfastly displayed my confidence and belief that she could more effectively meet her needs. The framework from which I consistently worked was that her problem was not an illness but a creative yet ineffective way to meet her needs and resolve the pain in her life. I did not want to excuse her from being responsible for her behaviors.

The homework assignments, which Jennifer continued and we reviewed for the first two months, served several purposes. First, they helped her to accept her feelings and become less critical of herself. Because Jennifer was not effectively meeting her needs, she naturally felt frustrated. She was thinking, "I can't go out feeling like this. People will notice and think there is something wrong with me." She was experiencing a natural feeling of frustration over unmet needs, but the fearful thinking produced an anxious feeling that only complicated matters. In effect, Jennifer was choosing to "anxietize." By telling her to use her feelings as helpful signals, I provided a new and more effective way of perceiving and thinking about them, as well as a different way of acting upon her feelings. Keeping a journal was also a totally different behavior that proved more effective as a response to her unmet needs than anxietizing. The journal became a way for Jennifer to take her counseling home with her and actively continue the sessions throughout the week.

While the journal and our work together acknowledged and accepted Jennifer's symptomatic "anxiety," in the sessions I focused almost exclusively on Jennifer's life situation, thoughts, and actions.

The second homework assignment was designed to help Jennifer get in touch with her personal wants and desires and look at her unmet needs. Anxietizing had become the focus of her attention and helped her to avoid the painful reality that she was not achieving her personal wants. I was attempting to get Jennifer to shift the focus away from anxietizing and to look at developing and expressing her personal wants. We could then assess how realistic the personal want pictures were and work at developing realistic plans to attempt to achieve them.

When we met the second week, Jennifer was pleased to announce that, for some unknown reason, she had not had any anxiety attacks. As far as she was aware, she had not changed anything in her life except to come see me and do the homework assignments. She was still confining herself to the house, afraid to go out, but somehow the tension was lessened. She did experience many anxious moments, but when she wrote in her journal she noticed that nothing negative or bad was happening in the real world.

What Jennifer did realize was that two main issues continually emerged in her thinking. The first issue had to do with career concerns. "What am I going to do with my life? My children are getting older. My oldest will be driving next year, and they don't need me as much. I hated the job as a nurse's aide and was relieved when the doctor told me I had agoraphobia and should quit work. I don't have any skills, and I should do something, but what? I'm not that smart, I'm just a housewife." As we discussed these issues, it became clear that Jennifer's need for power was not being met. Control theory defines power as the perception that we are making a meaningful impact on the world. Jennifer clearly did not perceive that she was doing this. In fact, she thought of herself as having nothing of worth to offer. I asked her what type of work she saw herself doing. Her answer was dealing with people in a helpful way that made her feel competent and working with office and business machines, which she enjoyed. She agreed to take a Career Assessment Inventory; which might help her develop a clearer picture of what she wanted. We would continue working on this area throughout the counseling.

The second issue of Jennifer's concern had to do with her dissatisfaction in her marriage. She saw her husband as weak and ineffectual. The children did not respect him. Jennifer fluctuated between feeling sorry for him and being angry at him. Like one of the kids, he whined and pouted when he did not get what he wanted. "I only have sex with him to keep him happy. Then I feel guilty because a good wife should want to be with her husband. Then I get angry at him because he's not meeting my needs. I just want out of the relationship, which makes me feel guilty."

Then, in a quiet voice, sounding ashamed, she admitted that for two years she had been "having an affair." I asked her if she thought this was okay. She said that it was not and that she felt terribly guilty about it, but she needed some love, affection and to be cared for. I told her I was glad that she trusted me enough to tell me something that was obviously difficult for her to reveal. I expressed my concern, saying, "If having an affair is not okay for you, we have to find another way you can feel cared for. If you're doing something you believe is wrong, you'll only end up hurting yourself more in the long run." Jennifer understood that she was running counter to her values and that she was already experiencing much pain because of it.

After two hours, Jennifer and I both realized she was not satisfactorily meeting any of the four basic psychological needs. I theorized that while her anxietizing was her best attempt to meet these needs and was probably maintained because it served a purpose, it also left her needs for fun and freedom unfulfilled. By confining herself to her house, she felt trapped, with little or no fun in her life.

Prognostically, control theory tells us that the more pervasively the needs are unmet and the greater the number of unmet needs, the longer the counseling will take. The affair had been going on for two years, an indication of how long the marriage had been lacking. This was not going to be a quick case.

My hope was that Jennifer would see me as a need-fulfilling person and take me into her personal picture album. My listening intently indicated to her that she was important. By meeting regularly with someone who would consistently express caring and concern for her well-being, she could sense belonging. The weekly sessions not only got her out of the house, giving her freedom, but feeling accepted by me gave her the freedom to express herself. When I interjected humor into the sessions, Jennifer was able to relax and begin to meet her need for fun. When she became a need-fulfilling person, a deep and meaningful relationship between us could develop. Through the involvement of a relationship with a caring, responsible person, Jennifer could begin to meet her needs responsibly and get her life under control and moving in the direction she wanted. In just three weeks, Jennifer had shown some relief from her symptoms and appeared to be feeling increasingly more comfortable around me. These developments indicated to me that a need-fulfilling relationship was developing.

By the end of the first six weeks, Jennifer reported that she had cut down from three pills a day to one. She rated her anxiety as having been cut in half. She had not had any anxiety attacks and had twice gone out to dinner with her husband. Jennifer had called her lover and found that he had been transferred to another office. While somewhat saddened by the loss, she resolved not to attempt to track him down and expressed pleasure that the affair was over. She did not love him, she said. She did not really even know him. They had had sex on and off for two years, but they had never talked or shared their lives. She stated she was in love with the idea of being loved and had kidded herself that sex was love. It was a way of avoiding the pain of an unsatisfying marriage.

At the end of the sixth session, Jennifer thanked me for having gotten rid of her anxiety.

"What do you mean?" I replied.

"Well, it's not totally gone, but you've gotten rid of most of it, and I'm feeling much better."

"How did I do that?" I asked.

Jennifer was taken back. "I really don't know, but I feel better."

"Jennifer," I said, "You have to stop giving away your

power. You're not taking responsibility or credit for doing things right."

She looked quizzical and expressed that she didn't know what I meant.

"The counseling is not magical. I gave you some new information, some different ways of looking at and thinking about your life situation, but you chose to believe what I told you. You chose to keep a diary. You chose to go out to dinner with your husband, not to track down your boyfriend, to cut down your medicine, and to start going out of the house again. It's the same way that you chose to anxietize. You're really a very powerful and creative person, and you have to start taking responsibility and credit for yourself and stop giving it all away." To explain this further, I gave her a copy of *Control Theory*.

The next four sessions would conclude our first series of ten meetings and bring us up to a two-week break over the Christmas holidays. During these sessions, we went through *Control Theory* and analyzed Jennifer's life according to control theory ideas. Part of our time was spent helping Jennifer develop a realistic picture of work and a career plan, and another part focused on her marriage and a marriage plan. A third area of focus was Jennifer's failure identity, particularly what she was doing in her life and what would help her meet her needs and take her life in the direction she wanted it to go.

Our identity, which is how we perceive ourselves, is directly tied to what we do to meet our needs. Jennifer described herself and what she did as wimpy, indecisive, putting things off, a fence straddler, and a worrier. In reality therapy, it is important to help the client develop a positive identity of strength. Control theory shows us that the pathway to this is by helping the individual develop pictures of herself the way she would like to be. These pictures are connected to the individual's innate psychological needs. Throughout the counseling, I would ask Jennifer such questions as, "If you were the strong Jennifer, how would you have handled the situation differently?" and "How would you have liked to deal with it?" and "What's your ideal picture of yourself?" As is almost always the case, in counseling, Jennifer described her ideal self (the picture of a need-fulfilling Jennifer) with words that were the exact opposite of those she had used to describe herself initially. She pictured herself as strong, assertive, decisive, tackling situations directly and immediately, having firm opinions, and not worrying. When Jennifer was describing her present life situations, we would analyze how she handled them and how effective she was. Then we would use the picture of her ideal self as a guiding image for how she would have liked to deal with a given situation. The picture of the ideal self becomes the guide for helping the client travel into her imaginative creative center and develop new behaviors for dealing with situations. In this way, the client learns internally to develop new ways of dealing, which is much more powerful and effective than having the counselor suggest, advise, or teach new coping methods. The client learns to empower herself instead of becoming dependent on the counselor.

In this type of counseling work with a client, it is essential to evaluate how realistic and reasonable the pictures of the ideal self are. For example, as Jennifer expressed how she wanted to be, it became clear that she wanted to be perfect so that everyone would like her and she could meet all their needs. As we evaluated these wants together, she realized that they were not realistic and actually led to pain. Jennifer was able to relinquish this unrealistic picture and replace her wants with more rational, functional, realistic ones.

Jennifer learned through her understanding of control theory that she could not meet other people's needs. She could only meet her own needs in a way that would allow others to meet their needs through interactions with her.

Counseling was moving along smoothly. Jennifer was accepting the ideas of the book and beginning to put them into practice. She had reduced her medicine by two-thirds. Although she experienced general uneasy feelings of anxiety, she had not had an anxiety attack since our first visit and was much less anxious about leaving the house, driving, and resuming her normal activities. She was beginning to develop a realistic picture of how she would like to be. She remained ambivalent about her marriage, uncertain if she wanted to try to turn it around or leave.

It was at this time, late in November, that Jennifer's lover resurfaced. He wanted to resume the affair. Jennifer had a panic attack, which I knew was a purposeful behavior ineffectively designed to help her cope with her life not being as she wanted it. I told Jennifer this was a good opportunity to look at how the anxietizing helped her and to use control theory to analyze it. In some immediate, short-lived fashion, the anxiety must be helpful or she wouldn't continue to use it.

We discovered that Jennifer had a need-fulfilling picture of herself as a strong Catholic woman who cared for her dependent children, met the needs of her husband, and was viewed as a good Catholic daughter by her parents. She had adopted the values taught by her parents and her Church and based her pictures of herself on those teachings. By having the affair, however, she was acting in opposition to those values. Unable effectively to live out her pictures of the good Catholic girl, Jennifer paid penitence for her transgressions by guilting. This self-criticism only weakened her more and left her further away from how she wanted her life. Since she was unhappy with her husband and had been ineffective at meeting her needs in that relationship, the affair temporarily gave her a feeling of love and belonging. Now that her lover had resurfaced, she felt threatened. While it is a natural biological response to experience some anxiety as a reaction to a threat, out of the fight or flight response designed to pump adrenalin so we can preserve ourselves from danger by fighting harder or running faster, Jennifer's perceived threat was self-created. She still had the need-fulfilling picture of making love to her lover in her head, a picture that conflicted with her other pictures. This caused a serious conflict that she dealt with through anxietizing and phobicking. Not wanting to take responsibility by making a choice, she shifted the focus away from the conflict to the preoccupation of both anxietizing and "suffering" from the strange illness of agoraphobia. However, she now had a strong enough need-fulfilling relationship with me and knew enough control theory that she would never be able to anxietize in the same way again. It was becoming increasingly clear to Jennifer that not only did the anxiety function to cloud the issue and avoid reality, but it also became a way to say no to her lover. It penned her in her home so that she could not go out to meet him as often as she would like. She was also saying no to her husband and children. Because she "had agoraphobia," they were paying more attention to her, being more considerate, and placing fewer demands on her. And she was also saying no to her job: the doctor had told her to quit being a nurse's aide because of the agoraphobia, putting that decision out of her hands. Finally, she was punishing herself to pay penitence for her sins.

After we had a clearer understanding of how the anxiety worked for her, I reinforced how creative and powerful she really was. Although she might have unknowingly stumbled onto the behavior of anxietizing, it was a very powerful and creative alternative to dealing with her problem. While nurturing Jennifer's unfulfilled power need in this way, I nurtured her belonging need by accepting her noncritically and expressing my concern for her. I let her know that while I thought her anxietizing was creative and powerful in the short run, it would continue to have devastating results on her life in the long run.

Gently, matter-of-factly, I urged Jennifer to take responsibility for herself. It was her choice whether or not to have the affair. If that went against her values, she needed to accept the fact that she was choosing to do something she thought was wrong. Guilting, thinking of herself as less of a person, was not helping her. It was, in fact, hurting her. She was still having the affair, and the guilting and self-criticism were not going to change that. She just felt worse about herself and more unlovable, which increased her hunger to be loved and resulted in thoughts about turning to her lover. Jennifer was creating a vicious, self-defeating cycle.

Jennifer understood and agreed with what I was saying. She decided to take responsibility for her behavior. She chose to continue her affair, but not at the same level of frequency. Instead of actively pursuing her lover, she waited for him to call and pursue her. Sometimes she would meet him for a romantic interlude; other times she declined his offer. She chose to take a middle path. The interludes with her lover were enough to feed her need for love and belonging and, to a lesser degree, her need for power and importance. By reducing the frequency of their meetings and at times refusing him, she felt closer to her values and less guilty. More importantly, she was starting to accept responsibility for her actions. With an increased awareness of her behavior, she was choosing to respond to breaking her values in a less destructive, more effective way. Jennifer never changed her values. She still felt that what she was doing was wrong, but she took responsibility for her actions and did not try to avoid her choice through misery and painful behaviors.

The affair continued for about six more months, and we talked about it from time to time in our sessions. I maintained the same control theory stance: it's your attempt to meet your needs; it runs against your values; you need to take responsibility for your behavior, and I'll help you try to find better ways to fill your needs. The affair ended for good when her lover was transferred to an out-of-state branch of his company. Jennifer handled it very well. Their interludes had become less and less frequent and she was meeting her needs much more substantially in other parts of her life, so the impact of the loss was virtually insignificant. Jennifer expressed relief that the affair was over and stated that she never wanted to make the same mistake again. It was too seductive and entrapping: it felt good at the time, but the long-term effects were too painful.

I was glad for Jennifer when the situation resolved itself. It had been a very painful choice to continue the affair, and I felt for her. As her counselor and a meaningful person with whom she was involved, I would have preferred that she had had the strength to end the affair immediately. Knowing control theory, however, I had to accept the fact that I could not make choices for her. I realized that although Jennifer was not doing what I wanted, I should not attach a negative value to that. My role as her counselor was not to control her and get her to do what I believed was best, but to help her learn to take the responsibility for meeting her needs by making the most effective choices she could.

We concluded our first series of ten sessions by focusing on Jennifer's specific concerns about how to deal with expected hassles during the upcoming holidays. This marked an important shift in the counseling process. Until then, the focus of counseling had been on general areas—the affair, her anxiety, a career plan, the ideas of control theory, and her identity. There had been a symptom reduction, along with a reduction in medication and an overall increase in functioning. Now Jennifer was beginning to look at the day-to-day specifics of her life, finally taking a close look at how she could live her life differently.

We continued this process after a two-week break. Jennifer reported that she was pleasantly surprised with how the holidays had gone, and we then picked up where we had left off.

In our sessions we used what I call a reality therapy/control theory method of problem solving and brainstorming. Jennifer would present me with a situation that was frustrating for her. Knowing that the feeling of frustration was a signal which tells us that the situation did not go as she wanted it to, I would ask her what she had wanted to happen. We would then develop a clear picture of how she wanted the situation. Next, we would review what was in her control in this situation and what was out of her control. This served as a reminder of a central teaching of control theory; we have direct control only over our own actions and thoughts. It was important for Jennifer to be continually reminded that, at best, we can influence others by acting upon them in ways which might increase the probability that, in fulfilling their needs, they will behave as we want them to, but we never have direct control over other people. After reviewing this central principle and determining if her picture of how she wanted the situation to go was realistic, I would ask her what she did about the situation. At this point I would break down the specific components of her total behavior: feeling, thinking, and acting. I would then ask her to make a value judgment about what she was doing. Was her behavior helpful? Did she handle herself in what she considered the right or proper way? Did her behavior take her in the direction she wanted to go?

If she judged her behavior not to have been effective, we would use the creative brainstorming process. We would suspend any value judgments, relax, and through a free associative type process, get in touch with the inner creativity within us and generate and verbally spin out alternative behaviors. I would write down the different choices and then we would start evaluating them and decide on a plan for how to use the different approach when a similar situation would arise.

I would always suggest that Jennifer could anxietize as an alternative, using the verb form to identify more correctly what Jennifer was doing. Using a noun to refer to an emotional action identifies it as an entity separate from the individual. By suggesting that Jennifer could anxietize as an alternative, that choice was clearly kept in her awareness and placed as a solution under her control. She was responsible for her behavior and had a sense of ownership of anxietizing, which reduced the probability that she would utilize it. I would actually say to Jennifer, "Let's take a look at how anxietizing might help you." We would review the power of anxietizing, such as enabling her to avoid doing work, getting her husband not to make demands on her, and keeping her anger under control. Anxietizing is effective because others frequently allow themselves to be controlled by it. However, we also discussed the long-term negative consequences of this behavior.

Again, this stance accepts Jennifer and points out what a creative person she is. It changes the picture of herself as a weak, ineffectual person into the picture of a strong, effective person with control in her hands. It diminishes the perception that anxietizing is scary. Viewing anxietizing as a choice reduces the fear of losing control because the emphasis is continually placed on the choice and her control over it.

In the comfort of the session, Jennifer was able to laugh at the idea of anxietizing. The ability to laugh at herself was an expression of self-acceptance and a crucial step toward a happier life. This is especially important for a person like Jennifer, who worries and takes life too seriously. Fun is one of our basic needs, and counseling should include moments of fun, laughter, and humor.

We also began to use control theory to gain a greater understanding of why and how others in Jennifer's life behaved. Jennifer began to see that she allowed her husband to control her with his moping and whining. When her husband wanted Jennifer to do something she did not want to do, he would resort to using a variety of moping, whining, pietizing, pleading, sulking type little-boy behaviors. She would respond to his childish behaviors by guilting, telling herself that she was doing something wrong as a wife if her husband was unhappy. We discovered that Jennifer pictured husband-wife relationships unrealistically. She had an idealistic picture of a husband who was always happy with his wife. This picture corresponded with her need for love and belonging. She also had an unrealistic picture of a wife always able to make her husband happy. This picture corresponded to Jennifer's need for power and importance. Consequently, when Jennifer's husband moped and whined, it conflicted with her picture of the husband-wife relationship. She would naturally experience frustration and behave by guilting, which she used to convince herself to give in and do what her husband wanted. Her husband would then temporarily stop whining and moping, which corresponded to Jennifer's picture of being able to make her husband happy. However, always giving in to her husband resulted in a loss of freedom and led to a feeling of being trapped and controlled. This conflicted with another of her love and belonging need pictures about marriage being a fifty-fifty proposition. Jennifer responded with anger and played the martyr role, which did nothing to enhance her own identity and resulted in increased discomfort and frustration with the marriage.

Jennifer realized that she was not responsible for her husband's emotions and that she was allowing herself to be emotionally blackmailed. When she wanted to place all the blame on her husband, I quickly countered by explaining that he was not holding a gun to her head: he was doing the best he could at the time to get what he wanted, just as she was doing by anxietizing and even by entering into this relationship pattern. She was able to see this and agree that the martyr role was her way of staying in control and meeting her power need. But in the long run, it had negative results.

Jennifer continued to evaluate the pictures in her head and came to the conclusion that they were unrealistic. We developed more realistic pictures of her marriage, which resulted in a decreased frustration. She also evaluated her guilting and

sentenced for rape or child molestation. He presented the image of a tough guy always ready to fight, in a group or as an individual, complete with prison-made weapons. Powerless and a victim of violence as a child, he did not trust or relate well to men. He used his good looks and charm with women to meet his need for power. His legendary reputation as a lady's man also gave him indirect power over men. Through letters, collect phone calls, and visits, Everett had as many as four women at a time believing that he loved them and would marry them upon his release. They, in turn, provided him with visits, attention, and varying degrees of financial support.

In the spring of 1985, as a resource teacher/counselor for behaviorally ineffective students, I took two groups of high-risk juveniles to an inmate-run program at the maximum security Massachusetts Correctional Institution at Walpole. This program, called "Point Blank," was conducted by psychologically screened inmates who had undergone a specific training program. The inmates led a tour of the prison, including cell blocks, library, educational facilities, hospital unit, new-man section, chow hall, and auditorium. A correctional staff member was present at all times during the three-hour program. The purpose of the program was not to verbally assault or intimidate, but rather to talk to the youths in a civilized manner and to let them know the realities of life in prison. This field trip, or one like it, is offered at my public high school annually. High-risk students are identified by concerned staff members and are asked if they would like to participate. Once parental permission has been obtained, rules, expectations, and guidelines for the experience are set up in a preliminary session. After the trip, there is a feedback and follow-up session, which usually results in the participants maintaining informal involvement with me or other faculty who attended.

After completion of the program, I write letters to all four of the inmates who conducted the program, both to express my appreciation for their efforts and to make them aware of the positive impact it had on the young men. Everett, who was one of the four inmates, responded to my letter and the friendship began. Through letters and visits, trust developed slowly, and he began to take some risks that involved sharing fears and goals and being honest about his behaviors.

Everett was granted parole to a halfway house in the Boston area in July 1985. He called every other day to let me know of his adjustment. Within a week, he had run, violating the stipulations of his parole. Clearly he was not ready and not in effective control of his life. When I had not heard from him for a couple of days, I called the director of the program, who knew of our friendship. I learned that Everett had run and then had called the halfway house and apologized for letting them down. I sensed his failure and felt powerless. Discouraged and frustrated, I chose depressing thoughts and feelings. But I knew that what I really wanted was to help Everett gain more effective control over his life: my depressing was not achieving that goal. Refusing to give up on him, I chose to do something positive. I wrote him a letter expressing my caring and my belief in his potential to be a responsible member of society. I sent the letter to his grandmother to give to him because she was a need-fulfilling person to him, and I knew that sooner or later he would be in contact with her. I had chosen to do all that I was in control of. The rest was up to Everett.

In August 1985, Everett called me, told me he had received the letter, and asked if we could talk. When we met, I saw and heard that he was tired, haggard, and afraid. I listened to him talk about what he had been doing for the past month. I asked him what he wanted, and he answered, "To stop running." I then asked if what he was choosing to do was getting him to stop running. He said no, but that he would not choose to go back to being locked up again. His plan was to go South, stay with relatives, and work for a moving company. We discussed pitfalls and potential consequences of being "on the run." I expressed my concern and caring for him and my belief in him. I did not agree with his plan, but I respected his right to meet and fulfill his need for freedom with his own pictures. He expressed his trust in me and our involvement and asked if he could call me once a week to let me know how he was doing. I said yes, hugged him, and left. Instinctively I knew that he would turn himself in because I believed in what he said he really wanted.

He wanted not to run, which meant he had to fulfill legal obligations and face the consequence of parole violation, which was jail. He phoned me for two weeks, then he turned himself in. His grandmother called, told me what had happened, and asked if I would work with him. I agreed.

Once back in the correctional system, Everett made choices that moved him from the Concord Classification Institution to Gardner Medium Security to Maximum Security at Walpole to the 10 Block Segregation Unit within Walpole for aggressive disruptive behavior. Individuals whose behaviors are viewed as threats to security are sent by classification boards to institutions that have progressively more controls. Everett started out being classified to a medium-security facility with an open campus. His behavioral choices while there resulted in his being classified to maximum security, which is housed in one facility, although there is movement within the confines of the prison. The segregation unit, the most restrictive security, is almost total confinement to one's individual cell. The time frame within which all this occurred was from September 1985 to March 1986. During this time, I had weekly contact with Everett, refusing to criticize him. We discussed the natural and logical consequences of his behavioral choices within the framework of a correctional setting and how they related to getting him what he wanted, which was release from prison and freedom. We identified his total behavior as follows:

- *Doing*—Assaulting inmates over disagreements; attacking child molesters and rapists; confronting correctional officers—verbal defiance; making shanks (prison-made knives)
- *Thinking*—Hate, anger, bitterness, failure, fear
- *Feeling*—Powerless and defeated
- *Physiology*—Tense, agitated, on edge

We focused on what he was choosing to do—the doing component of total behavior. Value judgments did not come easily. In fact, initially, they did not come at all. Again, I felt frustration over his choices since returning, but I refused to give up. I had given my word, and a person's word, especially in prison, is what he or she stands for. I sent Everett a copy of *Control Theory* to read. He responded enthusiastically and reported that it made a lot of sense. (That book, along with *Positive Addiction,*[1] has since become very popular within the system.)

Everett clearly articulated that in prison none of his basic needs was being met. In that particular external world or environment, he perceived that he had no power, freedom, or fun and was not loved or cared for. He still wanted out, but he was not at all confident of his ability to make it. He reported that the pictures in his head were jumbled, and all he really knew was how to survive in prison. He finally had earned his parole and had blown it, letting down his family, the people at the halfway house who had gone to bat for him, me, and himself. Not having made it on the run, he was back in the place he hated most but knew best. Everett was choosing classic "give-up" behaviors. He was "aggressing" to meet his need for power within the system. Our positive involvement and perseverance empowered him to make the following statement: "I want to gain better control over my life. What I'm doing isn't working. It's only gotten me to the most restrictive security within the system. I don't know how to go about this. Will you help me? I don't trust anyone here." I said that I would help him.

Up until this time, I had been asking Everett constantly what he really wanted. I must have asked equally often if what he was choosing to do was working. He continued to want his freedom. His evaluation of what he was doing ran from making excuses to recognizing that it was not working. But he was not willing to change and do things differently until he had "bottomed out" and ended up in segregation—further away from his picture of freedom than ever.

We got down to work. I was not concerned about parole or dealing with society at this point since Everett was in isolation and locked up twenty-three hours a day. The focus had to be on small, positive behavioral choices. Since the basic needs for power, freedom and love and belonging were too hot and in-

[1]William Glasser, *Positive Addiction* (New York: Harper & Row, 1972).

tense to work on, I chose to explore the need for fun. Given the obvious limitations of his environment, I asked what pictures he had in his head to meet his need for fun. He responded that he liked to work out, read, and draw. I asked if he was willing to operate differently for a week, and he said yes. We made a plan by which he would read and draw while in his cell behind the solid door. In the hour out of his cell, he would work out away from other inmates. I sent him some books, a drawing pad, and pencils. He committed to the plan with a handshake, and we made arrangements for him to call me collect midweek to let me know how it was going. Instead of being aggressive with other inmates and disruptive with correctional officers, Everett chose to isolate himself positively within his isolation.

One of Everett's first drawings (see page 70) typifies the drawing of a caged person with no needs being met.

The plan went well. After that first week in 10 Block, Everett had no disciplinary reports for any major or minor infractions and was recommended for 9 Block, where there was a little more freedom. He got three hours out of his cell every other day and no solid-door isolation. His plan was to continue reading and drawing. Now he chose to play basketball with other inmates. We talked about the potential for conflict, but he decided he could walk away and use his head to handle a problem instead of his fists or a weapon.

He continued to check in with me by phone midweek, and we evaluated his plan when I saw him every weekend. I lavished him with positive reinforcement and encouragement. Everett would just smile and shake his head. We continued to talk about his total behavior. We looked at what and how he was doing and thinking differently, how he was feeling, and the changes in his physical state.

- *Doing*—Reading, drawing, working out, playing basketball
- *Thinking*—More positively, hopefully, skeptically
- *Feeling*—Less angry and defeated, a little successful
- *Physiology*—Less tense

As we added to his plan, we brainstormed pitfalls and how he could choose to handle them. If he did not feel he could do it, then it was not included in the plan. We added two college correspondence courses: psychology and business. Everett did well in both. He was enjoying what he was doing and having some fun as well as success. He was also beginning to recognize that he had more power and freedom over his choices, if not his environment. He knew that his grandmother cared, and he was also beginning to see me as a need-fulfilling person. He was slowly getting stronger and feeling more effectively in control of his own life.

Everett spent thirty days in 9 Block and was recommended by the department for the Phase 2 Segregation Program at the medium-security facility at Norfolk. There Everett added to his plan and participated in a substance-abuse program and worked as a houseman in the kitchen, serving and cleaning for three meals a day. The substance-abuse program was a support group led by correctional staff for those inmates who were serving sentences on drug-related crimes. The program dealt with how they would handle drugs and alcohol on the streets and encouraged their involvement in Alcoholics Anonymous and/or Narcotics Anonymous when released from the segregation program. Everett went for three months without a disciplinary report. During the previous five years, the longest he had ever gone without such a report was one week.

Yahoo! Things seemed to be falling into place. I wondered if all this could be too good to be true and too easy to be possible. Everett had spent four and half months expending his energies positively. In three months, his contract in the Phase 2 Segregation Program would be up, and he would be classified to a medium-security facility in the general population. We had already begun to talk about the pitfalls of handling larger numbers of interactions.

Segregation	*Population*
Twenty inmates	Sixty in a block and six hundred to twelve hundred in all, depending on the institution
Small number of officers (the same staff)	Large numbers of officers who change frequently
Small, segregated recreation	Entire population in the yard
Twenty men at meals	Chow hall for hundreds
Lock-up time	Free to move about prison unless doing isolation time

Everett had done well in the segregation units. General population was a scary prospect. He had an "image" to uphold as a tough guy who was always ready. I continued to ask him what he wanted. This particularly annoyed him when he would give me excuses instead of a value judgment, and I would calmly ask him again what he wanted.

MARY: Everett, what do you really want?
EVERETT: I want my parole, my freedom, to be out of prison.
MARY: Has what you've done in population gotten you that?
EVERETT: No, it only got me D.S.U. (Department Segregation Unit).
MARY: What are you willing to do to earn your parole and freedom?
EVERETT: Whatever I have to do, but it's hard from in here.
MARY: Everett, you're not alone. Together we can figure out a way. Look what you've managed to do so far!

As it turned out, we did not have to plan for general population right away. As a result of an incident in the Phase 2 program, Everett went back to the maximum-security 10 Block at Walpole. He had been playing his radio loudly, and an officer told him to turn it down. When Everett refused, the officer returned with four other officers. They stormed the cell, physically cuffed and shackled him, and then moved him to Walpole 10 Block. Everett's perception was that it had not been necessary to take the radio or to "run" in on him. The officers could have asked him to lower the radio some more or even to shut it off. It was a power issue. I asked if the radio had been worth the price. He thought about it and said yes and no. No, because he was right back where he had started four months ago. Yes, because of the principle of his dignity and manhood. His perception was that for years, as a kid, he had been beaten while things were taken from him. As a young adult, he had fought for himself and what he believed in. Everett also perceived that even though this was a setback, he had handled the conflict with the officer more effectively than in the past. He had not been physically assaultive nor verbally abusive. From his perspective, this was growth. He recognized that in the long run he was farther away from his picture of freedom, but he had moved through the segregation system once before and was certain he could do it again. In retrospect, Everett felt more confident that he could effectively handle isolation than the challenges of population. He was in no way confident that he could face his "brothers" and the inmate population with "this control theory stuff" and still maintain his credibility as a solid con.

So we started from square one—or did we? The place was the same, but the total behavior was different.

- *Doing*—Reading, drawing, working out, college courses, writing
- *Thinking*—Control, basic needs, pictures
- *Feeling*—Quiet, content, hopeful, slightly confident
- *Physiology*—Relaxed

It was now August 1986, and Everett was scheduled to spend the next 107 days doing isolation time. An individual's record in the correctional system is cumulative. Disciplinary reports are reviewed by disciplinary boards that find the inmates guilty or not guilty as charged. Guilty pleas by inmates or guilty verdicts by the board result in disciplinary sanctions such as loss of good time (automatically calculated at sentencing meaning mandatory time of sentence—time is added during incarceration for disciplinary sanctions), isolation time, recommendation for reclassification to higher security, or a referral to the segregation unit for a hearing. The sanction can also be a combination of the above. All the incidents that had occurred since September 1985, when Everett returned to the system, resulted in isolation time, loss of good time off his sentence, and a segregation referral. His behavioral choices resulted in an accumulation of 107 days isolation, which an inmate can be scheduled to do at any time. When Everett returned to Walpole, he was on the ISO (prison jargon for isolation time) sheet. Isolation time in 10 Block consisted of twenty-three hours behind a solid closed door, no television or radio, one hour out a day, and a shower every third day. Food was passed through a slot in the door. He would do fifteen days straight, have one day off, and start fifteen days again until it was done. In the beginning, and up until about three quarters of the way through, he would tell me that he was benefiting from the quiet time alone. His pictures were becoming clearer. He continued to reiterate his goal of freedom and parole and his plan to continue choosing responsible doing behaviors. "I've finally begun to realize that by my choices, I've allowed the system to win and have power over me. I've fed into the power and control issues, and I've been the only loser so far. I'm tired of being here. I'm still uptight about being a responsible citizen, but I really am beginning to think and believe I can do it."

After about seventy-five days of isolation time, Everett began to talk about feeling tense and uptight. He was pacing in his cell and thinking about the consequences of "ripping out" (meaning, destroying as much of his cell as he could—ripping toilets and sinks from the wall, for example, are not uncommon). We spent some time on the phone on a day off from isolation.

MARY: Everett, it sounds like you are not feeling in effective control of this isolation time. What can you do?

EVERETT: I can rip out and get rid of my tension, anger, and hostility.

MARY: Is that what you want?

EVERETT: No. I want out of D.S.U. and here.

MARY: If you choose to rip out and that choice is yours, will that help?

EVERETT: No.

MARY: What else can we figure out to do?

EVERETT: I need a break. The isolation time is getting to me.

MARY: What are you doing to handle the isolation?

EVERETT: Reading, sit-ups, push-ups, drawing, walking, sleeping, writing. For the first time in a long time, I'm choosing to do the right things so I can get out of here. The screws [cops] never recognize or tell me I'm changing or doing well. They just keep throwing the past in my face. Why don't you just give up on me? I'll never make it.

MARY: First of all, Everett, I'm not giving up on you and that's my choice. I really believe in you and your potential. I know you can do whatever you have to do to get what you want. If you have managed to survive all you have in your life both in and out of prison, then you have the strength to hang in with this now. However, the choice and power are yours. It's up to you and what you really want! What do you want?

EVERETT: You know what I want. I want out of segregation and earn my parole.

MARY: Has what you've been doing been working for you?

EVERETT: Yes. I've gotten no D-reports, and I'm staying out of trouble.

MARY: Are you willing to continue what you've been doing that's been so awesome?

EVERETT: Yes.

MARY: Given the framework of 10 Block and the system, what can we come up with to relieve the isolation, tension, and frustration?

EVERETT: Besides ripping out?

MARY: Yes. What are the options, if any?

EVERETT: The captain is not too bad a guy. Maybe I could talk to him.

MARY: Will you?

EVERETT: Yes.

MARY: What will you say?

EVERETT: I'll tell him I'm starting to lose it with all this isolation, and I'm really feeling like going off. I'll ask if he can use his pull to suspend it for a couple of weeks.

MARY: How possible is it for him to do that?

EVERETT: He could if he wanted to.

MARY: When will you ask him?

EVERETT: Tomorrow morning when he comes on duty.

MARY: What about ripping out?

EVERETT: No. I'll do some more push-ups, and I'll get a shower tonight so I'll get out of here.

MARY: Suppose he says no?

EVERETT: I'll deal with it.

MARY: How?

EVERETT: I'll write down all my angry feelings and send them to you.

MARY: Okay. Anything else?

EVERETT: That's all I can manage now. Just talking it out helped, but if I go back in ISO tomorrow, it'll be another fifteen days before we can talk again.

MARY: If he can't suspend your ISO time for awhile, could he shorten it?

EVERETT: I'll ask.

MARY: So you're going to ask to have a couple of weeks suspension of ISO first and then shorten the days?

EVERETT: Yes.

MARY: I'm proud of you. You worked this out really well.

It worked out that the captain went to bat for Everett and suspended his isolation time indefinitely while he worked to transfer him to 9 Block, where there was no isolation. The captain commented that he had noticed how well Everett was doing and felt that he deserved to be where there were fewer restrictions. We talked, and Everett was pleased that doing things the "right" way finally paid off. He was transferred to 9 Block, and he continued to do well. He stuck with his previous basic plan, and it worked. Throughout his time there, we continued evaluating the plan, adding to it, and talking about what he was choosing to do differently and how he was feeling and thinking differently. Everett's drawings were changing with his success: a picture he drew at that time is reproduced on page 77.

In June 1987, at the segregation review hearing, Everett was given a choice. He could finish out his D.S.U. time in 9 Block and then be classified to population at Walpole Maximum Security, or he could recontract with the Phase 2 program out of which he had been shipped for the radio incident. Completion of the Phase 2 program would almost certainly guarantee a classification to a medium-security general population. It was Everett's choice to do Phase 2 again, not because he was fearful of handling population, but rather to prove to himself that he could complete the Phase 2 program successfully.

Everett went to the Phase 2 program at Norfolk and con-

tinued to be free of D-reports. He earned parole from his original state sentence. But he had a county sentence to serve as a result of a charge and conviction that had occurred in 1985, when he was on the run just after we met. Together we created an environment of hope and the beginning of a more successful identity. Everett continues to be incarcerated, but in a less restrictive, general population environment. He had handled the ups and downs in a more consistent and responsible way. He is currently preparing himself to be released in several months. If released, he will continue to be on parole for his state sentence for eight more years. Everett has begun to take more effective control over his own life and is looking toward the future in a positive way. This story is not over. The ending is not yet written. Let me share with you Everett's perception of his specific process for change.

> Before meeting Mary Corry and being introduced to reality therapy and control theory, I had served approximately four years in the Massachusetts Prison System—with one of the worst disciplinary records of its history. I received, in these four years, close to 250 Disciplinary Reports ranging from serious assaults on staff members as well as other inmates to minor infractions of the rules and regulations. This breaks down to about one or two tickets weekly.
>
> Two years ago I met Mary Corry, who gave me Dr. Bill Glasser's *Control Theory* book to read. She worked with me personally through some very difficult and trying times for us both. Many of those times I just wanted to give up, but Ms. Corry wouldn't hear of it and she pushed that much harder for me to use R.T. and C.T. to make a plan to get what I wanted and stick by it. Gradually, the D-reports I received were less serious and less frequent. I started thinking about what my actions would result in, rather than just reacting. Eventually, it became second nature to think through all situations automatically before reacting to a situation. I have now cut my D-reports down to one every four months—approximately three a year as compared to my previous sixty-two a year.
>
> Mary Corry told me when we first met that she believed in me and my ability to be someone besides a ripout tough guy. Through her guidance and continued work in R.T. and C.T., I now believe in myself and my ability to control my future.
>
> Everett, June 4, 1987

DR. GLASSER'S COMMENTS ON "VALUE JUDGMENTS SOMETIMES DON'T COME EASILY"

Our prisons are probably the fastest growing of all our institutions. One reason is the large number of people like Everett. At the time Mary Corry met him, he had been in prison for eight years, one third of his life. If left to his own devices, as most prisoners are, he would stand a good chance of spending most of his life behind bars. Having met Mary Corry, however, Everett has a reasonable chance of being able to find a life outside of prison.

One of the present trends in criminology is to believe that men in prison cannot be helped, a concept that I strongly reject and one that Mary Corry proves wrong conclusively. Not only was Everett helped in prison, but much of that help took place while he was isolated in segregation. There, difficult as it was, he worked with Mary Corry and began to learn the new behaviors that would eventually lead to his release.

Strange as this may sound, what Everett and those like him in our prisons have to learn is to depress, both in and, even more important, out of prison. Because all of us live in a crowded society and have a need to belong, we have to learn to get along with other people, many of whom are not easy to get along with. To do this, we must have a quick, effective way to restrain the anger we feel immediately when we are frustrated by another person. Depressing for a few vital minutes, or in extreme instances up to a week, is the most common way we do this. While it is painful, depressing restrains us verbally and immobilizes us physically. This gives us needed time to pull ourselves together and figure out how to deal with the frustration in a better way than lashing out in anger or continuing to depress. Used for too long, of course, depressing is counterproductive, but used for a short time, usually for less than an hour until we find a better way, it is an essential social behavior. If we did not depress, we could not survive as a society.

It is not that Everett did not know how to depress; he depressed much of the time in jail, especially in solitary confinement. But he had chosen not to use depressing often enough when he was frustrated by people, which happened frequently. Unwilling to depress when he was unable to figure out how to satisfy his needs, Everett frequently lashed out in anger. It was his angering that put him in jail, and if he had not learned to do something like depressing until he found a better behavior, he would have stayed in jail for most of his life.

Unfortunately, jails are filled with people like Everett, and they are especially difficult places for such people to choose the total behavior of depressing. In close, unavoidable contact with frustrated people who anger much more easily than they depress, many prisoners find themselves in a vicious cycle: the more they anger, the more they are incarcerated with other angry people, and the harder and harder it becomes to do anything else.

In control theory terms, Everett had not found any goal that he was willing to put into his special world and also willing to work for without angering. It was not that he had no effective behaviors, but that he did not have enough. He did not even know what to want that would give him the sense of the power, love, fun, or freedom he needed.

Everett had lived his life like a thirsty man who desperately wanted to get rid of the pain of the thirst, but who did not know that water, which was actually all around him, would relieve it. He had spent his life thrashing out at the world as if he knew there was something out there that he needed, but he did not have any idea of what it was or how to get it. Working with Everett, Mary Corry was starting from scratch. When she met him, it was as if he were a newborn. He knew how to anger but not much else. What she did was analogous to adopting and raising this newborn, teaching him how to do better than angering when he was frustrated.

At the end of this case study, Everett has probably reached adolescence. He still has a long way to go, but by the time he writes the letter that ends the case study, he knows what his needs are, he has some idea of what will satisfy them, and he has learned a variety of behaviors that are now working in prison to give him the beginnings of effective control over his life.

When Ms. Corry had made enough contact with him so that he was able to put her into his special world as a need-satisfying person, she gave him a copy of *Control Theory*. It pleases me that he was willing to make the effort to read it. From it, he was able to learn about his basic needs, the pictures in his special world, and then say to Mary Corry, "I want to gain better control over my life. What I'm doing here isn't working. It's only gotten me to the most restrictive security within the system. I don't know how to go about this. Will you help me? I don't trust anyone here."

What Everett then did, with her help, was to learn how to live with much less angering. Without her care and concern, he had no chance at all; with it, he still had to learn how to do what infants usually learn in the first few years of life. Of course, Everett was not an infant but a grown, intelligent, and talented (to judge from his art work) human being. He had a series of primitive behaviors, fighting and manipulating especially, that he used to gain a sense of power. But the power he gained did not last because it was only power for the sake of power: it did not lead to any lasting or responsible goal. If he had not gone beyond this and been able to find first one goal and then others that became pictures in his special world, he would never have been able to make any progress.

The first goal he actually admitted to himself was to establish a relationship with Ms. Corry. She became to him very much like Annie Sullivan was to Helen Keller. (I use this example because, to me, what Annie Sullivan did instinctively was to employ with skill and patience the ideas of control theory in a reality therapy setting.) As is clearly shown, Everett slowly began to learn to satisfy his needs with more effective total behaviors. Then, almost without warning, after he had gained a little ground, he made a sudden retreat from responsibility. He did not depress, which would have given him a chance to continue his progress, but regressed to "power for the sake of power," which had been all he had known for so many years. Again he was placed in isolation.

This time, however, due to his acceptance of Mary Corry, he decided that he did not want to show the world how tough he was. He began to figure out a series of behaviors to use instead of the "ripping out" angering that he had employed so often in the past. At this point, what comes across to me is the intense pain of Everett's effort to do his time in isolation successfully. Along with all else he was doing—reading, drawing, working out—he was also depressing to keep the angering restrained. He was able to do this because now he had not only an overall goal to get out but, more important, a day-to-day goal to show Ms. Corry that he could make it.

Prison is a tough place not only because of the other inmates, but also because of the guards. Many guards find it satisfies their need for power to assert their authority on the job. In the radio incident, Everett lost the power struggle with the guards and was placed back in segregation. This was an especially tough test because he had just gotten out. With the help of Ms. Corry and the kindness of a sympathetic captain, however, he passed the test. Here we see how painful depressing really is. To keep his anger restrained, he had to depress so strongly that he finally came to the conclusion that he just could not keep it up. The picture of a man struggling with depressing to avoid "ripping out" as he spent what seemed an eternity in isolation comes through powerfully in Mary Corry's description of this critical period in Everett's life.

Unfortunately, psychiatrists cannot predict the future. I can only hope that Everett has found enough effective behaviors (his art will help him if he uses it) to avoid angering when he is frustrated, as he surely will be. Going into the community at age twenty-four with few resources is hard for anyone; for a man leaving prison, it is much more difficult. Everett started further back than almost anyone I have ever heard about, but with excellent help he moved a long way forward.

We heard from Mary Corry that six months after he was paroled from prison, Everett was doing well.

5

A Priceless Gift

*A Child Succeeds in School Despite
Serious Problems at Home while
Her School Counselor Learns from
Her about the Strength of the
Human Spirit*

MEGAN G. FATES

T HE COURT awarded ten-year-old Rachel and her
little brother to their father, and the small group
in the judge's chambers felt relief. It had been a
long six years, but all four members of this unusual family unit
were now going to be able to take control of their lives—individually and collectively.

I first heard of Rachel through the high school secretary. For
her and for many other local people in this resort town at the
end of nowhere, the police scanner is an integral part of life. The
fire, police, ambulance, ministers, priests, harbor master, high-
way patrolmen, and so on all rely on these messages in order
to help their fellow citizens. Of course, this is also the source of
news and gossip in a sleepy winter town of fewer than five
thousand people.

For school personnel, the police scanner explains many of
the behavioral aberrations that cross the academic threshold.

The secretary's husband (also our lock-up man) had responded to the call that a small girl had been walking around town with nothing on but a raincoat in the early morning hours. (The lock-up man is the town employee responsible for jail security. The "jail" is a locked room with windows and toilet facilities in the police station. The lock-up man usually works nights. The next morning the "locked-up" persons are transported fifty miles by armed policemen and police car to the district court for arraignment. Because of the small size of each local town, the lock-up man is paid hourly as needed.)

Maybe, I thought, the little girl was an elementary student and I could "help" her. I had never heard of Rachel, but a few phone calls later I found out that she was four years old, that she lived with her parents, who were not married, and that her mother was pregnant.

Referrals had been made to appropriate outside agencies. I knew that in September, when she entered school, she would legally be "mine." When we hear of such things in the special-needs department, we have an inside saying. We tell the secretary, "Take out another folder." This time a fat one was forthcoming.

I said and thought no more of Rachel until the following year, when the perceptive and experienced kindergarten teacher asked to see me. Although she had exhausted her bag of tricks, Rachel cried frequently in class and was not adapting to the pre-readiness program. Several appointments had been made with Rachel's mother, but she had cancelled them. Telephone conferences, with a crying baby in the background, were difficult. On the positive side, the teacher stated, Rachel seemed bright, was liked by her peers, and did beautiful art work.

One unbreakable rule in our school is that no child can receive extra services or be tested without written parental permission. Because school (any school) seems threatening to so many of our young parents, I have made it a practice to meet some parents elsewhere: the donut shop, the beach, their homes, our community center, and in several cases, the church parish hall. By choosing an alternative spot, I find it sometimes seems easier to focus on helping the child.

I met Katherine, who was going to turn the knob on so many of my values and emotions, at the wharf coffee shop. She had taken a part-time job there to earn some extra money. Her baby son was playing quietly in a corner. She ordered coffee for both of us, and I let her pay for it. (Many years before, a parent had rightfully complained that I never let her do anything for me. I learned from her to let parents do such things for and with me.)

Katherine was a large, handsome woman with an alive and intelligent demeanor. Born in South America, she spoke several languages. Rachel had been born when she was sixteen, meaning that Katherine was now twenty-one. She had been living with Tony, the father of her children, since she was fifteen. She spoke of their financial difficulties as a real source of problems. They were not able to afford a car, babysitters, or any of the extras of life. She preferred not to be on welfare. However, she was on a waiting list for subsidized housing. This is a common story in Provincetown. Summer resort living makes buying a home impossibly expensive, and year-round rentals are unavailable. Many people are forced to find seasonal rentals and move every May and October. Summer arrangements for child care are difficult as parents strive to make enough money from the tourist economy to carry them through the next winter's bills and pay off last winter's bills. Children are often on the streets at all hours of the night; Rachel had been no exception. Unfortunately, welfare regulations further complicated the finances of women like Katherine. They are in a Catch-22 if they report that they live with their children's father.

I spoke to Katherine of Rachel and her problems in kindergarten. She had already recognized problems at home. Rachel cried easily for no apparent reason and was very moody. Katherine voiced concern about Rachel's poor self-image. I asked if I might work with Rachel and see if we could help her. I would need Katherine's assistance. She agreed to both.

My plan was first to spend time in the classroom. I would observe Rachel, especially her interactions with others, her daily work habits, and her response to direction. Next, when both Rachel and I were comfortable with each other, I would do some formalized testing. Katherine gave written permission, and I said I would get back to her late the next month.

My job entails myriad kinds of psychological interaction with children and their families from preschool through twelfth grade. It is always a treat to spend half an hour daily with the younger children, and also a good reminder that this is how the high school youngsters I see began in school.

I sat with Rachel in the classroom, observed her beautiful art work, and talked to her about the different toys she brought regularly to school. I sang kindergarten songs, played kindergarten games, and clapped for kindergarten running teams. By the end of the week, Rachel and I were friends. I asked her if she would like to work with me the following week and was not surprised by her response: "When?" and "Can I bring my doll?"

Through testing and observation, I found Rachel to be a child who wanted to do well, who tried hard to please adults, but who drifted easily from the subject at hand. I also found her to be a child who needed to be structured and focused. Otherwise, her own interests intervened. She would talk about the doll she brought (which was soon renamed Megan), ask about television shows she had seen the night before, or question the well-being of her little brother. All of this information and concern would make good meat for counseling, and I put it on my back burner. Meanwhile, I needed some good clinical testing, and for the moment I concentrated on getting the data I needed.

I gave my standard battery of tests:

1. Wechsler Intelligence Test-Revised (WISC-R)
2. Bender-Gestalt with Koppitz scoring
3. Wide-Range Achievement Test (WRAT)
4. Drawings—house, tree, person

Later I would update these with a Rorschach, additional achievement testing (the WRAT was being revised), readministered Bender-Gestalt, and continued drawings.

Visual motor/perceptual testing and related intelligence subtests showed Rachel to be in the bottom twentieth percentile for her age. However, intelligence testing showed her to have a full-scale score of 125. Many of the subtest scores were in the superior ranges, but those subtests involving motor/integration and time constraints lessened her overall score. The 125 IQ was only a baseline indication of her ability. And it did not measure her creative and imaginary talents.

Rachel had no idea of her many strengths. Her self-portrait was of a small child who cried a lot, was "dumb," and could not do well in school. She was also overwhelmed by her problems at home and felt responsible for them.

There would be so much we could do and work on together. I felt we had made that important bond for therapy. Rachel was creative, verbal, and knew she wanted things to be different. Also, I liked her mother, despite Katherine's difficulties. I felt confident I could make a difference in Rachel's life and enjoy it. I had many handles to work on.

For an Individual Educational Plan to be written and implemented, all those involved with the student's education must meet together, go over any findings, and come up with a suitable program. In order for it to be valid, both parent and appropriate school personnel must agree and sign the now-legal document regarding the new school program for the child. This group of people is called a team. A series of progress reports and follow-up meetings are incorporated into the plan. Usually, the school psychologist (me) is responsible for follow-up in such areas—many of the complaints about paperwork and not enough time with kids originates with all this mass documentation.

Rachel's educational plan was agreed upon by all team members. Rachel's team consisted of the school principal, the resource room teacher, the school nurse, the classroom teacher, me, and her mother. The plan consisted of the following items:

1. Regularly scheduled time one-on-one with the resource room teacher doing readiness and organizational tasks. This was to help Rachel with her distractibility and visual motor deficiencies. She would learn techniques for pencil grip, paper centering, and letter formation.
2. An eye examination. Rachel was found to have astigmatism and needed glasses. Both the exam and the glasses were arranged to be paid for by the local Lions' Club.

The president of the club is a high school English teacher who works easily with the special needs staff in such cases. With a written note from me, approval is quickly granted.

3. Regular sessions with me.
4. Promotion to first grade. This was a most important feature of the plan. Rachel's self-esteem was seen as a primary issue. Certainly a year with all the services being offered, the built-in checks, and the understanding of all concerned was worth giving her a chance at first grade.
5. Monthly meetings for Rachel's mother with the classroom teacher to discuss Rachel's progress in school. If babysitting was needed, twelfth graders would be used.
6. One afternoon a week placement in an outside art class. Provincetown is known for its artistic heritage and remains a haven for many well-known and aspiring artists. There are several art groups and associations in town, some of which sponsor children's groups. Rachel would be a prime candidate. I contacted a local agency that raises funds specifically for local needs, and financing was obtained. The parents were to provide transportation. That entailed Katherine and/or Tony walking several blocks either way. Later, a group of mothers formed their own pool. Rachel was given a ride on stormy days.

With help from community resources, school personnel, and Rachel's family, a strong, positive plan was created. Commitment to Rachel had been made.

When Rachel and I were alone together, she had a lot she wanted to talk about. We made a list of what was important, and she illustrated it. I made a copy for my folder and laminated the original for her. She elected to keep her copy taped to my pullout drawer so that she could refer to it when she needed it. Her list included:

1. Being smarter in school.
2. Helping her mother more so she wouldn't have to work so hard.
3. Seeing that her little brother was all right.

I made an addition to her list: having fun.

I taught Rachel how to play cards—Old Maid, Go Fish, Solitaire, and Fan-Tan. As we played, she talked. She caught on quickly to the games and rules and became a good player. The numbers and symbols on the cards were not confusing, and she seemed to have "card sense." When my own children were younger, I had spent many hours teaching them games and recalled the many happy hours and serious conversations we had had. This technique worked well with Rachel. I asked her about her work; she showed me stickered papers. She complained she didn't know her letters; I showed her that she knew some numbers on the cards and she realized she now knew her numbers through ten. Rachel responded similarly as she began to sort out some options. She knew she was not being "left back" (the horrible juvenile vernacular for being retained) and was enjoying her time with the lively young woman in the resource room. Her glasses were most attractive on her, and she was enjoying her art lessons. Her instructor felt she was particularly talented, and her classroom was now a storehouse for her completed art projects. She did not take them home because her brother would ruin them.

Rachel mentioned her choice for first-grade teacher, who was fortunately my choice as well. Her kindergarten teacher agreed, and arrangements were begun. I felt that Rachel was beginning to feel better about herself in school, and we could move to the second item—her relationship with her mother. I was not going to drop her school achievement goal, but it seemed time to start focusing on Rachel's concerns about her mother. And they were bigger than I had assumed. Rachel talked a lot about the amount of alcohol allegedly being consumed. The case had now taken a new direction, and I wondered if Rachel was being unduly neglected. Summer vacation would soon be here, and this could be a truly unstructured time for Rachel. I decided to talk with a respected colleague in the system (who happened to have taken a week of training in reality therapy) and together we decided:

1. There was no concrete evidence of neglect or child abuse.

2. The two major problems were putting some positive structure into Rachel's life and helping the family get through the summer.

I then had a conference with Katherine, who agreed to the following:

1. Let Rachel participate in the town recreation program. (I'd already spoken in general terms to the recreation leader to ascertain the appropriateness of the program.)
2. Become involved with our "road-show counselor mommy," a traveling therapist, who visited Province-town one day a week during the summer to help parents with parenting skills.
3. Do what she could about babysitting problems.

Tony had a new daytime job as a carpenter. I had no answers to the babysitting problems; my twelfth-grade students were earning more money as waitresses and chambermaids. My less-than-perfect solution was to work with Rachel about what to do, for example, how to use a telephone in case of emergency and knowing who her neighbors were. Then I let the "road-show mommy" know of my concerns. When I left school and Rachel in June, I gave her packs of cards with my phone number on them in case she needed it. I did not hear from her.

Rachel survived the summer, and first grade began. She was firmly settled in her remedial program. The crying seemed to have lessened, but she continued to exhibit "spaciness" and difficulty in focusing. She was bringing many toys and belongings to school. Conferences with Katherine and counseling with Rachel suggested that the relationship between Rachel's parents had deteriorated over the summer, alcohol being a large problem. Katherine had the appropriate AA and Al-Anon information, but I was not sure whether Katherine and/or Tony had the problem.

The small family structure, tenuously built, began to crumble. Tony left the house and moved thirty miles away, Rachel's beloved dog Ricco died, and I was now seeing Rachel twice a week, hoping her short-term plans would have better chances for success.

Over the next few months, we delineated which toys could come to school, where they "resided" in school, and the times they could be part of Rachel's day.

Rachel adored her new teacher. Mrs. Candleson is a highly creative, soft-spoken, energetic, maternal woman. Her room looks like a children's museum. Her husband, a talented carpenter, had put in closets, shelves, and hanging apparatus. She had decorated the room with homemade rugs, curtains, and children's sculpture and drawings. Books were everywhere, art materials were readily available, and there were all kinds of interesting activities geared to small children. Born to be a first-grade teacher, Mrs. Candleson spent most of her out-of-school hours happily fulfilling that dream. Rachel responded to this creative approach. Her special-needs teacher complemented Mrs. Candleson with firm and regular academic structure. The results were overwhelming. Rachel recognized her intelligence and wanted to learn. She now liked the academic aspects of school and put forth reams of decorated academic paperwork. Her teachers, in recognizing her value, had given her a lasting gift— and made my job easier.

But the death of Ricco became an overriding issue when Rachel accidentally overheard a conversation between her parents. The gist of the conversation was that Tony had put the dog to sleep. Rachel became inconsolable and cried continually. I tried to talk to her about her progress, her mother, and her brother, but with little success. She continued to cry about Ricco. I asked her if crying about Ricco would bring him back. "No, but it makes me feel better." I asked, "Does it help you learn?" We worked it out that she could choose to cry about Ricco in her time with me, provided she did not cry about him in class. Her teacher agreed to ignore any outbursts, to send her to the lavatory to clean her face, to redirect her to her academic task, and to let her do her crying with me.

This was not an easy choice for the caring Mrs. Candleson, who loved hugging and comforting her charges. In the discus-

sion to convince her to try an alternative to hugging and comforting, the turning point was asking her two questions:

1. Do you want Rachel to continue crying in class?
2. Is what you're doing working?

She agreed to my plan, and the classroom crying in time ceased.
But it was not so at home, and not with me. Finally, I scheduled
a conference with both Tony and Katherine. Rachel tearfully
told them of her sadness. We worked out a plan whereby Ricco
could be mourned in a more manageable way. Times and limits
were set. Tony agreed to take Rachel to the farm where Ricco
was buried, and Rachel drew pictures and made plaques for his
long-delayed funeral. The memory of Ricco started to fall into
place more realistically, and interference with progress lessened.

We had advanced to Uno, a rummy-like card game. Rachel
was able to read the words on the point and direction cards.
While she learned to understand the advantages and disadvan-
tages of being dealt high cards, I again queried her about what
she wanted. Her list had changed and now included world
peace, saving whales, and spending more time with both parents. Again we decorated and laminated her wishes. Two letters, well illustrated, were sent—one to the President of the
United States and the other to the Japanese Embassy. Rachel
received a reply from the office of the President, which included
a personal letter from the President's secretary and a booklet
about the U.S. effort for world peace. Unfortunately, the booklet
was geared toward a much higher reading level and was filled
with much military and political information. The Japanese letter, however, conveyed easy-to-read concerns about the whale
and enclosed charming pictures and information about Japan.
This information was delightfully shared with her classmates.
The class was encouraged to visit Japan and see the country and
Japanese people. Rachel enjoyed her time in the academic lime-
light, and Mrs. Candleson was in ecstasy. The class soon did a
Japanese skit with specially made costumes, decorated note

cards with Japanese brush strokes, and planned and cooked a Japanese meal. Rachel flowered in this creative hothouse.

Her third wish, more time with her parents, was not so easily filled. Katherine, unbeknownst to all, had been commuting at night to the local community college to work on her General Equivalency Diploma. She told me that she did not want Rachel to know her mother did not have a high school diploma. A classmate's daughter was babysitting, and she was pledged not to reveal Katherine's plans. I congratulated Katherine on her decision to advance her education and reassured her that she would pass, deciding not to discuss the secrecy issue. Rather, I concentrated on Tony's role.

Tony had joined AA but had not seen the children. Katherine and I discussed Rachel's desire to see him regularly. Katherine and Tony's relationship was poor at this time, so I asked permission to have Tony come to school to talk to me.

At this time, each parent was blaming the other for the difficulties in the relationship. According to Rachel, there had been much yelling and screaming by both parents. Katherine felt it was okay for Tony to see his children "if he's sober." I had my initial meeting with Tony in another school in the system so that Rachel would not see him accidentally. Charming, intelligent, and sober, Tony spent an hour with me. I talked to him about Rachel's concerns and behavior. I discussed how his cooperation during the Ricco episode had helped Rachel. It became apparent in this one-on-one meeting that he truly loved his children and did not know what to do. Because he wanted to be part of his children's lives, he was open to considering ways to do that. He voiced that he was afraid of antagonizing Katherine and did not want his children to have to choose between them.

Because Tony wanted to resume contact with his children, we worked out a plan to approach this problem. He decided to bring his AA counselor with him to Katherine's home. We planned the details of how to handle this, including the best way to contact Katherine, what to say, and when it would be convenient. A quick role play covered several contingencies. Katherine accepted Tony's invitation. I never heard the details except that after three months and the end of first grade, Rachel was seeing her father somewhat regularly for extended times and that summer looked more structured. She had begun to read and compute, even though not at grade level. When I gave her a book that summer, it was without my phone number.

Second grade began. I was eager to work again with Rachel, but she was upset. Her father, she told me, was very ill and was going to be hospitalized. I asked her how she knew this, and she said her father had told her. Her perceptions included a fatal heart problem, her heart being similar to his, and a great deal of medication. As I tried to zero in on the exact problem and its seriousness, the crying resumed. She was sure that he was going to die and that she, in the near future, would die in the same way. Her teacher told me that Rachel was crying often in class and was visiting the nurse frequently. Feeling I did not know the truth, I was at a loss for what to do next until I had more specific information.

First, I called Tony to assess the exact problem. He told me that he had been taken to the hospital this past summer for exhaustion, was presently on heart medication, and was now okay. He said he had talked to Rachel about his condition because she had seen the medication in his bathroom and he had missed some of their summer time together while he was hospitalized. We made an appointment for Tony, Rachel, her teacher, the school nurse, and me to discuss this together. Tony reaffirmed his health to all in front of Rachel.

Aware of the reality of the problem, I now could make a plan with the nurse and Rachel's teacher. The three of us devised a system: Rachel received one chit for a ten-minute visit to the nurse daily. The nurse would decide if Rachel was sick and whether her work needed to be made up. Rachel decorated her chits, and after two weeks decided she did not need them anymore.

Now, over Parcheesi and Sorry, Rachel explored alternatives to crying spontaneously. I knew we had made gains when she brought up Ricco's death again. "I don't need to cry out loud. I can cry inside and get my work done," she told me dry-eyed.

Rachel continued to receive academic remedial help and made slow but steady progress. She was an active participant in her class, with a penchant for projects and group work. Rachel volunteered for class chores willingly and was a good class citizen. Her new teacher's strengths were in the natural science field, and Rachel enjoyed the class field trips that centered on the marine wonders of Provincetown. At home she decorated soup cans with shells, and her homemade pencil holders were in demand from her peers. Her less-than-neat locker and desk had to be periodically cleaned of aborted art and science projects and unfinished art booklets.

I then talked to Katherine about enrolling Rachel's three-year-old brother in the local Head Start program in the hope that much of what had taken Rachel three years could be accomplished in less time for him. Katherine filled out the proper forms willingly, and her son was later accepted.

Meanwhile, Katherine told me she was now "on the wagon." Since Katherine was forever secretive, I had never really known she was "off" and had never explored that avenue with her. Neither had Tony mentioned it. However, I am well aware that I am often personally and professionally surprised when alcohol is found to be a major dynamic in relationships. Despite my professional knowledge, I am continually amazed at the extent and forms of alcoholism. (A year after this, I contacted the local AA and had an Al-Anon group begin in our school during the school day.) Katherine also had a new boyfriend, had completed her GED, and was looking for a good job. I complimented her, wished her well, and put all this information on my overflowing back burner.

The year ended well. When Rachel entered third grade in the fall, she had grown two inches, developed a young girl's body, and started wearing a bra. I was grateful that she had not been retained in second grade. Although Tony lived a hundred miles away, she and her brother saw their father regularly, every weekend. This involved a ferry ride both ways and Katherine's participation to get the children to and from the ferry at regularly scheduled times. Once at their father's, Rachel spent much time during the day with his new girlfriend while he worked overtime. Rachel liked the new girlfriend, Cora, who was a weaver. She spent time with Cora learning the intricacies of the loom. On Mondays, Rachel often brought to school yarn projects she had done with Cora. A vegetarian, Cora was also a superb cook. Rachel raved about the new foods she ate while she was there. She never verbally compared Cora to her mother, but it seemed to be a very comfortable relationship. She accepted her father's need to work as part of his caring for her and valued the time he spent with her. She would return knowledgeable about the construction he was doing.

In the meantime, Katherine's friend, Frank, had moved in and become a new source of problems. Rachel made no bones about her dislike for him. For a month we tried to develop plans for them to get along, which all failed miserably. Rachel knew that her record player and radio bothered Frank, so she tried to play them at a lower decibel, and when Frank wasn't home. She tried to clean up after dinner to help her mother. And she tried to play with her little brother to keep him out of the way. Frank, she told me, took her radio away for a week, complained about the way she did the dishes, and never mentioned how she helped with her brother. Discouraged, she discontinued her attempts. It seemed to me Rachel's good intentions were doomed if even childish efforts were not recognized.

Finally, I asked Rachel if it would be okay for me to discuss her feelings with her mother, with the understanding that Katherine might very well tell Frank. Reluctantly, Rachel agreed, but only after figuring that it might be a chance for resolution. She put little faith in any chance for success.

I called Katherine to school for an appointment. She volunteered quickly that Frank disliked Rachel, but he did like her little brother. Rachel and Frank clashed all the time, she admitted, and Katherine felt that she was always in the middle. I suggested that she bring Frank in and that we discuss methods of mediating the problem. She liked that idea, but she felt Frank would not come to school, especially to see a counselor.

Unfortunately, the next week Katherine was taken to the hospital on an emergency call, and she stayed almost a month. Tony could not be reached until the weekend, and Frank was in charge. Confusion reigned, and my usual technique of getting people together to work things out did not work. Meanwhile,

Frank punished the children by denying visitation with Tony and even visits with their mother in the hospital.

At a loss, I called the hospital social worker, hoping that a compassionate person would be able to help. I never did meet this wonder woman, but she managed to arrange for the children's visits as part of Katherine's recovery plan and even lined up babysitters. She had talked to Katherine and gotten the names of friends. Several were past students, and I knew them. I phoned them and tried to arrange an alternative place for Rachel to go at the end of the day. Although I found one responsible sitter, I was minimally successful because of the friends' problems and schedules. (Some enterprising people in this town could make good money and help kids and their families by opening an afterschool/evening day care center.)

This was a hard time for the caring school personnel, who had to balance empathy and concern with the responsibility of educating Rachel. There was little more the school personnel could do. They relied on time to help get through this period. Rachel's schedule remained structured and expectations reasonable. After a month, Katherine came home to recuperate. However, the Frank-versus-Rachel dynamic continued.

Weekends with Tony were a structured diversion, and he began keeping the children through Monday, to the consternation of the attendance officer. The attendance officer was also the head custodian, and he felt inconvenienced each time he went looking for "truant" children. Even though I explained to him that the children were not in Provincetown and he did not have to look for them, he resented the time spent writing the mandated reports and follow-up forms. Custodians can be wonderful friends to school personnel provided they are kept far away from administrative tasks. I don't think the head custodian ever forgave me for my role in the Rachel "truancy."

Rachel continued to discuss her desire to be with her mother, but not with Frank. Katherine and Frank fought, even as Katherine convalesced, and Rachel futilely tried to stop them.

Rachel and I spent much time playing cards and trying to create new plans. Any plans to make Frank happy were discarded as impossible. Those involving her mother were limited because of Katherine's illness. That left Rachel as the course of change. This was difficult for me as well as for Rachel. Finally, she said that if she got out of the house more, she would be happier. Now we both had a handle on the problem. We filled her afternoons: Monday was catechism, which was often missed because she was with her father; Tuesday, Brownies; Wednesday, gymnastics; Thursday, library/computer club, and Friday, visits with her father. All these activities minimized her time at home and gave her a chance to have fun. Once home, she could babysit for her brother, help as needed, do her homework, and try to avoid Frank.

Conferences with Katherine and Rachel were well meaning but unsatisfactory. These meetings reflected a strong bond between Katherine and Rachel. Each would say how much she loved the other and how she wanted them to be together. Katherine would try to explain how important Frank was to her, and Rachel would express her distrust of him. Simply, Katherine wanted both Rachel and Frank; Rachel wanted only her mother. Resolutions were fuzzy, well-meant. The meetings ended with tears and the desire of both to try harder.

As it became more obvious to Rachel in counseling that her relationship with her mother was what she wanted, and that Frank was a permanent part of the picture, Rachel started to come to grips with her own role. She realized that by doing well in school, helping at home, and not confronting Frank, she could have more of her mother's love and approval. For the most part, she started to become as successful as a nine-year-old could be under the circumstances.

School had always been a positive experience. Her academic skills were becoming stronger, and she loved sharing her progress with her mother. Every Thursday she gave her mother a beautifully decorated folder of her work. We spent time together preparing the folder every week so that she could give it to her mother before she visited her father. Often the folder was filled with lovely poems and personal letters to her mother.

At home, Rachel tried to help as needed, concentrating on keeping her brother busy so her mother could rest and/or get her work done. When possible, she ignored Frank. Some of the role plays we did were very creative. She decided that if confronted she would not argue but say, "I'm sorry. I'm going to my room to do my homework." There was always a book in her room that she could be reading for a book report. Rachel did many book reports.

As the weather permitted, we took our sessions out of doors. Our plans and discussions were in cranberry bogs, marshes, on beaches, and wildlife trails. We collected shells for projects, leaves for tracing, sand for art work, and assorted refuse. We even had a paper bag for discarded bottles and cans. She decided to give the money from redeeming them to the school library since she had found them on school time. We talked about the beauty that surrounded us and the changes the seasons brought. We also talked about the changes both in her and in her life. She began to talk about long-range goals rather than the short-term ones of the past. Rachel wanted to learn many languages as her mother had and to write poems and stories for children in the various languages. Of course, she would illustrate all of them. I told her such goals were attainable and talked to her about her talents and about how she might begin achieving her goals. Her folders could become her first journals. There was so much to help her find and so much she could learn.

It was time for Rachel's fourth-grade annual review meeting with her teachers and specialists, the principal, me, and her mother. For the first time, she tested at grade level. Her emotional demeanor was satisfactory, although she could be both strong-minded and dreamy. I was not so concerned about this; these were good survival and coping skills that she had learned to direct to her advantage. Her dreaminess was now more a part of her creative process and a source of her ideas, as well as a way for her to keep in touch with her inner world. And she would need to be strong-minded and stubborn to stand up for what she wanted and what should be hers. Her new educational plan was agreed upon by all present. She would see me as needed, and I would check on her periodically. She no longer needed remedial help. Rather, she could now devote that time to library club or art studio.

After the meeting, Katherine asked to speak to me. Her

illness had reoccurred, her relationship with Frank was questionable, and she was thinking of giving the children to Tony. She wanted only visiting privileges and the possibility of resuming custody someday. She wanted me to know because she would be telling the children that week. She and Tony had already discussed it.

My time with Rachel was now limited. I taught her a new game to take to Rhode Island; she gave me a poster she had made in art studio. The poster was filled with artifacts we had collected from the National Seashore, and there were hearts and rainbows all over it. She said she hoped I would come to her college graduation, an early invitation I accepted with pleasure. I was so proud of her.

Rachel was happy about living with her father and starting a new life in what she called "my other family," but she was not happy about leaving her friends, teachers, school, mother, and surroundings. She wondered what her new school and teachers would be like. I reminded her that she knew some children at her new home from her visiting, and that most small New England schools are fairly similar. Then she asked me to phone her new teacher and tell her about all the things she had learned. I could have added, "And all the things I have learned."

The last time I saw Rachel was at the district courthouse, where she waited with her parents and brother while a decision about her future was made. I stood as the judge gave his final recommendations, and I felt tears come to my eyes. I was saying goodbye to a "younger daughter" and friend—given to me for only a short time to love, cherish, and direct. I thought, "Thank you, Rachel, for your priceless gift. You were a validation of the strength and decency of the human spirit."

DR. GLASSER'S COMMENTS ON "A PRICELESS GIFT"

This case illustrates the process of helping a small child to cope with growing up in a tough situation. We all like to think of childhood as a time of parental love and support in an intact family with health and financial security. All too often, however, this is not the case, and for Rachel it certainly was not. If left to the care of her parents and to chance, there is some doubt as to whether she would even have survived. But Rachel was not left to chance, far from it. What happened shows how much a few highly caring people can mean to a child with much potential but in desperate need of enough care to get started.

It is remarkable how much Rachel was able to sort out the positive from all the negatives around her. This case brings out the basic reality therapy concept that when we teach or counsel, it is important that we not treat our clients as if they were victims. We do not deny that many of our clients have been mistreated, but our effort must be directed first at seeing that they are not mistreated, and second at teaching them that there is a great deal they can do for themselves despite what has happened to them. Since we all have to fulfill our needs in the present and by our own efforts, whenever we think of ourselves as victims we will be hampered in this process. Victims wait for people to do things for them. Effective people depend on themselves; any help offered is welcome, but they do not depend on it.

Neither Megan Fates nor any of the others who did so much with Rachel ever dealt with her or even thought of her as "poor Rachel who can't help herself." This spunky little girl illustrated so well the control theory axiom that what happens to us need not damage us in the long run unless we let it.

Everyone involved in Rachel's treatment recognized that what they had to do was to support her strengths. To do this, Megan Fates went into the kindergarten. "I sat with Rachel in the classroom, observed her beautiful art work, and talked to her about the toys she brought regularly to school. I sang kindergarten songs, played kindergarten games, and clapped for kindergarten running teams. By the end of the week, Rachel and I were friends. I asked her if she would like to work with me the following week and was not surprised by her response: 'When,' and 'Can I bring my doll?' "

In working with young children, ten years of age or less, it is best to start by seeing the child in her natural habitat. For young children, that is the classroom, not the counselor's office. Megan Fates knew that we build our strengths from need-satisfying activities, so she concentrated on doing what she could to see that Rachel had a good day in school. She knew that the better Rachel found school, the less she would withdraw and cry. Megan Fates also learned not to expend a lot of time and energy on what she could not do, which was to change what was happening at home.

It matters less where we satisfy our needs than that they are satisfied, and in the relationship with Megan Fates and her teachers, Rachel learned that she could satisfy her needs in school and in the community. It was from this school strength that she was able to cope successfully with an increasingly chaotic home life, as both her parents became sick and later separated. Remarkably, Rachel was able to learn to cope with Frank, her mother's boyfriend, who did not like her. She would not have been able to do this had she not had daily a solid school experience by this time.

Clearly Megan Fates is a dedicated counselor, and she very much knew what she was doing. Those who work with young children will see many Rachels. The world is full of children like her, and if these children meet a skilled counselor, much can be done to help them expand their strengths. What we should learn from this case is not to be discouraged if the odds seem to be stacked against the child. Children quickly become strong and resilient if they have any place at all where they can satisfy their needs. If not at home, it can be through teachers or counselors in school; it can be a neighbor, a minister, a coach, or even a close friend. It just has to be someone, somewhere.

As you read the cases in this book, I think you will be impressed by how well children learn to meet their needs in new situations. I believe this is because children are in the active process of learning new behaviors and find it natural to try something different. Adults, on the other hand, often find this difficult because they try to use the behaviors they already know in places and situations that require new ones. When we as counselors ask the core reality therapy question, "Is what you are doing helping you to get what you want?" we are trying to get those we counsel, both adults and children, to consider doing something new.

As counselors, it is important that we keep our minds open to what we can do to augment what goes on in the counseling office. Megan Fates helped Rachel get involved in a community art program, even to the extent of finding the money to finance it. She also taught her to play cards, taught her letters and numbers, helped her to get eyeglasses, got her into the first-grade class that she felt would be best for her, and saw that she was involved in a community recreation program during the summer. These are things that we do for children, but usually not for adults. We should encourage adults to do these things for themselves.

6

"I'm Not Going to Let Them Affect Me"

An Abused Child Finds a New Life for Herself

TERRI LEONARD

M Y INVOLVEMENT with Sarah Masters began when I became a guidance counselor in a coed high school in St. George's, a city of approximately 250,000 people in Newfoundland.

Several of Sarah's teachers had mentioned her, indicating problems, but stated at the same time that Sarah had no desire to see a counselor. I knew it was inevitable that we would meet, and we did in October 1986, in the halls of Thurston High School. Her teacher, Mrs. Joan Barry, had called me. Sarah had left class and was standing in the corridor sobbing, rigidly clenching her arms about her breasts. Mrs. Barry asked me to handle the situation because she had to return to her class.

Sarah Masters was tall, thin, and frail with blonde hair and freckles. As I approached, she acted distant and said she did not want to see me or any other guidance counselor. As I coaxed Sarah down the corridor to my office, my plunge into one of the most complicated and unusual cases in my ten years as school guidance counselor began. Subsequent counseling sessions revealed a frightened, timid, suicidal, and purging seventeen-year-old girl.

My first priority in counseling Sarah was to develop an involvement with her and to help her build trust in me. Previous counselors had contacted her home, and it was obvious that this was very threatening to her. In fact, one of Sarah's first requests was that I not contact her home. Over and over each time we met, she begged, "You won't talk to my mother, will you?" as she grasped her hands so tightly that her knuckles turned white. I assured her that I would not. I learned quickly that Sarah feared her mother more than anything or anyone else.

In my first meeting with Sarah, I tried to keep things light by discussing her school life and asking only general questions about her family. I never pressured Sarah to give specific information about her family: she cringed each time her mother and brothers were mentioned. It was going to take a long time to build a relationship with this girl, I thought. I acted friendly, but I waited for Sarah to tell me what she wanted me to know, pushing a little but retreating as soon as things became too much for her. I saw her more frequently than I usually do my clients, eventually daily. We went to lunch several times: I was concerned about her weight and wanted to see if she would eat anything. I made myself available after hours if she needed to talk to me on the phone. School in general had been a positive place for her, and this was helpful to me. Later I learned that one of the reasons she never missed school was because she was not allowed to stay home sick. If she did, her mother would beat her.

Little by little, Sarah began to trust me and talk about things that concerned her; her mother's lack of love for her, her brother's being on drugs, her own depression and suicidal tendencies, as well as her inability to eat and keep food down. Sarah mainly focused on what was happening to her, rather than on what her mother or brothers were doing. She never blamed anyone for what was wrong with her. Most adolescents blame everyone and everything except themselves for what is wrong with them, but Sarah never did. After discussing all areas, I asked her which area she would like to work on right away. She chose her inability to keep food down because for months she had been regurgitating what little she did eat.

Afraid her mother would find out, Sarah did not want to see a doctor concerning her regurgitation. Doing anything contrary to her mother's wishes frightened Sarah. Her mother had not let her go to a doctor even when she had been very sick. I felt it was necessary for Sarah to see a medical doctor: her regurgitation may have been life threatening, as Sarah was very thin for her height. Also, I wanted a second opinion on whether she might carry out her suicidal tendencies. I needed the reassurance that she would not commit suicide, and it would give me some protection if something did happen.

Getting Sarah to see a doctor was not easy, however. It required ingenuity on my part and trust on Sarah's part. Since she herself had chosen to work on this area, I confronted her with doing something about her problem: "Sarah, you've been talking about doing something about your problem. What are you going to do about not eating and throwing up all the time?" As if she could read my mind, Sarah replied, "I don't want to see a doctor!" I continued to pursue the issue, asking her, "What are you willing to do?" She persistently replied that she did not want to see a doctor. "Then will the problem go away on its own?" "No, it won't." I finally asked, "Is not seeing a doctor going to get you eating again?" She finally agreed to see a doctor when I told her that I would go along with her for support. This was a big step because Sarah was now doing something to help herself instead of just talking about her problem. It deepened her trust in me, and I could use this success in the future when things were difficult for her. A friend of mine, a pediatrician, agreed to see Sarah when I told her of the girl's circumstances. It was not necessary to inform the parents since Sarah was seventeen years old and could see a doctor without her mother's permission. With this assurance, Sarah agreed to see Dr. Parker.

At Dr. Parker's office, Sarah was very nervous and would not allow Dr. Parker to examine her. Sarah kept looking to me for reassurance as Dr. Parker asked questions concerning her inability to eat. But even though she was nervous, she cooperated by answering the questions and even smiled once or twice. Dr. Parker, sensitive to Sarah's present state, did not push Sarah beyond what she thought Sarah could handle. When Dr. Parker told her that she had to gain weight or be hospitalized, Sarah cringed. Sarah feared being put in hospital almost as much as she feared her mother. This proved to be advantageous in encouraging Sarah to gain weight. If she gained no weight in the next few weeks, Dr. Parker would have to place her in hospital.

Sarah's weight did stabilize, but her suicidal tendencies continued for several more weeks. During this time, I was never sure that Sarah would show up in school on Monday because she left each Friday saying that she would kill herself.

To keep Sarah focused on the next day, I arranged for her to draw pictures and bring them to me. She was talented, especially with pencil drawings. She was also very good at crafts, so I would have her make crafts such as bookmarks and Christmas ornaments for her friends and teachers. I would also give her an appointment for the next day. On one occasion, Sarah did take a blade and cut her arms. She refused to see Dr. Parker that week because she was afraid of being placed in hospital. She was also testing me to see if she could trust me and if I would take control by attempting to force her to see the pediatrician. I did not. Sarah herself told Dr. Parker the following week that she had cut her arms. This was a real sign that she was accepting responsibility for her own behavior and was beginning to trust us. Dr. Parker informed me that the cuts were not deep and had not been life threatening.

During the next month, Sarah made slow but steady progress. She began to smile a little and have good days. She talked less and less to teachers about the crazy things that were happening with her brother who was on drugs and acting very strange. She seemed able to vent much frustration in my office and had less reason to vent her frustration to others. To keep her thinking and doing rather than feeling, I asked her who was in control when she became upset. Did she or the other person make her upset? She said that she was not in control. I then had her evaluate what was happening by asking, "Do you want your mom controlling your emotions and feelings?" She answered, "No!" I asked her again, "Do you want your brother Ben controlling you?" She again answered emphatically, "No!" I would confront her, asking, "What can you do?" She then would reply, "I'm not going to let them affect me."

Sarah saw Dr. Parker once a week and managed to maintain her weight, sometimes even gaining a pound or two. She started to feel better and act more responsibly, so I decided to cut back on the number of times I would see her. I thought perhaps twice a week rather than every day would be enough. But as time went on and Christmas neared, Sarah started throwing up again and became very weak and sick. It was a downward trend, her strategies for coping taking a nose dive. She started depressing. Simultaneously, she failed her Physics and Math exams and her brother Ben, taking drugs, was seeing God on television and coming into her room at night. Sarah became immobilized by fear when her brother did these things. She reverted to her old ways, depressing. She could not commit herself to her new way of coping. She seemed unwilling to take control of her feelings and rationalize more.

We talked of having slips to her old way of behaving. "It is normal to swing from the old way to the new way, and vice versa, until the new way becomes a part of you." Her old way was to get upset in class and make a scene. We talked about the attention she would get from being upset in front of her friends. This was her way of controlling them and getting their attention, and it was also her way of trying to control me. It had worked for her in the past. Although Sarah admitted that depressing was her way of coping, she was not able to make changes. I decided not to let Sarah give excuses. I kept saying, "You have learned new ways to cope, and it is about time you used them." She eventually responded to this counseling. Using her new behaviors, she pulled herself out of her depression and started feeling better again.

With Christmas coming and the holidays beginning, I wondered how Sarah would cope away from school. I was going away for the holidays, so I would not be available. I suggested, with Dr. Parker's permission, that Sarah call her if she needed to talk to someone. She did call Dr. Parker and went to see her once over Christmas.

When Sarah returned to school in January, she was upset. Christmas Day had been good, but after that things fell apart. One of her older brothers, who drank excessively, started assaulting her sexually. Overcome by fear when this happened, she became totally immobilized. Her brother had molested her on three occasions, and her mother had beaten her once during the holidays. Sarah was again scared, frightened, and unable to cope. We discussed her options. She could leave home, she could stay and put up with what was happening to her, or she could tell her parents what her brother had done to her. Sarah decided that she could not tell her mother because she would beat her and call her a liar. If she went to her father, he would only tell her mother because he too was afraid. Sarah felt that her only way to deal with this situation was to stay there for now. This situation is very difficult for a counselor because students over sixteen years of age must leave home of their own accord before receiving help from Social Services. The Child Welfare Act protects children under age sixteen, but those over that age are left in limbo. Sarah was emotionally incapable of making the decision to move out because she feared what her brothers and her mother would do to her if she left. No assurance from me seemed to matter. We discussed this situation every day for a week until Sarah gradually realized what she must do.

Because Sarah was incapable of making this decision on her own, and I sensed that she needed to hear it from me. I finally told her that I thought she should get out. "Sarah, it is too dangerous for you to stay there." For the first time, Sarah wanted to leave. She also said that her father had suggested using her head and her legs. She took this to mean that he would understand if she left. Sarah agreed to talk to a social worker as long as her mother did not find out. She asked me to stay with her while she saw the social worker.

The social worker, Pat Arnold, explained to Sarah the consequences to her if she stayed in her home, which would probably be a nervous breakdown. The social worker agreed to arrange financial support for her and to help her find a place to stay. Sarah said she would move out, but she did not want Pat to contact her home concerning her or any other member of her family. Pat explained to Sarah that she might have to investigate her family because of younger brothers living there. I realized how far Sarah had come: a month ago, she would have gone into a complete panic at this thought. Sarah had learned to trust me, Dr. Parker, and now Pat Arnold. Our relationship had given Sarah the strength to do what would have been unthinkable a few months ago. Sarah had come a long way.

Pat Arnold decided to investigate Sarah's younger brothers, fourteen and fifteen, by going to their school, instead of their home, to determine if they had been abused. There were no signs of abuse. Pat Arnold reported that she would not have to go to Sarah's home concerning her younger brothers. Sarah was delighted and relieved that her mother would not be called. She did not want to be blamed for causing more trouble in her home. Sarah also stated that her mother would not mistreat the boys because as they got older and bigger, they would retaliate.

Sarah was placed in a foster home as a boarder. She was actually too old for foster care, but because she was so upset emotionally, it was decided to place her with a foster family. The foster mother was a wonderful, warm person who had three other foster girls younger than Sarah, a daughter who was twenty-three, and a retarded son who was twenty. This home seemed like a good placement for Sarah, who came from a large family with six brothers and a sister of her own. The interaction with the members of the foster family would let her experience normal family relationships, unlike the abuse she had received at home.

Each day during the week before Sarah left, she took extra clothes and things out of her home in her book bag. She now had a boyfriend, and she stored these things at his house. On Saturday, she was ready to leave and just walked out the door, telling her mother she was going to study at a friend's house. Sarah went to her foster home, never to return home again. No one involved made any contact with Sarah's parents. I notified the police that she had left and that she was being helped by Social

Services. But when Sarah did not return home, Mrs. Masters notified the police, who in turn contacted Social Services. Mrs. Masters was an aggressive and domineering woman, who became very abusive in conversation. Pat refused to give Mrs. Masters information about Sarah. Mrs. Masters was told by the police and by Social Services that Sarah was old enough to leave home and that she could do nothing about it.

Maybe now that Sarah no longer had daily contact with her family, she would have a chance at some real progress.

Extremely frightened and fearful after leaving home, Sarah was especially afraid of meeting her brothers on the street. She spoke of this constantly, and when she did meet them, she had anxiety attacks. Afterward, she regurgitated for long periods of time. Three times during this period from April to August, she was hospitalized when her vital signs became so low that she needed intravenous feedings to get them back to normal. Dr. Parker was a great support during those times. She was aware of Sarah's fears and did not force her into hospital for any length of time, even though the situation might have called for more medical attention. Dr. Parker was allowing Sarah to remain in control of her life by trusting her to get better without being in hospital.

When Sarah felt comfortable in her new home, I expected her to begin to feel comfortable in talking about her former family. She never did. She was unwilling to say an unkind word about her mother or her brothers, no matter what they had done to her.

From January to June, I tried many ways to help Sarah accept herself and feel positive about herself. I encouraged her with school work, where she had success in subjects like history, literature, and art. She felt very positive when she made good grades. I encouraged her to make plans for her future, talking about subjects she could take next year so that she would get admitted to the university. We talked of her getting a summer job. I thought as she experienced success now, she would see herself in a positive light and build her positive self-image rather than dwell on the past.

As the end of the school year approached, my counseling

strategy was to keep Sarah focused more on passing her exams and less on her fears of her brothers. When she became anxious, she again started to have bouts of uncontrollable regurgitation and to create crises by becoming extremely upset and nervous. These attacks occurred more frequently as school exams approached.

Anticipating this, I refused to accept excuses for her not writing exams, and I pushed her no matter what anxiety she felt. I would say to her, "Sarah I know you are not feeling that well right now, but this is a very important time for you. How will you feel if you don't write your exams?" She responded, "I'd feel pretty bad." I would then confront her by saying, "Then can you write your exams even though you are feeling sick?" She said, "I think so."

During exam week, Sarah saw her brother one day outside of school and thought he was following her. She was terrified at this thought and was experiencing extreme anxiety. After going to the school entrance with her to make sure he was nowhere in sight, I assured her that she was safe. I let her settle down, and then I asked her, "What is the best thing you can do right now to forget about your brother?" Sarah replied, "I don't know. I have to write my exam." I asked, "Will focusing your mind on your exam help you forget about your brother?" She said, "Once I start writing, I'll feel better." I asked, "Can you do that?" and she replied, "Yes, I think so." "I think you can too, Sarah. After all, you've come through a lot of difficult times this year, and you've handled them all." To get her to follow through, I asked her, "Do you want to go down to the exam room now?" She agreed, and I again reinforced her by saying, "I know you are scared, but I know you can handle it, Sarah. I'll walk down with you if you like." Sarah replied with a nod. She entered the exam room and never mentioned meeting her brother outside of school again. At other times, when the exam she was writing was not her best subject, she would panic. I would use relaxation techniques to settle her down and then ask her, "Can you write your exam?" She always replied, "Yes." She passed all her courses for the year except physics.

With school closing for the summer and my going away,

Sarah and I talked about the importance of relaxing and enjoying herself. I thought that with the pressure of final exams off, she would cope much better. She had planned to do volunteer work at the hospital where Dr. Parker worked. She was looking forward to taking a two-week holiday with her foster family at the beach and to riding the bike that her boyfriend had given her. I hoped that Sarah would have a good summer and come back to school more relaxed in the fall.

Up to this point, I have not mentioned Sarah's boyfriend much, but it was an interesting relationship, although not one we dwelled on together. George was a handsome fellow, with jet black hair and deep-set eyes. He dressed very stylishly and was overly polite. I was surprised that he had chosen Sarah as a girlfriend because he was much older, twenty-four years old to Sarah's seventeen. It seemed that he could have had anyone he chose to be with, and he did not appear the type to be overly concerned with people's problems. Sarah was a needy girl who required much time and attention. But perhaps this is what attracted him to her. Apart from his age, another concern I had about their relationship was that Sarah said they were not involved sexually. This I found strange for a twenty-four-year-old man. Why would he pick someone like Sarah when he could have a more mature relationship with a woman rather than a girl? George and Sarah had their problems over the summer, and when I saw Sarah, which was twice in two months, she was very concerned about these problems. They had had a number of arguments, and eventually she broke off the relationship with him. She learned that he was having a sexual relationship with one of her friends and that George had told this girl about a sexual experience he had had with Sarah. Again she had to be hospitalized for a couple of days because of regurgitation and very low vital signs. Sarah not only lost George and two of her closest friends, who had spread around what George had told them, but she also lost her health. The last few weeks of summer were lonely ones for Sarah.

On September 4, the first day of the school term, Sarah came to see me and said that she was glad to be back at school. She had a smile on her face and was well-dressed in floral jeans, tight jean jacket, and bright yellow shirt and socks.

During the first week of school, I saw Sarah every day. We discussed the courses she was taking and what kind of average she would like to attain in her final year in school. I also checked her courses to make sure she was fulfilling the requirements for graduation and entrance to the university. When we talked of her future, Sarah expressed an interest in becoming a guidance counselor, even though she was apprehensive about getting the marks she needed to get into the university.

I was feeling very positive about working with Sarah this year. I thought that she was on the road to recovery, that she would need less counseling than last year, and that time was on her side in her efforts to forget about her past. She herself talked about wanting things to be different. She felt that last year other students had treated her like a "freak." This year, she wanted to make new friends and have students like her instead of shun her. We talked about her making friends without revealing her past to them. I told her that one way people punish themselves is to tell people about their past. It is a test to see if others still like them after finding out what has happened to them. My counseling took the form of saying, "If they won't like you because of what happened to you, then those people weren't necessary for you in the first place." My approach was to show that I cared for her in order to give her a reason to move into the present and to emphasize the positive and worthwhile things she had done and could do.

The week that followed brought frustrations for Sarah. She found math extremely difficult to grasp, and economics equally difficult. She was upset about students not liking her and not being friendly to her. She also worried that she was upsetting her foster mother because she was still regurgitating her food. Sarah's nerves seemed to be on edge. She did not sleep most nights, and when she did sleep, she had nightmares. She would often wake up so frightened by her dreams that she would huddle, crouched in a corner. Strategies we thought would help when she woke up frightened were to go to her foster mother or to draw pictures of her dreams and bring them to me the next day. She phoned me late one night to talk after she had had a bad dream. I said, "I know you have these difficulties at night, but you are getting through the nights. Why don't you talk to me in the morning?" She had to realize that there were things she had to do for herself, no matter how hard they were. I thought if she could handle the nights on her own, it would give her confidence in herself. My plan was to diminish this kind of dependence on me. In the morning I would tell her, "You were disturbed overnight, but you handled it yourself." We would then look at any drawing she had done overnight.

Her nightmares continued through September. These nightmares, along with her inability to sleep, left Sarah looking frayed, drawn, worn out, and more anxious than ever.

It seemed like every day Sarah was coming to me with something new that was upsetting her. We talked at length about ways to cope with each situation as it arose. I thought she should be coping better now, but this was not the case. Her anxiety level seemed to have increased during the past few weeks. I could not understand why she was becoming so frustrated. I began to seriously consider that she should not be attending school this year at all. Little did I realize what was yet to come.

My suspicions were reinforced the following week. On Monday morning, Sarah told me that she had had amnesia for five or six hours on Friday night. She had left her house and did not know where she had been. When she came out of her amnesia, she was in an alley about ten minutes from her house and could not remember anything that had happened to her. This really frightened her.

The next week at school, Sarah had an anxiety attack. She hyperventilated and brought on a hypnotic-like state. These attacks, which continued for the rest of the term, seemed to happen only around me at school. They never occurred when I was not around. I was beginning to think that Sarah was doing this deliberately to get my attention. The attacks were extremely upsetting to me because I had never seen anything like them. The principal of the school was not pleased either: he had to call an ambulance each time it happened. After three such attacks, the principal decided not to let Sarah back in school without a medical certificate saying that she was fit to attend school. Dr. Parker wrote this letter, stating that the attacks were not life threatening and that there was no need to call an ambulance. Dr. Parker also agreed to be on call if I needed help when Sarah had another attack. Dr. Parker thought this might be Sarah's way of reliving what had happened in her past. It is not uncommon for children who have suffered great abuse to have anxiety attacks after they feel safe in a new environment. I realized the amount of trust Sarah must have in me to allow these attacks to occur only in my presence.

On October 15, Sarah had another bad attack at school. This was the first of a series of similar attacks. I sensed earlier that morning that an attack was coming. I knew when I had met with Sarah that her anxiety level was extremely high. She was very upset because her foster mother had been hospitalized the night before with severe pains in her chest. I talked with Sarah in the hopes of decreasing her anxiety level: "Sarah, your foster mom is in good hands at the hospital. She will be okay in a few days." This was to no avail. I held a paper bag over her mouth, as Dr. Parker had instructed if Sarah hyperventilated. In such circumstances, Dr. Parker agreed to take an emergency call from me, allowing me to remain calm. Regardless of my efforts, however, Sarah's breathing intensified and became very rapid. I was unable to hold her attention. One minute she would talk sensibly to me, the next minute she appeared not to understand what I was saying. At times she seemed like a six-year-old child, not the eighteen-year-old girl she was. Disoriented and confused, she would blink her eyes and shake her head as if trying to shake away the fuzziness in her head. I said, "Sarah slow down your breathing. Breathe to my counting. One . . . , two . . . , three . . . , four. . . ." But her breathing still increased; her eyes were rolling in her head.

I managed to get Sarah to the nurse's office, where she became very weak and continued to hyperventilate despite my efforts and hers to prevent it. She was drifting rapidly into a subconscious state. As she lay on the nurse's couch, she went deeper and deeper into her trancelike state. She held her arms tightly against her chest, fists clenched, causing her knuckles to whiten from the pressure. Her whole body remained stiff and tight as if she were doing an isometric exercise. As I tried talking to her, her body would twitch and jerk. I thought that if I could force her to think, maybe she would come back to reality. I asked her simple questions. "Sarah, where are you?" This question had to be repeated several times before she responded. I was astounded when she chanted in a childlike voice, "I'm hiding, I'm hiding, from Mommy and Daddy. I'm hiding." I asked her how old she was. In reply, she held up four fingers. Sarah was telling me that she was age four. My eyes widened with astonishment, as I tried to grasp the reality of what was happening. I was staring at an eighteen-year-old girl who was speaking as if she were four years old. In the next three hours, Sarah revealed to me some of the abuse she had experienced at that age. The reality was that her mother had abused her physically and sexually.

During these states, Sarah revealed abuses that had occurred to her throughout her childhood. These memories were barely accessible to her conscious mind. I believe that this is why she was never able to say an unkind word about her mother and brothers. She did not have access to these memories before the hyperventilating anxiety attacks. The hyperventilating brought her to a state where she relived the memories, and a few hours later the hyperventilating brought her back to reality. She would be very exhausted after these attacks and would sleep for a long time.

In this way, Sarah was both reliving and revealing the past, something she could not do until she had moved out of her home. She would even relive the pain that she had not been able to acknowledge previously when she had been sexually assaulted by four of her brothers. They had raped her repeatedly from age six to her present age.

Sarah would fight her fear of revealing these memories for weeks before she would let them occur. After they occurred, she discussed what had happened and wondered why. Sarah needed to tell me or Dr. Parker about the memories. This helped her to begin the difficult process of moving past what had happened to her. Now, no longer completely intimidated by her past, she was able to move on with her life. She would eventually feel better, sleep a lot, and be more pleasant until the next attack, which occurred a few weeks later.

During the good times, I tried to keep Sarah focused on school work and on attending school as much as possible. Even though she was quite sick, tired from not sleeping, and sore from the physical abuse she experienced in the memories, she came to school. She enjoyed some of her school work and never used her sickness as an excuse to stay home. It is ironic that the one positive behavior she learned from her home life, not to stay home from school no matter how sick, was now benefiting her. For even though life was difficult, she did maintain her routine. This kept her grounded in reality and helped in her fight. She fought to stay in the present as much as possible. We talked about her graduation, talked of ways to get along with the other members of her new family, and talked of staying involved with a few friends that she had developed during the year.

As time went on, the attacks occurred less and less often in school. She had several at home, and Dr. Parker was called to help. Sarah began to realize that it was not safe to have these attacks at school. The school principal was upset over them, afraid of what was happening to Sarah and concerned about the possibility of the school being sued for negligence. He wanted Sarah out of school. I found this very difficult to deal with. Again Dr. Parker came to the rescue by writing a letter saying that these attacks were not life threatening. It is not often that you find a medical doctor willing to put her job on the line by writing such a letter. It was obvious that Sarah was having the same impact on Dr. Parker as she was having on me.

As the attacks increased in frequency, Sarah went into the memories without hyperventilating. At the same time, the memories had become more violent and more severe. It seemed that the earlier memories were not nearly as violent as the later ones. It was as if she had to experience the early, less frightening abuse before she could relive the more traumatic abuse from her brothers and father. She had to become stronger in order to relive the more violent attacks. Nevertheless, no matter how bad the attacks were, Sarah was now recovering more quickly.

For example, one day she had an attack, and the next she wrote her final exam in literature. Even though she was still feeling the effects of the memory, she did not let it interfere with what she had to do. She had learned that life goes on, no matter what. She kept in her mind a vision of what she wanted in the future, which was to go to the university and become a guidance counselor.

A repeated theme in Sarah's counseling was that she thought she was a bad person who should be punished and that she deserved what happened to her. "Is this doing you any good?" I would ask her. "You can't correct the past," I emphasized. "You are not a bad person, and there is no need to punish yourself." I often used control theory to explain to Sarah what was happening to her so that she could understand why she thought she was a bad person who deserved to be punished.

Sarah's real world was that she was assaulted physically, emotionally, and sexually by her mother and brothers throughout her life. Today Sarah still believes that she is a bad person because her mother, who had all the power, told her so. Sarah believes she caused her mother to do terrible things to her. She is not yet able to accept the fact that her mother was a very abusive woman and probably incapable of loving her. As time goes on and Sarah gains strength and independence, she will probably be able to recognize what her mother was.

To deal with her frustration signal, Sarah organized and reorganized her behavior. Her picture of her mother was a loving and caring mom, but in the real world her mother mistreated her. Sarah created new behaviors to find a way to deal with the inconsistency and pain.

Organized behaviors that she tried were crying, becoming aggressive, attempting to fight back, seeking help from her father and brothers, and pleading for God to help her. When none of these behaviors worked, Sarah tried other organized behaviors, which were more creative, like counting by twos so that she would not have to think about what was happening to her. She learned to say it was not happening to her, but to another little girl. Finally she would say, "I'm going, I'm going, I'm gone." As she lived and grew in this environment, this behavior allowed her to believe that her mother was loving and caring and to maintain control in these traumatic situations.

As the pain intensified and Sarah got older, she developed other organized behaviors such as being sick, regurgitating, cutting her arms, and developing a picture of herself as a bad person who deserved to be punished. These were her attempts to deal with the pain and have control. These behaviors were purposeful, flexible, and creative—not crazy behaviors that had no meaning. At present, Sarah needs much attention because she received such negative attention in the past. This girl is more needy than most people. I compare her to the people in concentration camps, who were treated horribly. They did not want this treatment, but they had to live with it. Those that survived moved on. I emphasized to her, "You can't correct the past, and if you focus all of your energies on the past, then you have no energy left to focus on school or university." I tried to get her to focus on the good that would come when she was not dealing with the past. Sarah has had so many bad experiences in her life that it is going to take her a long while to become convinced that her life has changed.

I have been encouraging Sarah to move ahead, but I have listened to the past because in this case remembering was necessary. Sarah cannot move ahead until she tells someone she trusts about the past and from this trust gradually begins to accept that she is now safe; the past will not be repeated.

We have now gone through every age, and at every age something horrible happened to her. As she came close to the end of her memories, they seemed to be more traumatic. In the last memory, she realized that her father had abused her as well. She had thought all along that he did not know about what her mother was doing to her because his job took him out of town on a regular basis. Sarah was shattered when she learned that her father had assaulted her. She always thought that he would never harm her.

Sarah is a very needy person who has had a bad life for nineteen years, but the harshness of her life does not necessarily mean she cannot get over it. I have told her, "Once you start getting over things, you get over terrible things as well as not so terrible things. I don't think there is a relationship between how bad your life has been and the time it takes to get over it. If you have a slightly bad life, it doesn't mean you will get over it faster. It doesn't work in that proportion. You were mistreated, but you can still get over it. It is to your benefit to get over it. Human beings have great recuperatiye powers. Whether you are very sick or a little sick, when you are better, you are better."

Sarah and I have been working together for two years now, and she has come a long way. She will, however, continue to need counseling next year. Sarah has passed her twelfth year in school. She dropped two credits to allow her more time to work on the subjects that she had to pass in order to graduate. She did not think she could handle the math exam, and she had enough credits to graduate without it, so she dropped it. She also wanted time to see me without interfering with her class time.

As a result of her taking charge and accepting what she could possibly do under the circumstances, Sarah got an 80 average in the subjects she took. She graduated with high enough marks to apply for university when she gets her math credit.

When Sarah graduated from high school, I knew that I would see her less and less as time went on. I expected to see Sarah once a week over the summer and into the fall. She also planned to come back in the fall to do math at night school.

I helped Sarah get a summer job by writing to Social Services and explaining the importance of her having employment over the summer to keep her mind in the present rather than in the past. She went for an interview and landed a job looking after autistic children at one of their centers. Sarah was very happy about this job because for the first time she would be making her own money and have some independence.

Sarah enjoyed her work very much. While it was frustrating because she did not make friends with her co-workers, she seemed to have a real understanding and sensitivity for the autistic children she worked with. "I can understand where they are coming from because for years I couldn't communicate with anyone either, although for a different reason." She continued to have difficulties dealing with memories over the summer. When I was not there to help, Dr. Parker saw her.

I discussed with Dr. Parker the fact that I would not be available for counseling with Sarah after the fall, and we agreed that Sarah would continue to need counseling. I explained to her that a reality therapist might be the best type of counselor for Sarah, since that was what she was used to.

In August, Sarah finished her job. Within a week, she had another job as a teacher's aide for preschool children. She landed this job on her own after several interviews. Sarah really enjoys this work. She appears to relate to these children very well, and can use her art in the class. She also finds it much easier to make friends with teachers than she did on her previous job.

Sarah and I are gradually pulling away from each other. Sarah continues to see Dr. Parker and plans to see one of her colleagues at the health counseling center. Sarah is finding others she can trust and who can help her, and she is also taking more responsibility for her life. Having just finished and passed her final math course, she plans to attend the university next September.

It has been three years since Sarah had any contact with her family, and there are no signs that she will have contact with them. She is not interested in prosecuting them. Although legally that might be the right thing to do, it would probably have a very negative influence on Sarah herself and do more harm than good.

While Sarah was at school, I did the best I could for her, using reality therapy as my method of treatment. As a high school counselor, I work within a limited period in students' lives and thus have to let go of them when the time comes. I feel my counseling duties are now over with Sarah. While Sarah's therapy is not complete, I think she has made tremendous gains and growth through our relationship. Most important, Sarah is on the road to recovery, and I do not doubt that she will eventually make a full recovery.

I think Sarah has had an influence on me as well. She has shown me how a person, almost destroyed by significant human beings in her life, could let her creativity trigger behaviors, such as memory blackout when her survival was threatened, and how these behaviors could permit her to maintain control. She has helped me understand the recuperative powers of the human spirit.

DR. GLASSER'S COMMENTS ON "I'M NOT GOING TO LET THEM AFFECT ME"

Reading Terri Leonard's description of her work with Sarah, I could not help recalling a cartoon, published in a magazine more than forty years ago, which is now a classic. Two emaciated prisoners are chained high on a wall, looking as if they have been hanging there for weeks. In what seems a totally hopeless situation, one leans over and says to the other, "Here's my plan." I am sure that during the time she struggled with Sarah, Terri Leonard felt much the same as the man in the cartoon: we're in a pretty bad situation, but let's not give up; there must be something we can do.

The advantage of reality therapy as practiced by a counselor who knows control theory is that, as bad as the client's life has been and may still be, the counselor always has some idea of what to try. Terri Leonard knew that she had to help Sarah satisfy her needs right then, no matter what had happened and was still happening to her. She also knew that Sarah's self-destructive behavior was her best attempt to do this, but if she could be helped to figure out some better ways, this aberrant behavior would stop. Despite the ups and downs of this difficult and puzzling case, this is finally what happened.

Dr. G. L. Harrington, the great psychiatrist who taught me so much as I began my career, would have approved of what was done with Sarah. Over and over he emphasized, "When you don't know what to do, be sure not to do anything that might make things worse." On many occasions, Terri Leonard and Dr. Parker probably did not know what to do and perhaps were tempted, despite what they had promised, to dig into Sarah's home life, present and past. Fortunately, they kept their promise

124 CONTROL THEORY IN THE PRACTICE OF REALITY THERAPY

and stuck to basics: help her to get a little more love, a little more power, a little freedom and, once in a while, a little fun. Then be patient; wait and see what she does.

Pushing Sarah to talk about her family before she was ready in the vain hope that this might lead to some sort of therapeutic breakthrough could have been disastrous: she might even have committed suicide. Doing what they did for about a year, they were able to help Sarah make the slow but steady progress that served her well later in therapy. This progress helped her make the choice to discontinue the bizarre "attacks" that she had started so suddenly at the beginning of the second school year that Terri Leonard saw her. These attacks became the real test of whether or not therapy was going to succeed.

When Sarah started these attacks, the principal was so frightened by this strange behavior that he wanted to remove her from school, the only haven she had ever known. Confused themselves by what Sarah was doing, Terri Leonard and Dr. Parker managed to hold fast and continue doing what had helped her to get this far. They persuaded the principal to keep her in school, where they could help her to satisfy her needs. Despite the pressure of attack after attack, they did nothing new.

It is necessary now that I go into what I promised in Chapter 1, how control theory explains human creativity. Sarah's attacks are vivid examples of this amazing capacity. When I explained in the first chapter where all our behavior comes from, I also said that whenever the picture we want is significantly different from the picture we have, we feel an urgent desire to find a behavior that will reduce this difference and restore more control.

First we take a quick look into the behaviors we have. In these urgent situations, however, we usually do not have any that would be of use. But because we must do something, we will almost always create a completely or partially new behavior that we hope will work. We do this by tapping into a creative process that is continuously going on inside us all. Try to picture that each of us has inside of our brain a cauldron of creativity that is constantly bubbling like a pot of boiling oatmeal. While we cannot predict the time, place, or size of the next creative bubble in this pot, we can predict that it and others will continue to appear. Ordinarily, we pay little conscious attention to this constant source of creativity even though our dreams, when we are asleep and our attention is withdrawn, are a vivid example of the fact that it is there. While our dreams confirm its existence, most of us are not aware that we are constantly tapping into it. Large or small, there is a creative aspect to all of our behavior.

Parts of even our most ordinary behaviors, like the expression on our faces, the timbre of our voices, the motions of our hands, our whole retinue of physical expressiveness, are derived from this creative cauldron. I doubt that we ever express ourselves twice in exactly the same way: each expression is a small creation that we use to help us get across what we want to say. We tend to pay little attention to this vital capacity until we lose it as, for example, through the ravages of Parkinson's disease, which makes faces masklike and bodies stiff, mechanical remnants of once fluid, expressive people.

We are very aware of this unique capacity for creativity in star athletes and leading dancers who, as they perform in creative ways, astound us and seem at times even to surprise themselves. More than most of us, writers, musicians, artists, actors, and scientists learn how to tap into this cauldron continually as they create, and impromptu comedians are especially gifted at the same process.

This process is also capable of creating behaviors as bizarre as multiple personalities. Because of their extensive training, psychiatrists, more often than other mental health professionals, have traditionally dealt with these aberrant behaviors, traditionally called mental illnesses. The most common of these is labeled schizophrenia. As control theory explains, however, these are not illnesses. They are total behaviors that have as their thinking component bizarre creations like hallucinations and delusions.

To those who create them, the hallucinations and the delusions seem real, and because of this, traditional mental health professionals judge those who exhibit them to be insane. But reality therapists do not believe that the unrealistic thoughts, and even the actions and feelings, that people like Sarah choose makes them mentally ill in the sense that they are no longer capable of doing anything else. Had Sarah been hospitalized and treated with drugs as though she were mentally ill, instead of continuing in school as she did, it is my opinion that she would have found it difficult to trust Terri Leonard, and her progress would have been slowed down or stopped.

Sarah's attacks were so unexpected because they started after she had made so much progress and seemed able to trust the people who had been helping her. From their standpoint, she was out of the home she feared so much and well on her way to a new life. Not only were they perplexed, but I doubt if Sarah was even completely aware of why she used these attacks (technically best described as fugue states).

Terri Leonard's explanation is that it was Sarah's way of dealing with her belief that she actually was the bad person her mother had repeatedly told her she was. Sarah felt she should be punished and had repeatedly asked Terri Leonard to punish her. Since she had not been punished by her counselor, her attacks were her way of telling Ms. Leonard how bad she really was. Maybe then she would finally be punished.

This may be true or partly true; we are all conjecturing here. I think that it was even more Sarah's way of testing whether or not her counselor and the others could care for her if they knew how "bad" a person she was. If they still cared for her even after she revealed all the things in which she had "participated," she would know she was not really bad. They would not still care for her if she were.

If, on the other hand, they did not care for her as much as she had hoped, they would start to care more when she revealed her past. I believe that Sarah figured out that she would still be fairly safe because she had not told them anything directly. She could tell them what she wanted them to know while hiding behind the screen of the attacks she created. While she was hiding, she could continue to tell them how bad things had been and maybe they would finally care.

While both of these were possibilities, I think that by the

time Sarah decided to create the attacks, she was almost certain her counselor and the others would continue to care for her no matter what she revealed to them. By then, she trusted them more than she had ever trusted anyone, but she did not trust that they would continue to protect her for as long as she felt she needed protection. She panicked because she believed that they now saw her as much stronger than she saw herself. While she was aware that she was getting stronger, she feared that now as she was approaching adulthood (graduation), they would withdraw their support and protection before she was ready to be on her own.

Sarah created the attacks as an ingenious way both to tell them of her past and to ask them to continue to protect her. In a particularly creative twist, she did it as a little girl so that they could not fail to see that she was still far from being a capable adult. It worked. As she continued the attacks, she became more and more convinced that their support was real and would last. As this confidence developed, she no longer needed the attacks. But having done this once, she is capable of doing it or something very much like it again. If she panics again, as she likely will because she has not learned how to cope as well as a child raised in a normal home, she may again invoke the fugue states that seemed so useful to her in this situation. If she does, the attacks should be dealt with in the same way, and her progress, while slowed, will not stop.

What Sarah's attacks illustrate is how we are all capable of creating substantially new behaviors when we are living a frustration-filled life. Sarah was about as far from satisfying her needs as anyone I have ever worked with or even heard about, and what she created was truly remarkable.

While the creative process is always purposeful in that we attempt to use it to help us to satisfy a need, the creativity itself is always random. We will never know why or how Sarah's cauldron created the fugue attacks. If her cauldron had not created these, either it would have created something else, or she would have continued the anxietizing or other symptoms that she had created years before. But in some way that is not yet understood, her cauldron created these states, and in some way that is also not understood, she tried one and it worked for her. It is the same way that Thomas Edison created the electric light bulb. The idea came to him, he tried it, and it worked. Whether the creativity is crazy or sane, whether it is constructive or destructive, whether it has value or is merely whimsy, it is all the same process.

It is also the same for us all that the greater the frustration, the more we tend to look into our creative cauldron for an answer, but often no good answer is forthcoming. There is no guarantee that we will come up with anything that we will judge worth using. On the other hand, some of our most creative thoughts come when they are not particularly needed and when we least expect them. Perhaps the difference between highly creative people and ordinary people is that the creative people are willing to consider a creative idea when it appears, and the less creative let the opportunity go by. Lothar Meyer, the father of organic chemistry, dreamed of a snake swallowing its own tail and discovered the basic configuration of organic chemistry, the benzene ring for which he had been searching so long.

What psychiatry focuses upon and calls mental illness is the most bizarre of the creative feelings, thoughts, and actions that are part or parts of total behaviors like fuguing, hallucinating, phobicking, obsessing, compulsing, catatonicking, paranoiding, depressing, manicking, anxietizing, and guilting, to mention the most common. Medicine focuses on creative physiology that is called psychosomatic disease, such as heart attacking and peptic ulcering, and especially on creative immune system functioning, such as rheumatoiding and lupusing. I will discuss these creative diseases separately in the chapter, "Finding Your Own Way," which considers the case of Susan, a peptic ulcerer.

One of the indications that this creative process exists within us is provided by the results of the widespread use of psychotropic drugs like phenothiazines, which seem to shut down the bubbling of the creative cauldron. "Mentally ill" people, heavily dosed with these drugs, can no longer create in an acting, thinking, or feeling sense. This means that they cannot add expressiveness or fluidity to their motions or voice. Their actions become mechanical, their thinking concrete and slow, and their feelings flat.

As a result, they can no longer hallucinate or delude, but the creativity, which I believe is the essence of humanity itself, is blocked by the drugs. Their whole minds become as mechanical as their physical movements, and they look as though they have Parkinson's disease, which in a sense they do. But these drugs also have effects similar to what happens after a lobotomy in that those who take them also lose their psychological motivation. They care little about love, power, fun, and freedom: their main concern is survival, and many of them become interested in eating more than anything else.[1]

From the standpoint of therapy, the counselor should be aware that whatever creativity the client comes up with is always the best total behavior that the client could figure out at the time to satisfy his or her needs (actually pictures in his special world). No matter how bizarre, counselors must realize that they are dealing with a very creative total behavior, such as Sarah's attacks. They are not dealing with a mental illness.

The task of counseling, illustrated so beautifully here, is to avoid being distracted by the bizarre creation and continue to focus on the aspects of the client's behavior that are still sane and functional. Accept that the client needs whatever he or she has created, but do not let the client control you with it. If you allow that control, you are encouraging the client to continue what will be self-destructive if it continues for too long. To the extent that you can, encourage the client to continue satisfying his or her needs in sane and ordinary ways. If you do this, the bizarre behavior will stop, as it did with Sarah. This is not easy to do, and many counselors do not understand the need to do this, but it is by far the best way to deal with these kinds of creative total behaviors.

As we will see when we come to the case of Susan, creativity can also be expressed in the physiologic or somatic area. When this occurs, it often takes the form of what we accurately

---

[1]For a scientific review of this destructive process, see Peter Breggin, *Psychiatric Drugs: Hazards to the Brain* (New York: Springer, 1983).

call psychosomatic diseases. They are psychosomatic because it is the psychological component that must be addressed as much or even more than the somatic. For example, when Susan was helped to satisfy her needs, her total behavior of ulcering (the ulcer is somatic) stopped. Almost every case in this book reveals examples of this process and what the therapist did that was helpful. Review Jennifer's phobicking as described in Chapter 2 for another particularly good example. Also see *What Are You Doing?*[2] for examples of how to deal effectively with psychoses and other creative behaviors not dealt with here.

[2]Naomi Glasser, *What Are You Doing?* (New York, NY: Harper & Row, 1980).

7

The Little Girl Wakes Up

Becoming a Survivor of Incest

JANET A. THATCHER

JUNE HAD "fallen asleep" to cope with the intense pain from the realization of what might be in her past. "I don't know what happened. I'm still asleep." I heard this repeatedly in the early months of therapy before we both learned that there were incidents in her life that were beyond her toleration to face at the time. "Falling asleep" had been an effective total behavior for June from the time that she was ten years old. Now, at age thirty-five, she was uncovering the grim details of her past and experiencing this past in the present.

June came from a struggling working-class background in the Midwest. Her father had to move the family often in order to stay employed. In later years, he became an alcoholic, attempting to recover by himself. June's mother was a homemaker who assumed the once-traditional role of being passive and dependent on her husband. June had four older siblings, two sisters and one brother, all of whom had moved away from home by the time they were sixteen or seventeen years old. Her brother was aloof, but she formed close relationships with her sisters, especially Elizabeth, who portrayed the mother role for June. June's mother often confined herself to bed, spending much time aching and paining. Elizabeth became fairly protective, attempting to guide June through the maze of childhood and adolescent experiences by telling June what to do, rather than teaching her reasoning and thinking skills.

During childhood, the family had become very involved in a fundamentalist church. June used those religious beliefs to enable her to cope with the tremendous physiologic pain that she was experiencing—debilitating headaches and ringing in her ears. Her perception was that she had done something evil and was being punished. It was important to her father that she become actively involved in the church by witnessing—declaring her evilness and sins to God during the Sunday services in the presence of her family and the congregation. She wanted to be forgiven and thus accepted by God and the congregation as a worthy, loving individual. Although unable to pinpoint exactly what she had done that was evil, she continued to witness, never feeling either successful or forgiven. The pressure to continue this witnessing left her feeling frustrated. She later realized the tremendous impact of those experiences and expectations upon her perception of the world and of herself.

As June grew to adulthood and graduated from high school, she began to realize the restrictiveness of her parents' home. The religious restrictions, social restrictions, and parental requirements became overwhelming for her, and she decided to follow the paths of her siblings and leave home. After her high school graduation, June realized that she enjoyed writing and creating, and she chose to pursue a college education and career in the theatrical area. She became active in a community theater and found recognition and friendship from her involvement.

In the community theater, June met Ted, with whom her sense of belonging was strong. He provided support, security, and a challenge to her intellectual skills. They were married soon after meeting. The marriage seemed to serve several important purposes for June: breaking away even more from her parents, rebeling against her parents' value system because the marriage was racially mixed, and developing a sense of emotional and physical security.

June became pregnant soon after the marriage and gave birth to a daughter, Johanna. As June prioritized her energies toward her daughter, her spouse became more and more active in his theatrical career. June perceived that her husband treated her much the same way her father had treated her. He tended to take charge of their lives, to dictate their life style and values, and to maintain his independence while encouraging her to become more dependent on him. Although she sought and perceived the dependence as her security, she resented it. She started to withdraw from Ted, and the marriage deteriorated. Ted became verbally and physically abusive in his attempts to create the role of a wife that he desired. As neither of them had the effective behaviors to maintain a good marriage, the marital relationship became less and less need-satisfying for both. They decided to divorce.

While Johanna was still very young, June lived with her in a small community of a large metropolitan area. The treatment that they experienced was perceived as prejudiced, negative, and hateful. Scorned by both races, their lives were even threatened at one point. Throughout this time, June's perception of herself, based on her fundamentalist religious beliefs, was that she was continuing to be evil and was doing something wrong. However, she was never able to pinpoint her unacceptable behavior or why she deserved to be punished. Throughout these years of being a single parent and dealing with her confusion, June worked and struggled to fulfill several roles: mother, father, homemaker, and breadwinner. She received little financial aid or emotional support from anyone as she attempted to be a "good" mother and provide a "good" home for her daughter.

When Johanna was four years old, June married Jim, a school teacher. As part of his commitment and love for June, Jim adopted Johanna. But because of his perfectionism as a parent, the father-daughter relationship developed only in a limited way. Both June and Jim believed that because of her mixed ancestry and the racial prejudice of the community, Johanna had to excel—be a high achiever. They exposed her to the creative arts, encouraging her to develop her own talents. Johanna took piano lessons, June read her poetry and stories, and together they drew and created pictures.

June and Jim had two more daughters. Despite the ten-year age difference between Johanna and the older of the half-sisters, she became very close to them.

After the birth of her youngest child, June began to experience physical discomfort and eventually had a hysterectomy. With this surgery, she experienced much emotional pain and grief because she had hoped to have more children. She frequently experienced depressing feelings and had severe difficulty in coping with her various roles. She wanted to be a "perfect" mother and parent her children so that they would become responsible and not have to deal with fear and guilt. Although she devoted most of her time and energy to her children, however, she did not feel that she was accomplishing her goal as a parent. Nor did she know which direction she should take or what changes to make. Being a wife was difficult since her only role model was her mother, and she could see the difficulties in her parents' marriage. She also felt a lack of purpose in her life regarding a career because she no longer worked outside the home. Overwhelmed by what she perceived as a lack of knowledge about parenting, being a good wife, and providing for the emotional needs of her family, she would retreat to her bedroom, as her mother had done. This retreat gave her relief from responsibilities and gained her attention from family members.

At this point, Johanna was experiencing difficulty with her adolescent growth and role, and June came to the counseling setting with her concerns about Johanna. June had studied various counseling approaches in her college course work and had attended a one-day workshop where Dr. Glasser talked about control theory and reality therapy. These concepts were parallel to many of her own values, such as individual responsibility, allowing consequences, not accepting excuses, and emphasizing actions. She sought a therapist in private practice who used reality therapy techniques. Johanna did not view herself as having difficulties and tended to project much of the blame and responsibility onto others, especially Jim. Viewing him as a perfectionist who could not be satisfied, she had given up being involved with him. They neither talked nor did things together, and she refused to invest energy or time to work on this relationship.

Johanna was having difficulty identifying herself as biracial. She viewed herself as either black or white and alternately tried to gain acceptance from one group or the other. Living in a situation where the two groups stayed segregated, not knowing any other biracial adolescents, she thought she had to choose between the two. To address these issues, I did both individual counseling with Johanna and family counseling with Johanna, June, and Jim. The focus in family counseling was on helping Jim and Johanna develop their relationship by creating time together, learning to talk and listen to each other's wants and behaviors, and helping June to determine her role as mother. With Johanna individually, I tried to help her define her racial identity. After several months, Johanna changed her priority of wants from what her parents requested to her own wants of acceptance and involvement with peers. As she did this, we became less involved in counseling.

Seeing the changes in her daughter and perceiving that she was at fault for the family's difficulties, June questioned her skills as a mother. Her depressing became a flag for June that she needed individual time with the therapist, but she was having trouble asking for therapeutic help. I presented the idea of giving Johanna a break to see if she could implement the ideas we had talked about and doing individual therapy with June.

Once we started, it became evident that June had many more problems than were discussed in family counseling. She seemed immature and uncertain about her identity, and her relationships were limited both in depth and in numbers. She perceived herself as a person who had little to contribute and distrusted herself in social situations. Her excuse for the lack of interaction was that she did not possess a college degree. June's family interactions varied from frequent and intensely involving activities to avoiding her family and family projects, at the same time depressing and withdrawing. This pattern was especially true of her relationship with her husband and children. However, the involvement with her parents and siblings seemed consistent and intense.

Although June developed a trusting relationship with me, she was still reserved and evasive at times. She avoided areas of conflict and wanted to talk only about her depression. Her physiological behaviors included headaching, experiencing heart palpitations, and shaking.

We discussed what June wanted from her family, the professional and personal aspects of herself, her roles as wife, mother, daughter, and sister, and her spiritual beliefs. She shared her attempts at achieving these wants and her frustrations, but she always returned to the depressing behavior with both her family and me. June seemed to be stymied in her progress in therapy and thus began to weaken in her commitment to help herself. I decided to confront June with her lack of investment in therapy and to help her see the consequences of this choice. The relationship between us seemed strong; by now, June viewed me as a need-fulfilling person. "June, we have been talking for several months. I have noticed that you show up for your sessions, we talk and develop plans, but you do little more. You seem to want to go along without really figuring out what is going on and to avoid telling me and yourself some truths. I am unwilling to continue in this way, so you have a choice—to begin to really work in therapy or to stop counseling. I will not continue to see you if you are not willing to trust me with what is really going on for you, and I cannot make you tell me." June's picture of herself as a growing, developing person who would be rid of these difficult struggles and who would be functioning as a wife and mother was a priority for her. She decided that she would invest more energy in therapy by placing her mental health and growth as a dominating picture. She made a decision, during this emotion-filled session, that she did not want to lose this therapist, the only person with whom she could talk and who understood her. It was at this point that June began to "wake up."

Her perceptions of herself and her situation began to clarify. In examining her present behaviors, she was able to understand the total behaviors she chose as a way to meet her survival needs. The behaviors consisted of physiologically losing awareness of her surroundings, feeling scared and numb, thinking "I'm scared and can't face this," and acting immobilized, talking and moving very slowly. During sessions, June would use these behaviors to avoid facing and acknowledging her situation. I would point out to June that her observable behavior was that she was "going to sleep" in therapy. Although effective in protecting herself, she began to realize that the long-term consequences were devastating.

Once June was able to perceive these behaviors as ineffective in getting her need for belonging met, she began to make some significant choices about her life. Through her "waking up," she began to become aware of some of the memories in her perceived world that she had not wanted to recognize. Deciding to question her sisters, June listened hesitantly to situations in the family that neither she nor her sisters wanted to acknowledge. With this information from her sisters and through my slow and persistent probing, June was able to remember many past events and behaviors. She remembered that she had never liked sleeping alone. (If her husband was away on business, she would ask one of her children to sleep with her.) She remembered that her father had answered the door while not completely dressed. She viewed this behavior as normal and could not understand the behaviors of her friends upon seeing her father. During therapy, June asked, "Is this how other fathers act?" She was now questioning many of the events in her life. Ultimately, through her questioning and probing, she was able to walk back through her past to discover many significant events.

During a therapy session, June was able to reveal one of the painful memories.

JUNE: I feel as if something happened to me as a child, but I don't know what. My sisters have told me about times that Dad was weird, but I don't know if he was with me.
JANET: What do you mean, "Dad was weird"?

JUNE: Well, he would bother them, but they told me that he didn't bother me. But I don't know. I think he did, but I don't think he did.

JANET: Is it that you don't want to think he did or to find out?

JUNE: If I find out, I don't know what I'll do. [She begins to "fall asleep."]

JANET: June, what's going on right now?

JUNE: I'm scared, and I don't want to deal with this!

JANET: June, remember this is a safe place, I'm a safe person, and you want to get past this. Is it going to help you to avoid this memory?

JUNE: No. Oh, I'm scared. [Beginning to cry.] You know, my Dad may have treated me just like he did my sisters.

JANET: May have?

JUNE: No, I think he did. He did bother me!

JANET: June, it's important for you to tell yourself and me what he did. Will you do that?

JUNE: [After a long pause, crying, and "going to sleep" several times as I was trying to help her stay in the present behavior.] He *did* sexually molest me.

June had realized the horror that her father had sexually molested her. She had "stayed awake" and had begun a journey from which she could not return easily.

As she maintained herself in the present, she was able to safely recall many of the incestuous incidents by her father. She revealed that her feelings in and about the past seemed overwhelming to her, but I told her that it was paramount to focus on these feeling components as they directly affected her wants, her perceptions of herself, and subsequently her total behaviors. The feeling components that she was able to bring to the present included terroring, loving, angering, and frustration. Her thinking regarding the past (but very much in the present) included "I don't count," "I'm accepted only sexually," "I love/hate my father," and "I am okay only as a little girl." Her thinking and feeling components were sometimes contradictory, and her acting was inconsistent. At times, her present acting behavior could be that of an adult woman performing the roles of wife, mother, and working person or the behavior of a little girl by using "baby talk" and being dependent and helpless.

Her past or memory in the perceived world was filled with painful, negative events. In order to resolve the vast discrepancy between her wants and her perception of what she had, she used helpless, childlike, sometimes psychosomatic behaviors. These behaviors had been effective for survival in her childhood, but they were becoming increasingly ineffective. In her present situations, these total behaviors allowed her to avoid emotional intimacy, to maintain her status quo, and to avoid the decisions about her father's role in her life. In examining her memories and past, June was able to realize that these behaviors were adversely affecting her opportunities to create the life that she had said she wanted. The behaviors that she was using to avoid facing painful memories also isolated her from appropriate relationships with her husband, children, and friends. Her attempts to maintain the functioning of the family without changes became ineffective because of her family's desire to grow and to be involved in many activities outside the home.

When June decided to stay awake, she accepted the effectiveness of talking with others about the incidents that were affecting her present being. Her first discussion, outside of therapy, was with her sisters. She realized that her sisters had desired to protect themselves and her. They expressed shame and helplessness in not accomplishing this responsibility. Having the confirmation that they were victims of their father's behaviors, June began to recall even more incidents. Several times, she wanted to stop remembering because of the pain that accompanied these visualizations. I helped her to realize that the process was essential, using the analogy that she would "vomit up what the mind alone cannot digest." As the therapist, I would help her to handle the poisonous recollections. With this reassurance that these feeling behaviors were now within her control, she made the decision to share even more openly.

June also entered an educational support group for victims of incest. There, able to share what she felt and thought, she began to realize that she and the others had feelings and thoughts that were, for them, normal. June began to reevaluate her perception of herself. She realized that these behaviors were her way of protecting herself from the emotional devastation of losing the naivety of her childhood and of losing the trust and safety of a parent's protection. The perception of seeing herself as a child who was sexually attractive to someone was overwhelming, but she was willing to examine this perception. By changing her self-perception from negative and painful to positive and by changing some of her total behaviors, June was experiencing more and more control. She was becoming the woman she wanted to be. She continued to have many questions about what normal behavior was. Because of her father's sexual behaviors toward her and her mother's lack of acknowledging this behavior and her protecting her daughter from it, June had not experienced appropriate parenting. She was confident of very few of her behaviors and chose frequently to be creative in her behaviors, especially in reference to parenting. She would develop intense and involved emotional relationships with all of her children by spending much time and energy on their projects.

June was now ready to confront her parents with her memory of the past, the process through which she was going, and her statement of her feelings and thinking about them. Getting the family secret verbalized, at least within the family, was essential to June. We examined the possible consequences. She realized that if she changed the family roles by her own assertiveness and openness about the molesting incidents, her father might reject the actuality of the incidents, he might return to drinking heavily, the family might reject her, she might have to talk with her children about their grandfather, her mother might be devastated and return to her psychosomatic illnesses, and she might be rejected by her parents and siblings. June grew stronger and clearer about her decision to discuss the past. In her mind and during therapy, she rehearsed what she wanted to say, how she wanted to say it, and when this situation would occur. In actuality, the confrontation occurred after she heard a sermon in church (which she had recently begun to attend). The minister made the statement that families need to be honest and to communicate, and June knew what she wanted to do. The sharing with her parents was calm but emotional on her part. Her father stated that he had already admitted his behaviors, said his apologies, and would not do so again. June, with a firmness and clarity and awakeness that she had never experienced before, stated that he had not apologized to *her*. Her mother continued to protect herself emotionally by asking June not to discuss the past.

June had difficulty coping with her father's avoidance of facing the reality of his behaviors, his tendency to minimize the impact of his behaviors, and his refusal to address his relationship to her. She was very assertive with him and told him what she wanted, but he was unable to address her wants. The conversation ended with no compromises or commitments. Nevertheless, when the interaction was over, June felt peaceful and confident.

June continued to examine her recent behaviors, to compare and contrast them with her remembrances of past situations and behaviors, and then to more clearly determine a direction for her future. With the continual recollections of incidents, her angry feelings emerged more frequently. She was angry not only with her parents, but also with her sisters for not being more effective in their protection, with her brother for not suspecting what was going on, and with her husband for helping her to stay "a little girl." She began to ask for the things that she wanted and to express those thinking, feeling, and acting behaviors of which she had been previously unaware. For example, she asked her husband for his time without feeling guilty about needing attention, she learned to express her thoughts with increasing confidence, she learned to express her feelings about being a woman even though she might sound naive and possibly ignorant, and she took risks by attending functions at her children's schools. All of these behaviors were considered high risks by her, but she was determined to stay awake.

The responsibility of the sexual abuse was placed with her father; she stopped blaming herself. This transition was accomplished by giving her father long stares, during which time her thinking behavior was "It was your responsibility," and her feeling behavior was angering.

At the same time, June was experiencing some sadness

about the "little girl" within her. She was sad because the little girl was familiar and a significant part of her organized behaviors—how she related to people. We talked about having a symbolic funeral for the "little girl." June felt that if she held onto the little girl, she would not handle adult responsibilities and behaviors effectively.

The "little girl" had been her steady companion and, she thought, the only way of securing her father's love, but June now wanted the challenge of continued growth. By saying farewell, she would be able to relate to adults as equals, to relate to her children as a parent, and to relate to her parents (even though they would not reciprocate) as an adult. She decided to accept the adult role and had a symbolic funeral only in her thinking. The grief was short-lived as she was excited about the challenges ahead of her.

June continued to experience periodic dreams and recollections of the incest: she saw these as regressive—disappointments to her and to me. I reassured her that to me they were neither regressions nor disappointments. In fact, I viewed them as progress—her way of continuing to wake up.

June's confidence began to flourish. She joined another support group who called themselves survivors of incest, identifying strongly with the label of survivor. That label helped June to perceive herself in more effective control, less responsible for the incestuous acts, and more responsible for her future. With that strength, she decided to return to college and complete her degree. She also decided to volunteer her expertise and sensitivity to the organization sponsoring the survivors' support group. Combining her volunteerism with work toward her degree, she developed a pamphlet for the survivor of incest.

Although she thought that her parenting skills were effective, she realized, as most parents do, that those skills could be improved. She secured a part-time position teaching parenting classes, hoping to learn as she taught. (This position had not previously been filled by anyone without a college degree.)

The little girl was wide awake, and she had become a confident and competent woman.

Summary

My role in June's awakening was to be need-fulfilling by being consistent, available, listening but not always blindly accepting of her behaviors, challenging, and caring. Many times, it was important to confront June with those behaviors (which she held onto for her survival) that were becoming increasingly ineffective in fulfilling her other needs. The needs for belonging and importance were not being met effectively, so I needed to teach and challenge June in these areas. Establishing a role model for effective ways to communicate and relate to others was important. She needed feedback about her present behaviors, such as being asleep. As she attempted to block out the real world, I frequently had to inform June of the societal expectation for various roles and to correct some of her perceptions, for example, that a "father may touch his daughter anywhere as an expression of love." Through the therapist and others, June was able to establish a network that provided a reality check.

The relationship between us became very close but not dependent. In times of crises, June looked to me for assistance, but she was able to function generally on her own. Although there were sometimes telephone calls between the weekly sessions, June was able to cope by herself or with the help of her growing network of family and friends. On the Mother's Day following our final session, June sent a card with the following message:

In the time we have spent together, you have been like a mother to me. In many ways, I am like your child. On the outside, when we met, I was a grown-up woman with children and a husband and a job, all the grown-up things. But on the inside, controlling that grown-up woman, was a frightened little girl hiding in perpetual darkness from terrors she could neither face nor understand, hating herself and trusting no one.

With you, for the first time, that little girl felt safe and nurtured, cared for, and accepted. And as she began to grow, I began to take control. I grew up again, this time learning how to face the world, how to love myself, and how to share myself with others. I continue the growth process as I move on through life. And you helped me lay the foundation, to learn these important skills that are a good mother's highest priorities for her children no matter what their age.

During the time I was facing some of my greatest challenges while learning and growing, you were there. You helped me to hold on and to continue to mother my own children at times when I didn't think I could even go on trying. You were there with support and guidance above and beyond the call of professional duty. My children have benefited greatly from your influence. You have helped me to become more of the mother I have always wanted to be for them.

And so, on this Mother's Day, I'm thinking of you with respect, gradtilitude (spelled this way it means EXTREME gratitude) and love.

In receiving these feelings and thoughts from June, I grew in my love and respect for her and her strength and for that of other survivors of incest.

DR. GLASSER'S COMMENTS ON "THE LITTLE GIRL WAKES UP"

Basic to control theory is the concept that our behavior is our best attempt to satisfy one or more of our needs. Our needs become operational at birth and continue unabated throughout our lives. When we are little, if we are fortunate, we are raised in a home in which we learn how to satisfy our needs in responsible ways. We learn this mostly through examples set by all those with whom we live, but the example set by our parents is the most important. If they do not set a good example, we often fail to learn what we need to know as we grow older and must satisfy our needs on our own.

The tragedy of being sexually mistreated as June was is not only the mistreatment itself, which the child does not understand but almost always knows is not right, but the fact that the child frequently stops learning what she needs to know to grow into a competent adult. June grew into an adult and went through the act of marriage and raising children, but from the standpoint of knowing how to behave as an adult, she was still a "little girl."

The question of whether June could have been helped through counseling to grow into a competent adult without confronting her past is hard to answer unequivocally. Some people need to confront a traumatic past; others find it better to leave it alone. For example, Sarah in the last chapter, who was more extensively molested than June, barely revealed her past and did not directly confront it at all. Despite what happened, she still was able to move on to adult behaviors.

June could not do this. Perhaps her fundamentalist religious upbringing had inculcated in her the sense that she had been involved in something wrong and had to correct it. Whatever it was, she made up her mind that she had been wronged by her father and that she was going to stay a little girl until this wrong was corrected. What was harmful about this decision was that, until she entered therapy, she had dedicated almost her whole life to staying a little girl. To do this, she created a wide variety of symptoms that she used to escape from adult responsibilities; she only went through the motions of being grown-up. She could not grow up because she had not learned what it was that adults do with their lives.

For a long time before she entered counseling, June had nurtured a semiconscious fantasy that if she only confronted her father, she would be absolved: he would take all the blame, and the rest of the family would admit that they had not protected her as they should have. I am sure that many who see themselves as victims have this fantasy, but in real life it hardly ever works out this way. Abusers or even those in the abuser's family don't want to deal with it anymore. It is as important to them to let it drop as it is to the abused to bring it up.

In therapy, June began at first to gain the strength to be more aware of this fantasy, but she still did not have enough strength or trust to tell the therapist what was wrong. Later, in therapy without her daughter, she thought, "Now I have a chance," but she also increased her symptoms as her way of saying to her therapist, "See how I'm suffering. Help me!" But like the little girl she still was, she was evasive about what she wanted help with. It took great skill for Janet Thatcher to bring out the incest problem. June's choice to increase her symptoms was also her way of keeping her anger restrained, because the closer she got to dealing with the incest, the more angry she became. Unlike Everett in Chapter 4, June had kept her anger totally under control, but to do this she had to sleep, headache, palpitate, and strongly depress.

In reality therapy we do not deal with the past unless it is strongly related to the present. In this case, June's past was very much a part of the present: she wanted some admission of guilt from her father now for what he had done to her in the past. But like many victims of incest, when she confronted her father, she could not get the kind of admission of wrongdoing from her father or anyone in her family that she wanted. Still, she bene-fited from the confrontation in that she was able to make a statement he could not deny: "Whether you will admit this now or not, you did this to me!"

After this, with the help of Janet Thatcher and the survivors of incest support group, June was able to move on. As Dr. Thatcher says, she finally decided to "wake up" and begin to live as an adult in the adult world. It was when she realized what some victims of incest and other family deficiencies never realize, that the past can never be rewritten but only survived, that she made this decision.

Dr. Thatcher will probably hear from her occasionally, since June still has much to learn about being an adult. She will learn a great deal of this on her own because she is now ready and even eager to learn. Teaching the parenting class is a good example of how she will accomplish this. From experiences like this, she will gain much of the confidence that she needs to be a more effective adult. But June was a little girl for a long time, and her childish behavior and her painful symptoms did give her control over her life. When she behaved childishly, she was cared for and helped, and this will be hard to forget. She should therefore keep in touch with her therapist. She has come a long way, but she is not quite finished.

June would need help again if, for example, her father got old and needed her care. I doubt if she will ever be strong enough to do this on her own, and she should be counseled not to attempt it.

8

Why Bother Going On?

A Mother Is Overwhelmed Dealing with the Death of a Son and Irresponsible Behaviors of Others in the Home

THOMAS J. SMITH

IN LATE SUMMER 1984, I received a call from JJ, a depressing-sounding woman, who asked if I could help her with her problem and immediately answered her own question by saying that she doubted it. She said that no one could help: she only called because a friend had suggested that she do so. I asked her, in a caring manner, what was going on with her right now, who the friend was who had suggested she call, and what she saw as her problem.

I listened to JJ's sad story. Her eldest son had died as a result of a high school football injury only thirteen months previously. Her husband, John, did not understand her two surviving sons, Carl, a sixteen-year-old in eleventh grade, and Bill, a thirteen-year-old in ninth grade. Carl, especially, who was "into pot," was giving both JJ and John a hard time. I also learned that this was a second marriage for both and that both had brought children into the relationship. John's son, Tim, had recently come to live with the family. He was seventeen years old, not in school, and also causing problems. Because she sounded so desperate and in pain, I asked JJ how soon she could come to see me. She came the next day.

I always write or call to thank anyone who refers a client, and so I called JJ's friend, a former client, who had made the referral. She told me what she knew of JJ's situation and her perceptions of JJ's behavior and attitude: JJ had been acting more and more depressed during the past several months, keeping more to herself, and looking more tired than usual. She was very worried about her son, Carl, and his unacceptable behavior. The friend expressed her concern that JJ might "do something foolish." I interpreted this comment to mean suicide, although at the time I did not ask the question directly.

JJ arrived on time for her appointment, and we spent the first half of the session learning about each other. I encouraged her to ask questions about me in an effort to establish a friendly, trusting relationship. She asked how long I had been doing this "counseling business" and whether or not I had a family. I could tell she was a bit nervous and apprehensive, so I discussed how I had gotten into the counseling business, the type of clients with whom I worked, and what my regular full-time job was—working with victims and perpetrators of family violence. I also told her that I was the father of four boys and the grandfather of five children. This information helped her to feel more at ease and began the process of establishing a more trusting relationship.

I explained to JJ some of the basic concepts of reality therapy and control theory. I told her that I was not a magician who had all the answers, but I would help her to find what she wanted. We talked about pictures, being in control, being out of control (or the feeling of being out of control), communication difficulties, wants, basic needs, and how we get these needs met. Having had only several months exposure to control theory, I felt somewhat inadequate explaining it. JJ seemed to understand quite well, however. The more we talked about control, perceptions, and pictures, the better I seemed to grasp the concepts as well. I told her how helpful it was to have a bright, open, and willing client like her.

JJ described her situation as hopeless, out of control, and desperate. Since his brother had died, Carl, her sixteen-year-old son, had become very disruptive and belligerent. He was having discipline problems in school and in less than a year had gone from being a good student to being a poor one. JJ was feeling that Carl's problems were due to her failings as a mother and wife.

This was a longer-than-usual first session because JJ seemed to want to talk, and I felt it important to encourage her to do so. Her concerns and frustrations went beyond those she had for her son. She felt that her husband, John, was "picking on" her son, blaming him for everything, and not understanding her and the problems she was having with Carl. The situation was further complicated by John's seventeen-year-old son, Tim, who had come to live with them a few months earlier and was creating chaos in the house. Tim came in at all hours of the night, picked fights with Carl over money, house rules, and use of the family car, and argued with JJ and John over just about everything.

As I listened to JJ outline her problems, I came to believe that she felt these problems were insurmountable. According to JJ, nothing was working. No one really cared about her problems; no one could help her; she did not want to bother anyone with her troubles. Sometimes she spoke sensibly; sometimes she rambled and seemed terribly confused and distraught. JJ needed help sorting through these problems to determine which ones were hers and which ones were not. I assured her that I was concerned and would do whatever I could to help her understand how she could get better control of her life. I also told her that I believed her to be a very caring, intelligent, and worthwhile person and that she had convinced me of her potential to do well.

JJ expressed her frustration with her husband who, while being caring and loving toward her, was not treating Carl the way she would have liked. He blamed Carl for everything that went wrong and criticized him constantly. I asked her if she would be willing to discuss with John some of the information we had talked about in this session, and possibly do the same with Carl. (It should be noted here that the only reference to her youngest son, Bill, was at the beginning and the end of the session. He seemed, in her opinion, to be doing fine. Her husband, too, seemed to have no problem with the thirteen-year-old.)

Reluctantly, JJ agreed to do this, but she did not want to make another appointment. She wanted to wait and see how things went before deciding. Although I did not agree with this choice, I respected and supported her decision, encouraging her to call me if there were any difficulties.

During this session, JJ disclosed more information about her attempt to handle the loss of her seventeen-year-old son in a very tragic high school football accident. She stated that after a period of time and with the help of several friends, she had become involved with an organized group that focused on dealing with personal loss. She felt that the experience had helped her considerably. The group, composed primarily of parents who had lost children, spent time examining their behaviors in a supportive way to show that they had done nothing to contribute to their children's deaths. They met monthly to support one another during their mourning. I commented to JJ that her decision to take that step was a significant one that helped her build the strength to survive a very tragic time. She told me that she stayed with that group for about six months and then left because she did not want to keep recalling the tragedy that caused so much pain. I commended her for that action as another indication of her strength. However, it was clear that she was still experiencing a great deal of pain associated with this tragedy. Her decision to seek therapy was a good one. She agreed about the pain, but she was reluctant at that point to comment about the therapy.

JJ wanted advice on how to make her sixteen-year-old son give up drugs, stop staying out late, and obey the rules at home. JJ felt that her son was hanging around the "wrong kids," not communicating with her or her husband, and doing poorly in school both in grades and behavior.

The recent addition of John's 17-year-old son to the home had further complicated their lives. JJ had agreed to have Tim stay with them, but she was now feeling that it was a mistake.

I asked her to explain and give me more information. Tim, too, was in trouble, unwilling to follow house rules, smoking both pot and cigarettes, and being verbally disrespectful to people in general. Most of the problems JJ outlined had started shortly after the death of her oldest son thirteen months earlier. It was apparent to me that the entire family was experiencing the pain of this loss. While JJ was outlining all of these issues, I was attempting to help her realize what she had control over and what she needed to let other members of the family control. JJ was playing the role of "super mom" by attempting to manage everything. In the process, she was taking the blame for everything that went wrong. It was no wonder that she felt overwhelmed.

JJ described her relationship with her husband of seven years as reasonably good. Although their communication was satisfactory, John did not seem able to communicate effectively with her sons. Before the oldest son, Paul, had died in the accident, he had been the scapegoat, but now Carl was the one to get all the "flack" while John praised Paul. The youngest, Bill, seemed to get along well with his stepfather. JJ believed that she and John had a good working agreement regarding discipline: each would discipline his or her own children and not interfere with the other. The agreement was fine, but the kids were not cooperating.

In this unusually long session of almost two hours, I encouraged JJ to disclose as much as she was comfortable with in an effort to understand her better. When she said that nothing seemed to be working right, not even her job, I asked her to explain. She was an X-ray technician in an office with several doctors but was also expected to act as a receptionist. Despite the excessive workload, confusion, and too many bosses, she felt she did her job well and liked it. I helped her to look at her responsibilities, what she was hired and paid to do, and who had the responsibility for permitting the overload to occur. It was clear to me that her picture of her life was out of balance; she was in pain and confused.

JJ alluded repeatedly to the possibility of suicide, and I was concerned. For example, when she talked about the confusion at work she said, "Why bother? No one cares. Why go on?" When she talked about the problems at home, she said, "Maybe they would be better off without me," and "No one really cares." I encouraged her to focus on her strengths and the positive things that were going on. She was able, at least, to agree to call me if she felt things seemed to be getting worse. I think the reason she was reluctant to make another appointment was because she really believed that no one could help and she was at that time overwhelmed with information about these problems and her ability or lack of ability to solve them.

I did not hear from JJ for about nine days. Then I received a letter, an excerpt from which follows:

> I did approach my husband and my son in the manner we discussed. I was utterly destroyed by their reactions. The cure seems worse than the disease. I need time to see the results of my communications with them, then I will call you.

This was related to our discussion of responsibilities. JJ was not to take responsibility for her son's choice of behavior, nor for her husband's son's choice of behavior. After setting rules that were acceptable to them, she was to let them understand the consequences of their actions and then to be consistent in enforcing them. The brevity of the letter concerned me since she said nothing else about her status, feelings, or problems. I immediately called her to see what was going on. I wanted to know more about her son's and husband's reactions, what she actually said to them, and how she was doing. I also did not want to lose a client. (There was probably a bit of ego involved here, but I liked JJ and was genuinely concerned about her.) When I reached her about four days after she had written the letter, she said she was in a better place and was glad that I called. (Four years later, when I interviewed JJ for this case study, I learned that she probably would not have called me because of hassles from her husband and son about getting counseling. I also learned that she was reluctant to make another appointment because I had my office in my home, and she was concerned for her safety meeting me alone in my home office, a fact of great importance that I had never considered.)

JJ later told me that the phone call was a "lifesaver" for her. Although she still says she believes that I saved her life, she now knows that it was really her own behavior, strength, and willingness to change that saved her life. During the phone call we discussed what JJ was doing, what was and was not working, and how things in general were going. I did not want to push too hard for fear of pushing her away. She said she could feel that I was genuinely concerned. Some of the things we had talked about in that first session were working, much to her surprise, but she would not elaborate. She asked for more time to sort things out and attempt more of the new behaviors (my words, not hers) before setting another appointment. I said I respected that and she should call if there was anything I could do to help. Her last comment was that she and her husband were having major problems with Tim (his son) and that she was attempting to discuss with John the information we had covered in our session about behavior, consequences, and responsibility.

Three days later, JJ phoned to set another appointment. It had now been three weeks since our first appointment. She definitely sounded better on the phone, and I was looking forward to our next session with a much more positive feeling.

In this next session, JJ told me that she had internalized all the information we discussed at our first session. I asked her what that meant, and she said that she is a thinker; she had taken the information and applied it to possible situations and that everything we discussed made sense to her. No matter how hard she tried to find flaws in the information, she could not. And the more she thought about and tried things like making rules and sticking with them, and not taking responsibility for her son's delinquent behavior and poor school work, the better things got for her. At first, however, there was great resistance from both husband and son. We spent a little time talking about the power and control need, which made perfect sense to JJ as she had already been aware of how she was attempting to exert power in controlling her son. We discussed how she could maintain the power and control she needed and at the same time let her son experience power and control. This was difficult at first because the bottom line for her was his use of drugs in her home—the consequence of that behavior would have to be his departure from their home. We worked out a way for JJ to do this. Carl had to feel he had a part in the final decision. JJ said that in part she had already begun the process by talking with Carl, outlining the rules she wanted followed, and asking for his input. It was here that she got stuck. His rules were not quite what JJ wanted. However, the process had begun, and I commended JJ for her gallant effort and the strength to follow her beliefs.

Carl was using the loss of his brother to get his way by saying such things as, "If Paul were here, things would be different for me," or "You always let Paul do that, but not me." Carl seemed to be covering his feelings about the loss of his brother with acting-out behavior, and JJ was willing to confront him about this in a way that allowed him to talk about those feelings without fear of being criticized. But Carl still wanted his own way, lots of freedom, and the right to make his own decision about school and his future. It was obvious to me that JJ was beginning to take more effective control of her life just by the way she talked in this session. For example, when I asked her what she would do the next time she and her son discussed these issues (drugs in the house, school truancy, coming home at a reasonable hour at night, plus whatever topics he might have) she said, "Well, it's his life and I can't live it for him. He'll have to decide how important it is and what he really wants to do with it. All I can do is show him that I love him and tell him what I'd like him to do, but I can't do it for him!" I was elated at this response. What a wonderful experience, to have a client both verbalize and experience the concepts of reality therapy and control theory so quickly after the first involvement.

JJ was ready to set the limits for and with her son with all the love and concern a mother could muster and allow him to experience the results of whatever actions he chose to take, including moving out. JJ was also willing to let Carl experience expulsion from school for truancy or inappropriate behavior, failure if he did not do his work satisfactorily, and grounding if he chose not to live by what they agreed upon as reasonable rules of the house.

Exploring these ideas, especially the consequences regarding Carl, was very painful for JJ. It was all the more wrenching because of the recent loss of her oldest son. However, when we further examined what she had been doing the last eight to ten months and how it had not been working (and according to JJ, nothing has been working), it was easier for her to see that a new approach to life was necessary. It was very helpful that she had tried most of what we had discussed in the first session and had seen the positive results. She recognized that it was time to change. JJ also knew that once Carl made an agreement with her, he would live by it and the consequences because, as she said, "He makes very few promises, but when he does, he lives by them. He is a person of his word."

It was about at this point that JJ confided to me her feelings of not wanting to go on any more. Things seemed too complicated and unresolvable. This despite the beginnings of some success and the seemingly positive first part of this session. My picture of what happened during this session apparently did not match JJ's, so I asked her to help me. I explained that I was confused because I thought things were beginning to jell for her.

She first stated that she had agreed to meet again with her son, Carl, in about three days to finalize some plans about these rules, and that was creating some severe anxiety. Then she said that her husband was doing something similar with his son because of continued inappropriate behavior that was unacceptable to both of them. I asked her to explain.

Tim had been taking money without permission from his Dad and JJ. Then a credit card disappeared. Tim denied that he was involved in any way. All this had happened in the past three weeks, after my first session with JJ. Not only was JJ attempting to work things out with her son, but with her husband and his son as well. No wonder she was anxietizing! Then she told me that she was trying to help her husband with his son in the same way that she was trying to help hers, based on the limited information we had discussed in our first session. This was what prompted that desperate letter a few weeks ago, because no one was at that time accepting any of JJ's ideas. She was feeling rejected, unloved, and depressed, and she did not see how anyone could love her because of the way she had been acting the past several months. At this point I explored the basic needs with her, and she identified that the one she was not meeting was the fun need. Although she expressed the feeling that she could not see how anyone could love her, she acknowledged after some discussion that her husband really did love her, and later that her two sons did love her, but she just did not see how anyone could, given her recent choice to depress.

I asked JJ to think about things she could do to have fun and to bring the ideas to the next session so we could discuss them. She readily agreed. I also asked her to call me if anything happened that confused her or that could not wait until the next session.

As we discussed basic needs, she identified that her job was generally satisfying her need for power and control and that she would like more of a feeling of that at home. She also recognized that her freedom need was not being met. Although that, too, was important, the fun need seemed to her to be the most important at that time. She thought her need for love and belonging was in better shape than all the others, but it could be better. She was reluctant to talk much about her relationship with her husband.

Our next session was about five days later, and JJ came in ready to work. She talked about how she had discussed all the elements of our last session with her husband. Tim's behavior was not acceptable: John would no longer permit him to remain in the house, and he had given his son three days to move out. John had discussed this with JJ in the context of having his son take responsibility for his own actions and living with the consequences. She was elated with the results. John's son had moved out and was now on his own. Also JJ reported that the discussion with her son had gone very well, and he had agreed to a plan regarding drugs, school behavior, curfew, and reasonable house rules. In fact, his input, according to JJ, was surprisingly appropriate. His only objection concerned the use of pot in the house, and JJ refused to budge on that issue.

I asked JJ to tell me more about how John had set the limits with his son and her part in this process. She said that she told John how she was going to sit down again with her son and outline her expectations of him and ask for his input. The main issue, the use of drugs at home, was not negotiable, and the choice of behavior was his. Should he choose to violate their agreement, it would be his action that would prompt the consequence, not hers or anyone else's.

Her husband said that sounded fine, and he would do the same with his son, but he would repeat the rules once again as he felt that his son, who was eighteen, had already had enough chances to shape up. One more incident of any kind would constitute expulsion from the house. That did not take long—the next day Tim was given three days' notice to move. This was for taking money from his dad's bedroom dresser without permission, an act he admitted to.

JJ and I talked again about her ideas for fun for herself. She had a list that included tennis, river rafting, swimming, going to the movies, walking, and exercising. We explored all of these at some length, and JJ decided she wanted to race walk, something she had done years ago and liked very much. She developed a plan to begin doing that immediately. I asked her to call me after she started race walking to let me know how it went. I did this because I felt she needed support for taking this first step even though she had readily come up with this plan. I did not want her to sabotage it with excuses for not having done it. Just a gut feeling that I had and I felt another success experience for JJ would be most helpful. Also, at the last session, there was certainly evidence that JJ was still choosing to depress, although less, and I was concerned that any excuse to fail would be a serious setback. I wanted her to experience success as much as possible, and my concern over her recent attitude about life, suicide, and feeling out of control was still very evident in my world.

Over the next three weeks, JJ and I met two more times and some remarkable changes occurred. I had first seen a woman of thirty-nine, depressing, feeling old and out of control, and believing that life was over, change to a vibrant, active, alive, in-control-of-her-life young woman who was having fun, happier, and on the road to a loving life experience. JJ began race walking on a regular basis, started reading much more in her spare time, and was spending more time with her kids doing fun things. Despite the fact that her son, who was now seventeen years old, had chosen to move out of their house, things between them were much better than they had ever been. He had moved in with another high school friend, and they both worked, went to school, and shared expenses. JJ visited regularly and brought "care" packages and occasionally some money. She was also doing more things with her husband now, and they, too, were getting along better. JJ reported that communication was now so much better, and the entire family relationship had improved. She had not realized until now how good it could be.

Our last session was about three months after our first meeting, and a new woman was definitely in my office. I expressed my pleasure and feelings of happiness at the tremendous accomplishments she had made. While JJ told me how she believed that I was at least partially responsible for her success, I reminded her of our discussions about control of one's life, choices, reality therapy, and her strengths. She laughed and said, "Well, you sure helped a lot."

During the last two sessions, we worked on how she was taking control of her life by making appropriate choices for herself and providing the opportunity for her children to do the same. Although her youngest son was at that time presenting no problem, her fear was that he, too, soon would follow in his brother's footsteps. However, with her new attitude for living and her new learned behaviors, she was reassured (and I helped her with that picture) that that was not likely to happen, but that if it did, she was in much better shape to face it. And she knew that she and her husband were now providing a much more positive environment for young Bill.

We also spent some time talking about the unfortunate accident her eldest son had had and how her fear was contributing to some of her overprotective behaviors toward her children. She still felt that her husband had been scapegoating the oldest boy, and that after he died that behavior had been transferred to the next oldest. She feared that now that Carl had moved out, the scapegoating would transfer to the youngest. JJ stated that she felt she needed to "side" with the one being picked on in order to balance things. That, coupled with the feeling of wanting to show her love for her boys because of the underlying fear that she might lose them, she said, had caused her to act in such an overprotective manner. We discussed the ways she could modify that, using the control theory and reality therapy concepts we had discussed in previous sessions.

JJ decided to spend more time discussing these concerns with her boys and assuring them that she was not dwelling on the thoughts of their brother's death, that she had really resolved that, at least as much as anyone can. She wanted the two boys, Carl and Bill, to know that her concern was a genuine one for them and had nothing to do with their brother, now deceased.

About two months after our last session, I received a letter from JJ:

Dear Tom, Thanks to you I just celebrated my fortieth birthday. There was a time when I was sure I would not live to see another birthday. Most of the days are calm now, and as crises arise, they are met head on and with confidence. I sincerely hope you are doing well. I thank you for this wonderful life.

Epilogue

In the process of creating this case study and meeting with JJ again, I learned that she has given up her job and is now doing volunteer work and is much happier. Carl is in college, about to graduate. Her youngest son did, in fact, begin to act out some of the negative behaviors of his older brother. These were quickly dealt with appropriately and resolved. He, too, is now in college and doing fine. JJ says that she truly is in effective control of her life and is happier than she has ever been.

DR. GLASSER'S COMMENTS ON
"WHY BOTHER GOING ON?"

The client who threatens suicide directly or indirectly is the most difficult for any counselor. Once the possibility that the person you are trying to help may commit suicide creeps into your mind, it does not leave. But it is important not to let this thought lead you into lengthy discussions on the subject; do not, no matter what the client says, discuss the pros and cons of suicide. Acknowledge that you are aware that it is on your client's mind and show your concern, but then do exactly what Tom Smith did: do not alter your basic counseling strategy because of your fear that she will kill herself. By focusing on what JJ could do to solve her problems, he quickly helped her to regain the effective control over her life that led to the successful resolution of this case.

JJ's problems were tangible. She had lost a son in an accident, and she feared that another son was in the process of ruining his life with drugs. She did what almost all parents do when their children are struck with tragedy or impending tragedy: she blamed herself. While there was nothing she could do about the son she had lost, she felt that she had to do something about the son who was using drugs. She could not sit by and let him ruin his life. She had the further problem of her husband's irresponsible son who had come to live with them, and she felt that she had to solve that too.

But as much as JJ wanted to tell them all what to do, she felt helpless when it came to dealing with them because she really did not know what to do. It was this helplessness that led to the hopelessness that caused the suicidal thoughts to surface. She said, "Help me," to Tom Smith but in the next breath revealed her hopelessness by saying, "There is nothing you can do to help."

Fortunately for her, Tom Smith knows that the problems that bring people to counseling, no matter how dark they seem, have tangible solutions. Simply stated, needs are not being satisfied, and it is the counselor's job to help the client to satisfy them. Once her needs are being satisfied even a little better than before, and she realizes that it was what she did that accomplished this, she will feel better and suicide will no longer be a problem. That was the approach Tom Smith used from the time JJ called, and in three months' time, she had turned her life around.

JJ was a capable woman. If she were not, she would not have been helped so quickly. In fact, it was her capability that was working against her when she came to Tom Smith. She probably thought, "I am capable and still I can't deal with my problems, so how can anyone help me?" But what Tom Smith pointed out to her, which became the core of the successful therapy, was that *capable* does not mean taking responsibility for what others, even adolescent children, choose to do.

Things turned around for JJ when she learned the basic control theory concept, so hard for parents to learn, that *we can control only our own lives.* Parents especially need to accept that we can satisfy only our own needs and that it is not selfish to concern ourselves with satisfying these needs in a responsible way. At the same time, we can and should treat our children with love and respect. But this does not mean that we should accept less from them when we ask them to follow reasonable rules (such as no drugs in the house) when we are their sole support and they live in our house. There is no guarantee that this will get us what we want from them, but there is some guarantee that if we do not do this, neither child nor parent will get the life they want.

For a parent, this is difficult to learn, but JJ seemed to learn it during the first session. That she did not learn it completely is shown by the letter she wrote after she had tried to explain what she had learned of control theory to her husband and son. When they did not fall into line, she wrote the following to Tom Smith: "I did approach my husband and my son in the manner we discussed. I was utterly destroyed by their reactions. The cure seems worse than the disease. I need time to see the results of my communications with them, then I will call you."

JJ's husband and son did not see things her way, and she thought that they should. As the capable person that she was, JJ tried unsuccessfully to impose the ideas she had gained in counseling on them instead of just letting them know what these ideas were. She did not realize that it did not matter what they thought of what she told them. What mattered was that she had also begun to behave in a way that backed up with actions what she had told them. In the end, it was her actions, not her words, that would tell them the story. What she had learned would soon work beautifully when she put it into practice in her dealings with them.

By the time a worried Tom Smith reached her on the phone four days after she had written the letter, her actions had already started to pay off. To her surprise, some of the things that they had talked about in the first session were, in fact, working. What she also had discovered was how much better it felt when she stopped trying to control the others in the house.

In fewer than a dozen sessions, this competent woman gained effective control of her life. She set reasonable limits for her son and stopped thinking that she was responsible for what he chose to do with his life. He learned that it was his choice to do what he did, but he had to live with the consequences of his behavior. And one of those consequences was that he could no longer live at home if he brought drugs into the house.

JJ also began to concentrate on her own needs, especially her need for fun. To do so, she went back to race walking, which she enjoyed. It all seems so simple when you read the case, and even simpler when it is summarized here. But from the standpoint of Tom Smith, to do this with a client who was thinking about killing herself is not simple; a great deal of skill is involved. And even though she did it, and Tom Smith says so, JJ thinks it is all because of him. Looking at it from her standpoint, I can certainly see how she came to this conclusion.

9

Finding Her Own Way

Breaking Away from the Family Mold and Developing a Strong, Comfortable Identity

SHELLEY ANNE BRIERLEY

M Y FIRST CONTACT with Susan was in 1979, before Dr. Glasser had formulated his ideas on control theory. I worked with Susan using the eight-step model of reality therapy with a complete understanding of why it worked. When I saw her again several years later, my approach was similar, but I was able to be more focused as I had developed an understanding of control theory.

When I first met Susan, she was a shy, quiet-spoken girl of twenty. For the previous three years, searching for someone who could help her, she had seen five different counselors. She was living with her parents and had had only one significant relationship outside her immediate family.

During the first visit, I asked what had been most useful in her experiences with her previous counselors. As a reality therapist, I see little value in knowing what was not useful, but take great stock in finding out what was. In this way, I immediately know something that I can do to build trust and a positive experience. Susan indicated only one thing that stood out: one of the counselors had been less critical than the others and had helped her to look at better study habits at a time when she was stressed because of university exams. Since the criteria for being a good reality therapist include the ability to be nonjudgmental and to work with people to help them gain greater competence and comfort in areas they decide are important to them, I had a hunch that Susan and I would work well together.

Years later, I asked Susan what she remembered about our first meeting. "I felt such relief. I was safe. I knew I was going to make it—that I wasn't a hopeless case. Up until that time, I had thought I was really different and 'weird.' I assumed that everyone else was 'normal'—able to figure things out on their own and feeling good about themselves. I always felt awkward, uncomfortable, and unacceptable. I never seemed to be able to think of the right thing to say or the right way to act. I spent most of my time trying to be the way everyone else was, behaving so that people would like me. Unfortunately, I really disliked myself but had, until that time, never admitted it to anyone else but myself." She remembers our sessions as being a "good, fun time, with someone to talk to, confide in, someone who could help me. You didn't have any grand expectations of me—to give or be a certain way."

As we worked together, it became clear that Susan had spent much of her life trying to please others, especially her parents. When asked what she liked to do, believed, or thought about different topics, Susan would often answer, "I don't know. I never thought about it. My parents say you should . . . My friends say . . ." She also often used phrases like "One should . . . ," "Others say . . . ," "I've always been told . . ." She seldom had quick answers to my questions and, though laughing, would say how difficult my questions were for her to answer. Helping her to question, explore, and make her own decisions became a major goal of therapy.

The precipitating issue for Susan's seeking counseling at this time was a breakup with her boyfriend of four years. She felt he had been her mainstay, and without him she did not perceive herself as being able to cope. He had been the focal point of her life; they had done activities that he liked to do and had spent time with his friends. She now found herself isolated and felt stranded, anxious, and resentful. She found herself blaming others and resenting their social skills, but, at the same time, lacking the confidence and knowledge to make new friends and get her life on track.

Susan had few friends and was passive in the friendships she had. She waited for others to initiate outings or activities, such as going to pubs and parties. She was involved in no groups or clubs—social, athletic, or otherwise—and therefore had few means of meeting people her age. She did not know how to make friends, as the people she knew to be her friends had always approached her and done most of the reaching out. Susan's only planned and personally initiated activities were appointments with counselors and doctors for treatment of her recently developed ulcers.

Talking with Susan, I learned that she had several strengths: she was athletic, bright (maintaining consistently good grades at the university), frugal, witty when relaxed, musically inclined, and enjoyed being teased. It seemed to me that most people would perceive this petite, young woman to be fully functional, if somewhat shy.

When asked what she wanted, her first response was, "I want to feel better about myself, to be able to relax with people, to have some real friends, to know what to say or how to present myself in social situations." Later, she added that she did not get along with her mother; there were always hassles, and her mother was critical of everything she did. She did get along well with her father, but hardly ever spent time with him. Her mother was always around. What Susan wanted was to have a better relationship with her family. She described herself as a "chicken," but she wanted to learn to take risks and try new things rather than always "playing it safe."

During our appointments, we explored Susan's past and potential strengths, successes, and areas of interest. We also shared my experiences, interests, and those activities that had been helpful to me in developing new friendships. A good rapport developed quickly. We enjoyed similar interests, such as athletics and outdoor activities; we appreciated each other's sense of humor and generally liked one another.

Of all the things Susan had mentioned, relationships seemed to be of the greatest interest to her. I believed that if Susan could get more of what she wanted, not only would she be happier, but she would have more confidence, get rid of the ulcers, and feel better physically. I asked her what she was doing in her life to create friendships. She described herself as rather shy, not knowing what to say to people, especially when she first met them. She behaved passively, letting others initiate conversations and activities, and rarely suggested activities or shared opinions. She spent most of her time worrying what others thought about her, criticizing herself for being "so dumb, shy, and tongue-tied." She tended to go along with the crowd to bars or dances when invited, rather than reach out individually to meet people. I asked her if being passive, going to bars and school dances, and letting others initiate was working to help her meet the kinds of friends she would like to meet. Susan said clearly, "No. Jocks don't hang out at bars!"

We talked about the types of people she wanted to get to know. She wanted them to be athletic, health-conscious, fun, sensitive, good communicators, thinkers, and intelligent.

Having established these standards, we were able to discuss what might help her to meet such types of people. When she had no ideas or suggestions, I would suggest things she might try. If she thought they would help her, she would try them out.

SHELLEY: Where do you think people who are athletic, health-conscious, fun, sensitive, good communicators, and thinkers hang out?

SUSAN: I don't know, or I'd be there! [Giggling.]

SHELLEY: Well, let's take athletic, health-conscious and fun types. Where might they spend their time?

SUSAN: Skiing, playing tennis or volleyball, . . . maybe hiking?

SHELLEY: Sounds good to me, especially the activities that are in nature, like skiing and hiking. Maybe it was just the people

I hung around with and happened to meet, but skiing, camping, hiking, and wind surfing are all activities through which I've met athletic, fun people. The same with most team sports. These are all activities I see as conducive to meeting people. With skiing, you have to share chairs to get up the mountain, and if it's three to a chair, you can always volunteer to be the odd person with two others. Camping and hiking work because there aren't as many people, so it's easier to start up a casual conversation about the place, the weather, or good spots to check out. Team sports attract people who want to be with others. Where do you think you'd meet people who are also sensitive, good communicators, and bright and intelligent?

SUSAN: Gee, I don't know . . . unless maybe it was helping people less fortunate to do some of these activities.

SHELLEY: What do you mean when you say "helping people less fortunate"?

SUSAN: Well, maybe helping handicapped kids play volleyball or young people learning to ski . . . or just helping kids that don't have as much money to do new things.

SHELLEY: Okay, so could you see yourself joining a volleyball group, hiking club, volunteering to help kids, or any of these things at this time?

SUSAN: Gee, I wouldn't know where to start. I don't think so.

SHELLEY: Okay, so how about if we start small? Would it help if you knew more places that people you'd like to be with hang out? How they communicate to get things going?

SUSAN: Yes, sure.

SHELLEY: So, would you be willing to not change a thing, but just keep a list of all the people you see, observe, meet, or talk with this week whom you'd like to know better?

SUSAN: Sure, I can do that.

SHELLEY: Okay then, would you also note what it is that attracts you to them? Be specific about what they say or do that you like or would like to be like.

SUSAN: Sure! That will be fun.

SHELLEY: Do you think it will help you to know more about where you can go to meet people you want to be around and what you are attracted to in friends? If you get a better idea of what it is you like in people's behavior, it will help you to figure out some new things you can do to attract and initiate relationships with people you'd like to have for friends. What do you think?

SUSAN: You make it all sound so easy. I don't know why I never thought of that.

SHELLEY: You will—it's kind of like a child learning to walk. First you have to decide that you want to walk; then you have to observe closer to see how it's done; then you try it out, figure out what works and what you want to change to improve it, and then try again. Then it's just a lot of fine tuning to get the walk exactly the way you want it. Now, what are you going to do this week?

Some of the things Susan took on as assignments were:

1. Make a list of people you like.
2. Indicate what you specifically like about each of them.
3. Note where you met these people.
4. Make a list of places where jocks "hang out."
5. Watch and listen for people starting conversations and note how they initiate a conversation.
6. Initiate three conversations a week, being aware of what you say, and note on a scale of 1 (poor) to 10 (great) how effectively it works.

When I asked Susan what she would say to start conversations, it became clear to me that she was being too direct, too indirect, or trying too hard to find something interesting to say. Susan was using the following lines to start conversations, trying unsuccessfully not to be too obvious:

1. Do you like sports?
2. Are you alone?
3. I don't know the bus system.
4. Can you help me?

Part of the counseling strategy I used was to help Susan become more involved in the present moment instead of trying to end up with the goal—a friend. We would brainstorm possible comments in different situations: "It sure is busy/slow here tonight. Do you happen to know which person is our waiter?" "Hi! Do you happen to know what's the house specialty?" or ". . . who's performing tonight?" Or when skiing: "Hi. Do you mind if I share your lift chair?" "Great weather, isn't it? Nice skis. How do you find them? I'm looking for new skis and don't know much about the different types. Any tips?" Whenever I asked Susan to try a new behavior, we would first practice it in the office. This was one of the key aspects of counseling she was to remember years later when I approached her about doing this case study. She remembered our "practicing" the things I asked her to do. Sometimes I would demonstrate, and she always had an opportunity to try things out, building her skill level so she knew she could succeed.

SHELLEY: Okay, Susan, I'm a single skier waiting in line at the chairlift. You try starting up a conversation. [I would whistle and look around.]

SUSAN: Hi. Do you think I could share your chair?

SHELLEY: Pretty good. Now, I'll be the initiator and you be the skier, and you tell me which of these ways you'd be more interested in sharing your chair with me:
"Hi. Do you think I could share a chair with you?" or
"Hi. [Pant, pant.] Mind if I share a chair?"

SUSAN: The last way, for sure.

SHELLEY: What was different?

SUSAN: The last one's casual and you sound like fun—like it's not too important. The first one made it sound like you were pleading!

SHELLEY: Okay. You try it and see if you can make it sound casual and fun!
[She does it.]
Okay. Now, what do you do and say if he says, "I'm waiting for my partner?"

SUSAN: Oh God, I'd be so embarrassed!

SHELLEY: Would you? That's interesting! I'd probably say something like, "Oh, okay," and ask the next person. Or I might
say, "Okay. If they don't show up, give me a shout," and
smile and move on. Or I might say, "Mind if I go ahead of
you then?" and ask the next person I see who looks available. You try it. . . . "Oh, I'm waiting for my partner."

We worked hard to set tasks Susan could do and succeed at,
whether or not she got the desired response.

SHELLEY: Susan, let's assume you're not actually going to meet
anyone the first time. Let's just look at it as a chance to
practice getting comfortable initiating a conversation.
Would that help you take some pressure off?
SUSAN: Yes! !
SHELLEY: Okay, so just keep track of what you do that seems to
work okay, or that feels okay for you. It doesn't really
matter what the other people say—you don't know them
anyway and probably won't see them again!
SUSAN: Yeah, that's true.

Gradually, because we refocused on practicing and succeeding at trying skills, rather than succeeding with outcomes
and goals, Susan's self-confidence grew—it's hard to fail when
all you have to do is something you know you can do, you've
practiced, and you are able to do regardless of others' behavior.
She was making friends and feeling good about herself. In fact,
she started noticing how boring some people were, and how she
became the initiator and leader in relation to these people. She
started choosing the people she wanted to spend time with and
what she wanted to do so that she enjoyed that time and felt
good about herself. As she got more confident, she joined a
hiking group and later a volleyball team. Both these groups gave
Susan a social outlet, as well as some means to meet the types
of people she wished to meet. She did not meet Mr. Wonderful,
but she did meet lots of interesting, fun, athletic, intelligent,
sensitive people with whom to build friendships and relationships. Gradually, through our examining the different relationships she had developed, Susan realized that every friendship

is different. Rules, expectations, limits, trust levels, communications, interests, and so on change depending on the relationship.

During this time, Susan's ulcers came and went. We worked to help her identify things that seemed to keep them in check: diet, relaxation exercises, visualization, exercise, eating regularly. Susan remembers that she would come to a session with a terrible pain in her stomach and that it would be gone by the time she left. However, because of my own limits and lack of understanding as to why reality therapy worked, I was unable to help her resolve the issue regarding her ulcers entirely.

Susan eventually took a huge risk: she left the university and signed on as a trainer and camp counselor at a coed volleyball camp, where she taught kids how to play the game. This proved to be a major turning point for Susan. Friends and family had advised against it, suggesting she would be wasting her time. She heard: "You might not be able to get another job." "How are you going to plan for a future?" "Susan, this isn't like you. You're usually so stable and consistent. Throwing caution to the wind and making a rash decision such as this is something you may regret for years, especially if you can't get back into the work force." Friends from her hiking group and volleyball teams added that they needed her on the team and that "you can't really make a career out of volleyball—not earning money." It was true that the economic climate of our Canadian province was such that jobs were hard to come by. Susan's parents were concerned that she would not be able to gain future employment, as she had to quit her job in order to join the volleyball camp. When we discussed her options, we both understood enough about the recurring ulcers to realize that if she continued working at her previous job, she would have more trouble with ulcers. It was her decision to do what she believed was good for her health and maturation, instead of doing what everyone suggested was best for her. But she was very much concerned that her parents did not approve of her decision and that, if she failed, her mother would say, "I told you so."

SHELLEY: Susan, if you stay at your present job, what will happen?

SUSAN: I'll keep getting sick and lose all the confidence I've gained.

SHELLEY: And what will happen if you keep getting sick and lose your new-found confidence?

SUSAN: I'll have to quit my job anyway, and then my mom will just say I can't stick to anything—but it will be worse because I'll feel like I failed me: chickened out again!

SHELLEY: Do you think you will ever please your mother?

SUSAN: No, I really don't think so. I never realized it, but I really don't think I'll ever be able to please her.

SHELLEY: So, will it be better to keep trying to please her and continue failing, or will it be better to do what you believe is best for you?

SUSAN: Definitely I have to do what's best for me—but what if I fail?

SHELLEY: How can you fail? You're exploring different life styles in order to determine how you want to live, just like you tried out different friendships in order to decide on the kind of people you wanted to develop friendships with. If you decide that the life style of a coed volleyball training camp has nothing to offer, you can go on with the knowledge and experience you gain to try something else. Does that make sense to you?

SUSAN: Yes, it does.

SHELLEY: You see, Susan, I often use an analogy of a turtle when I'm talking to groups about trying new things. A turtle gets ahead only when it sticks its head out of its shell, and we're the same. Unless we try something new that we believe might move us in the direction we want to go, we never move forward or feel successful. So, I look at the little risks I'm taking in trying new behaviors—and the big ones—as a barometer of how much I'm potentially going to succeed. Then I can give myself credit for taking a risk and trying something new, rather than worrying about whether or not it will work out perfectly. Would it help you to look at this risk in that way? Going to the job at the volleyball training camp is a way of sticking your neck out and moving toward something you know is better for you than where you are right now.

SUSAN: Yes, it helps a lot to think of it that way. Oh, I feel so much better. I'm still scared, but I know it's the right thing for me to do. Will you write me?

SHELLEY: I'm a terrible writer. As you can see by my desk, paperwork is not my forte, but I will drop you a postcard from time to time, and I'll certainly be thinking of you and looking forward to hearing from you!

Susan did go to work at the volleyball camp, and that decision allowed her to begin to find her own way in life, to choose and succeed for herself.

We maintained loose contact. She wrote from time to time, and I sent an occasional postcard, as promised. When in town for a visit, she would always call or come for a visit to let me know all the new things she was learning and experiencing. To her surprise, she found that the more she made her own decisions, took risks, and landed on her feet, the more her mother began to respect her, seek her advice, and initiate activities in order to spend time with her. Her father and mother became more human in her eyes.

Susan worked at the volleyball camp off and on for a couple of years. Due to seasonal changes in the numbers of people attending the volleyball camp, Susan was able to take periodic breaks from her work in order to travel, attend classes at the university toward her teaching degree, and explore other areas of interest. It provided her with an exceptional amount of flexibility and change, which seemed to be important to her health and well-being.

A few years later, Susan returned to counseling complaining of severe anxiety. She was again suffering from ulcers. She had earned a teaching degree and was employed full-time as a teacher in a regular academic system. She was single, had traveled extensively, and had explored and developed a variety of relationships. By this time, Dr. Glasser had developed control theory, and I explained the basic needs to Susan. We talked about the importance of meeting all of one's needs, although not all at the same time, and the fact that what we do is always our best attempt to do this. Ulcering was the physiologic component of the total behavior she was choosing that was not at this time successfully meeting her needs. To stop ulcering, she had to learn some better total behaviors than she was using now.

A colleague of mine, Diane Gossen, had taught me a useful technique, the "needs tray," to zero in on the target areas most relevant to the client. I tried it with Susan: "If I had a tray, and you could have one or more of these needs today before you leave, which would you choose: love, personal power, fun, or freedom?" Freedom and friends were her answers. This helped me narrow my field of questioning.

SHELLEY: What would you like your life to be like if you had a magic wand and you could do whatever you chose?
SUSAN: I'd be teaching kids in a small school.

Susan and I worked to identify in great detail the exact situation she would like.

SHELLEY: You've been teaching kids in school. What would be different in order for you to enjoy it?
SUSAN: It would be smaller.
SHELLEY: How many students and what ages?
SUSAN: Maybe two hundred kids in the whole school. My group wouldn't be teenagers!
SHELLEY: What ages would they be? It's much more useful if you can say how you want it to be than how you don't want it to be.
SUSAN: They'd be younger—maybe six to nine years of age.
SHELLEY: You dislike teaching five days a week. How many days per week would you teach in order to have lots of freedom and time for friendships?
SUSAN: Three would be best—Tuesday, Wednesday, Thursday—or five days, but mornings only.

Many of the changes Susan wanted involved the use of her time. "I'd have a part-time teaching job, three days a week working with children between six and nine years of age in a

smaller school (two hundred students). The rest of the time, I'd
be involved in sports activities: volleyball, basketball, cycling,
and swimming. I'd have a place to live that I liked, small and
cozy, by myself for now (people living upstairs, though). The
rent would be two hundred dollars a month so that I could save
for traveling, and I could come and go as I wish and have friends
over."

SHELLEY: What's going on right now?
SUSAN: I work eight hours; by the time I get home, I'm too tired
to do anything active. I spend a lot of my time off planning
lessons or reading, but I just feel anxious all the time. My
ulcers are getting worse, so I have to take more time off
from work, and I spend more time worrying about how sick
I'm getting."

It was May, so the obvious plan was to look at what Susan
would do in the present to get more control over her time and
her body until the end of June.

SHELLEY: How does spending time alone help you to get more
freedom and friends?
SUSAN: It doesn't, really.
SHELLEY: Okay, so when was a time in your life when you were
happiest and had lots of friends and freedom?
SUSAN: It was when I was at the volleyball camp for children;
it was a great summer.
SHELLEY: What was different? How did you spend your time?
SUSAN: I had friends in the other counselors. They were there all
the time. There was always someone to do something with,
and people to talk to.

I was still trying to figure out what it was that Susan really
wanted.

SHELLEY: Which of the needs—belonging, personal power, fun,
freedom—did you have more of than you do in your present
life?
SUSAN: Freedom!

The pieces started to fall together for both of us, especially when I went over the concepts of control theory with Susan. I explained that the needs are like the motor of a car and that when we do not meet them, they drive us to behave in order to satisfy them. I explained that each person has different ideas of what freedom is. We call these the wants. For instance, her mother's ideas of how she wanted to get freedom might be to live a clearly routined life—to choose whether to make sausage or spaghetti for supper. Susan's idea of freedom was to have variety in her life style so that, rather than doing the same thing every day, she could choose how to spend her time—whether she would do physical or mental activities, by herself or with a friend. She wanted to have a loose routine with lots of unknowns and options. Susan could see the patterns emerging. Whenever she was meeting her freedom need, she seemed to be well, felt happy, had friends, and enjoyed lots of fun. Whenever she locked herself into obligations and heavy mental workloads with no physical outlet, she felt anxious, saw few friends, was unwilling to take risks, and had difficulty with her ulcers.

We worked to help her find a job three days a week teaching children six to nine years old, to find the activities she was interested in, and to create a living environment that was small and cozy with people living upstairs. Sometimes Susan would start to panic.

SUSAN: Maybe I should just take a full-time teaching job, if I can get one.

SHELLEY: What will happen then?

SUSAN: I know it won't work. I'll get sick and hate myself again.

SHELLEY: How do you know there aren't any three-day teaching jobs with students six to nine years of age? Have you asked anywhere? Have you let anyone know that's what you'd prefer? Do you know anyone who might have some knowledge of the inner workings of the school system you could talk to about this?

SUSAN: I don't know. It just seems too good to be true. Do you really think I could get the exact thing I want?

SHELLEY: I don't know, but you definitely won't if you don't try.

Ask around to find out if it's possible, or let people know it's what you'd like.

SUSAN: Well, I could ask my old vice-principal and some of my friends who are teachers.

SHELLEY: Good. The information you bring back will help us. What can you put on application forms for the school board so you say what you want, but don't close out any options?

SUSAN: I could say I'd prefer to work with . . .

All the work to identify her specific idea of an ideal life style for herself paid off. Susan managed to find a teaching position that she shared with a friend who wanted more time to spend with a sick mother. Susan worked three days a week with children eight years of age.

This scenario has been repeated with many of my clients over the years. When people identify exactly what it is they want and need, they can often find, create, or simulate a situation close to the hoped-for outcome.

For the first time in several years, Susan found herself well. She had learned to pay attention to her stomach: she now recognized that tightness, acidity, and cramping were her body's signals that she needed more freedom than she was getting at the moment. As road signs give us visible cues—slow down, caution, danger ahead, sharp curve ahead—Susan's body was sending her cues that she could either note and attend to, or ignore and carry on. Eventually, if she chose the latter, an ulcer would develop. The ulcer is just a stronger push from the body to get the individual to attend to the style of life, which is the way in which an individual is meeting his or her needs.

Susan learned to increase her awareness to initial cues her body sent her, to identify what need she was not getting enough of, and to make a small plan that was within her control in order to meet the need. Because she is getting some of the need met earlier, she is never as desperate in her attempts to address it and does not have to make such major shifts in life style. The changes she makes these days seem much subtler, which is easier for her as well as for those around her to accept.

When I showed this case study to Susan and asked her what I had left out, she stated the following:

> It was so important that you never looked at the past like all the other therapists I'd seen. You usually said, "Let's look at what you're doing now and what you can do to get what you want." You always emphasized the positive and helped me learn to laugh at myself. You had imaginative and creative ideas that seemed fun. I never felt weird going to you. You just accepted all the things I thought were weird about me, and you taught me it was okay to quit something if you decided it wasn't really what you wanted. Others never took me seriously—my stomach, and so on. They placated me rather than hearing my request for help. Now I think they just didn't know how to help me. Your humor, acceptance, and positive focus were at least 50 percent of what worked for me. I guess I always thought of you like my older sister or the mother I wanted that my mom didn't know how to be.

Susan and I still see each other from time to time. As a counselor in the helping profession for the past twenty years, I find a client every now and then who, for one reason or another, is still a friend long after our counseling relationship is over. I know enough about control theory to realize that it becomes a friendship because we are able to meet some of our needs with the other person.

To move toward closure of a counseling relationship that has carried on over an extensive period of time or where I perceive it will be difficult for the client to let go, I usually increase the time period between visits from once every two weeks to once every month, then to every couple of months. The individual is always encouraged to cancel the appointment if he or she feels it is not necessary. If the client wishes to pursue a friendship with me, I generally let him or her know that I do not spend a lot of "social" time visiting people. I suggest that we take a break from counseling for six months and that the client then call me and suggest doing something that we would both enjoy. I am clear in stating that if the client calls and a new relationship develops, we will both have to work at defining the limits of the friendship. If the client does not call, I usually do not pursue it. This has proved useful as a means of closing and/or changing the relationship.

Susan grew extensively in our counselor/counselee relationship. She earned both my respect and my sincere friendship through her willingness and ability to find many people, activities, and channels through which to meet her needs. I am not the only person with whom she can meet her needs. In fact, I am probably a very small part of her "want" pictures. She is in no way depending on me, and neither am I on her. Our time spent together these days is for a few hours every couple of months. It is a time of reconnecting and equal sharing about our past learning and future hopes and plans, as one would with an old and dear friend with whom one has experienced successes and failures, pain and growth, the willingness to be oneself and, thereby, the experience of being loved. When this happens in a relationship between a client and a counselor, I perceive it as a healthy interaction, one to be cherished.

There are far more counselor/counselee relationships in which the client wants only to meet his or her needs with the counselor. This is a very different type of relationship; I believe it would be irresponsible of me, as a helper, to encourage or allow such a relationship to move to a friendship, as it would inhibit the client's growth, rather than enhance it. It would also indicate that I, as a therapist, was meeting *my* needs at the expense of the client. Therapists and counselors deal with the relationship between clients and themselves in different and numerous ways. I believe that I cannot be a good therapist, nor can I judge responsibly my ability to assist my clients, unless I am meeting my own needs in my own life outside of therapy.

It's interesting to recognize that Susan and I have somehow moved our counselor/counselee relationship to one of equality, fun, and activity. This transition came about because of our honesty with one another, a sincere like, and a gradual move from therapy to doing activities together. The activities we spent time on were generally ones in which Susan was more physically apt than I. She became the teacher, and I the student.

Having had the opportunity to work with Susan using reality therapy both before and after control theory, I have observed

how powerful teaching people new ways to perceive and understand their own behavior, as well as having them do and try
new behaviors, is in helping them gain more control in their
lives.

DR. GLASSER'S COMMENTS ON
"FINDING HER OWN WAY"

Shelley Brierley concentrated on how Susan could take more
effective control of her life, not on her ulcers, because she knew
that this would lead to their healing. This is why she does not
mention them prominently in her narrative. It is, however, on
these ulcers, the psychosomatic part of Susan's problem, that I
wish to focus. The reason many doctors (including me) classify
ulcers and similar diseases as psychosomatic is because it has
been known for centuries that these illnesses seem both to grow
worse when the sufferer's life is not in good control and to
become quiescent, perhaps even cured, when the sufferer has
effective control over his or her life.

Psychosomatic disease, as I define it, is a chronic illness
that is a direct result of a life that has not been in effective
control—usually for a long period of time. It is also an illness in
which there is not only pain and discomfort but also tangible
damage to some tissue or organ of the body. Susan's life before
counseling fits these conditions perfectly.

Duodenal ulcers, such as Susan's, are a psychosomatic disease because the ulcer causes considerable tissue damage to
the wall of the duodenum, the beginning of the intestinal tract.
However, migraine headaches, for example, usually associated
with a life that is not in effective control, are painful and often
disabling, but by my definition would not be classified as a
psychosomatic disease because no one has demonstrated that
any tissues are damaged.

Assuming that there is no serious disability, which in many
cases like Susan's there is not, the main treatment for these
diseases should be counseling. If, through counseling, clients are
able to increase their need satisfaction significantly, they often

are able to live in relative comfort with only mild episodes of illness, or the disease may even be quiescent, as long as their lives stay in effective control. Susan's needs were well satisfied, and by the end of counseling her ulcers were quiescent.

While no one knows exactly what causes these diseases, control theory provides two explanations, one for diseases in which the immune system does not seem to be at all involved or is very little involved, and the other for diseases in which the immune system is the main problem. To understand both explanations, it is necessary to focus on the physiologic component of our total behavior because it is the malfunctioning of this component that is the source of all these illnesses. First I will deal with the group that includes ulcers like Susan's and coronary artery disease, the two most common examples of psychosomatic diseases in which the immune system does not seem to be involved. Then I will deal with the group that involves the immune system because I believe that counselors will deal with these as much as with the first group.

Ordinarily, the physiologic component of any total behavior is under the automatic and completely nonvoluntary control of an unconscious part of the brain called the hypothalamus or, as I call it, the physiologic brain. Except for a few unusual people (for example, yogis who have worked for years to gain voluntary control of aspects of their physiology such as heart rate), the rest of us have almost no direct or voluntary control over our physiologic brain. Whatever total behavior we choose, this part of our brain senses our actions, thoughts, and feelings and simultaneously adjusts our physiology to what it has "learned" (through millions of years of evolution) is the correct physiology for this total behavior. When it does this perfectly, as it does most of the time for all of us, our physiology is healthy.

An example of this healthy physiology is that when we choose to exercise, our physiologic brain causes us to perspire. If we did not perspire, we would become overheated and sick. But suppose you find yourself perspiring profusely when you are not exercising. This happens to many of us when we find ourselves in a very embarrassing situation. Something has gone wrong with how our physiologic brain is regulating our perspiration. And I believe this "something" is also the cause of psychosomatic disease.

One theory for why we sweat when we are embarrassed is that our physiologic brain that has evolved over millions of years has not yet "figured out" what the correct physiology should be for complex civilized behaviors like embarrassing (to use the control theory language for this total behavior). What our physiologic brain does is pick up on the strong resemblance between embarrassing and running and, in doing so, activates our sweat glands.

When we are embarrassing, the thinking component of that total behavior is the specific thought, "Right now I wish I were almost any place but here. I'd like to run out of here as fast as I can." This thought may be so similar to the thought of running itself that our physiologic brain turns on our sweat glands as if we were actually running.

To carry this a step further, if you embarrassed a great deal and if excessive sweating led to tissue damage, then embarrassing, a painful total behavior, would lead to a psychosomatic disease called something like "perspiritis." The best cure for this hypothetical disease would be counseling to help you deal with uncomfortable personal situations better. The medical treatment while you were being counseled would be a prescribed drug (if one existed) that reduced the perspiring. This drug might be dangerous to any user who also engaged in strenuous physical activity, so it would have to be prescribed carefully. Another helpful and much safer substance, not a drug, that you might consider using would be an antiperspirant.

The previous hypothetical explanation serves as an analogy to explain Susan's ulcers. It was clear that Susan had attempted for long periods of her life to live in a "civilized" way that pleased others much more than it pleased her. Shelley Brierley says, "I believed that if Susan could get more of what she wanted, not only would she be happier, but she would have more confidence, get rid of the ulcers, and feel better physically." The thought processes of the passive, frustrated life that Susan was attempting to live were being misread by the physiologic part of her brain, and because of this mistake, it provided a physiology that was neither appropriate nor healthy and led to her ulcers. The result of this misreading was that her physiologic brain "decided" that Susan needed more digestive juices as if she were continually getting ready to eat a big meal.

Perhaps when some of us are frustrated in modern life, the physiology of the thoughts that accompany these frustrations is similar to the physiology of the thoughts we have had for millions of years when we are hungry and worried about where our next meal is coming from. The sayings, "hungry for love," "hungry for power," or "hungry for freedom" give a folklore confirmation to this speculation. Susan was certainly "hungry" for a life different from the one she had made for herself. Was this psychological hunger being misread by her physiologic brain to the point where it was overloading her empty stomach with digestive juices?

The accepted theory for ulcers is that too much acid and other digestive juices lead to their formation, although why the normally protective duodenal lining breaks down adds complications to this theory, which I will mention shortly. But simple or complicated, there was no outside cause for Susan's ulcers; it was what she was doing in her own stomach and duodenum that resulted in her disease.

A confirmation of this theory is the fact that her ulcers healed when counseling led her to begin to lead a much more need-satisfying (less hungry) life. Susan is not unique; almost always a more need-satisfying life is the best cure for ulcers. Although it is not mentioned, I am sure that Susan received some medical treatment and medication for her ulcers. Although this may have helped, medication, unlike counseling, is palliative not curative. If the source of the client's psychosomatic illness is in the way she is choosing to live her life, then good counseling supplemented by good medical care is the most sensible and safe approach.[1]

The other group of psychosomatic diseases, those involving the immune system, have puzzled physicians for the past fifty

[1]For a discussion of how a similar scenario may be involved in most coronary artery disease, see Chapter 12 of *Control Theory*.

years. Doctors first became aware in the 1940s of the fact that in many common chronic diseases such as rheumatoid arthritis, the sufferer's own immune system seemed to be the culprit. The immune system seemed to be unaware that a normal body tissue or organ such as a joint, a nerve sheath, the skin, or a kidney belonged to its own body. The immune system then attacked and injured or destroyed this tissue or organ, as it does anything it encounters that is foreign to its own body. This leads to these diseases being labeled autoimmune, or immune to oneself.

The diseases involved are quite widespread. Millions of people suffer from rheumatoid arthritis when their immune system attacks one or more of their own joints. An equally large number suffer from eczema: their immune systems attack their skins. Large numbers of people suffer from multiple sclerosis: the sheath that covers their nerves is similarly attacked, and the nerve impulse is disrupted. Lupus is another example of such a disease: kidneys are attacked and often destroyed. There is also the possibility that in people who suffer from ulcers, the immune system may attack the protective coat that normally protects the duodenum and, in this way, may also be involved in diseases like Susan's.

A dramatic example of an autoimmune disease that was treated by the patient taking more effective control of his life is the case of prominent American Norman Cousins.[2] Cousins suffered from potentially crippling rheumatoid arthritis of the spinal column. With his doctors' permission, he moved out of the hospital to a hotel, took over most of his own treatment, and paid special attention to his needs, especially his need for fun, and he recovered completely.

My control theory explanation of what causes these autoimmune diseases has to do with the ability of our physiology to do as the mind does when we hallucinate—become destructively creative. This happens most often when effective control is lost for a long time. As I described in Chapter 5, constant creativity is characteristic of the way we are. But the more our lives are out of control, the more we begin to add some of this

[2]Norman Cousins, *Anatomy of an Illness* (New York: W.W. Norton, 1979).

always available creativity to all four components of our behavior. As long as this creativity is restricted to our actions, thoughts, and feelings, our physiology or health is not affected. But when creativity is added to any part of our physiology, it is our immune system that seems to become the most creative.

Somehow the newly creative immune system is wrongly alerted by the thoughts that are associated with a frustrated life and attacks its own body as if it were the cause of the problem. As with ulcers, there is a misreading by the physiologic brain, only now it turns on the immune system instead of the digestive juices. This misreading literally induces the immune system to become insane; it looks for an attacker that does not exist and, in doing so, harms the body it is designed to protect.

The immune system now behaves in a creatively crazy way and becomes an enemy to its own body, just as a crazy person might want to attack a friend or relative who is creatively misread by the crazy person as an enemy. But the difference is that the crazy person knows what he is doing and can, if he wants to, choose to restrain himself from the attack. We have a great deal of control over our actions and thoughts, even if they have become very creative and very crazy, because we can recognize that we are doing is wrong.

The creative physiology of a psychosomatic disease is much different from the creative thinking just described because the immune system has no way of recognizing that it is doing wrong. If I give the immune system conscious motivation (which of course it does not have), in some insane way it "thinks" it is doing right. Once it begins the attack, the new and self-destructive immune system begins to operate without restraint within the physiologic component of our total behavior, and disease is the result. The sufferer is not aware of what has happened until he or she is sick. Because all this goes on in the physiologic brain completely outside of consciousness, there is little or nothing that can be done to prevent these creative diseases; we can only find out about them after they occur.

It is important to keep in mind that no matter how creative our actions, thoughts, or feelings are, this creativity never extends to tissue damage. But when our physiology becomes creative, especially when the immune system is involved, there is almost always tissue damage. If, for example, a finger joint is damaged, as it may be in rheumatoid arthritis, this damage may not be reversible by anything that the sufferer can do. Therefore, counseling, even in the acute early stages of many of these diseases before there is significant permanent damage, is strongly indicated. In these diseases, counseling must be intensive because the sufferer may have to make major changes in his or her life to arrest the disease. These changes are much more possible before the disease has taken its toll, for example, before the person becomes crippled with arthritis. This is another indication for early and intensive counseling.

Anyone who suffers from an autoimmune disease should seek good medical care, but for some of these diseases, like multiple sclerosis, there is no accepted treatment. For others, like rheumatoid arthritis, the cure is mostly restricted to pain-killers and to antiinflammatory drugs in the cortisone family, which reduce the ability of the immune system to attack. But because these drugs have other health-endangering effects, they do not lead to a complete cure.

Medical researchers are working on all these diseases, and in several of them, they believe that some sort of primitive virus exists deep within the cells that are being attacked. It is this "hidden" foreign virus, which the immune system seems able to detect, that triggers it to attack the tissues involved in the disease. So far this virus has yet to be discovered in human beings. It may never be discovered or, if discovered, may not lead to the cure that we all hope for.

For now, good care for all psychosomatic diseases means seeing a medical doctor who will not reject the idea that the disease could be the result of chronic frustration and who will insist that the sufferer get counseling from the start to supplement the medical care. Throughout, the medical doctor must work cooperatively with the counselor, the patient must observe this cooperation, and the counselor and the medical doctor must be supportive of each other.

An excellent example of the kind of cooperation advocated here is shown in the work that Mary Corry and Dr. Parker did with Sarah in Chapter 5. Sarah had a variety of psychosomatic symptoms, if not diseases, and both women contributed to their becoming quiescent. I am also sure that Shelley Brierley would have been cooperative had Susan's ulcers flared to the point where a medical doctor was concurrently needed. The usual problem is not that counselors will not cooperate, but that many medical doctors find it hard to accept that treating these diseases requires the skills of the counselor as much or even more than those of the physician.

There is a bright side to this creativity that I would like to mention: there is always the possibility that when our physiology gets creative, what it creates will lead to increased health instead of illness. We tend to think more about illness because sick people, not healthy people, ask for our help. When a person whose life is out of control gets strong and healthy, either on her own or with help, no one except that person and those close to her pays much attention.

But we should pay attention to Susan, and she should pay attention to what she has accomplished. Ms. Brierley gives full credit to her client for the hard work she has done, as do most of the counselors in this book. Susan is now strong and healthy and has learned the control theory reasons for why this has happened. If she continues to use what she has learned, she will get stronger and healthier, in part because her physiology will continue to make constructive, creative contributions to her increasing health.

10

Becoming a Certain Man

An Immature Young Man Sets Realistic Goals and Learns to Value Himself

SUZY HALLOCK

A<small>N EMPLOYEE</small> in a well-known state association in Vermont called me one day and asked whether he could make an appointment for his son to see me. He said that his son was a college graduate, still living at home at twenty-six, not doing much in the way of work, being incommunicative with his parents, and spending much time alone in his room. His father was quite frankly frightened that his son was suicidal. They lived nearly an hour away, and he would be glad to drive his son to the office to see me. Although the son had a driver's license, he did not own a car, and his father did not think his son was competent to find the way alone.

This initial piece of information fascinated me: was it possible that a twenty-six-year old college graduate could not "find his way" to a destination one hour away? Was the son truly incompetent, I wondered, or did the father have an interest in infanticizing the son and keeping him dependent? The following week, when Phil came to see me, I thought perhaps both hunches contained some element of truth.

He was small, about five feet two inches, very slight, red haired, and balding. He wore coke-bottle glasses, his face was covered with pimples, and his fingernails were dirty. His hair was greasy and laid in wisps across his head. He wore a polo shirt, jeans, and sneakers, and he smelled of body odor. His behavior was odd; his movements jerky and nervous. Although he appeared quite anxious, he was eager to talk. And when he talked, all the history of his torment was unleashed, and I wondered whether I might just as well be a computer or a parrot who occasionally nodded and added "Um" or "Oh, really." Eventually, I came to see that his time with me was indeed his only intimate conversational time, and he was eager for it. He was a social isolate and could not envision authentic conversation with his parents, whom he characterized as "Archie and Edith Bunker."

When I was finally able to get a word in edgewise, I ascertained in a preliminary way that Phil perceived himself as a failure and that his personal failures were more frequent and of more consequence than the failures of other people. He was choosing to drink wine, often a full bottle in the evening, and he told me "that is how I get relief from a pervasive sense of powerlessness and despair." He felt sad most of the time, had contemplated suicide several times in the last two months, and discussed possible plans for doing so. While he did not feel especially guilty about anything, he nevertheless thought the world would somehow punish him for having trespassed an unknown or unwritten code. He further believed that perhaps he was presently being punished for something and perhaps he was just a bad person. He was disappointed in himself and critical of himself. Dissatisfied and bored, he was annoyed with everything and everyone and acted irritable in his relationships with others at home and with co-workers. He said he cried a lot. His appetite was good, but he tired easily and was sleeping more than the average.

During the first two sessions, I learned that Phil had several unsettling dreams every night, some of them about torture. He was underemployed and not satisfied with his work. His parents were "getting to" him, and he didn't even know if he liked them. He said he had enormous feelings of being sexually inadequate and had never dated a girl nor had any sexual experiences other than masturbation. He perceived himself so sexually and psychologically impotent to handle adult life that one morning in what he described as a "desperate, crazy, and self-destructive moment," he poured battery acid on his penis. As if to test the limits and efficacy of craziness, Phil immediately showered off his stinging member and remained sober and subdued the rest of the day. We talked about this incident as indicative of a fantasy wish to "make it go away" and not present sexual inclinations with urgency, and also to "feel" something in his genitalia other than frustration, since he had never been "satisfied" through a "fully sexual" experience. Protesting both his sexuality and his state of virginity, it appeared to be a desperate cry for help, but no one could hear the call of course, since it was so crazy an action that he had been unable to share it with anyone safely until now.

We began to talk about the choices Phil had and the ways he could effect change in his life. After listening to recollections of painful experiences in school, from his earliest years through his time as an economics major at the state university, I told Phil that while I appreciated his fears of facing his situation honestly and effectively, he could not use those experiences to stop him now or allow them to provide an excuse for living half a life. We talked about individuating out of his family, about choosing life, and about choosing one's own life. (It had been his father's plan that he major in economics as a prerequisite to a career in banking or business.)

Once he had decided not to kill himself and to try to change some of the parts of his life that were not working, I told him that unless he bathed before the next appointment, I would not see him because it was unpleasant to sit in the same room with him. If he wanted to spend time talking with me, it had to be satisfying for me too. I told him one of the behaviors most adults in our culture used was daily bathing, and I was going to expect him to act like an adult even though he did not feel like one. Part of the daily shower included shampooing his hair and washing his face. If his complexion did not clear up with increased cleanliness and the addition of a daily vitamin-mineral supplement, I would ask him to see a dermatologist. I checked with both Phil and his father about the date of his most recent physical examination. It had been a couple of years before, but he was said to be "normal."

Phil began to look better and take more pride in his appearance. He hated his job and said he was getting crazier and crazier at work. His mind would wander, and he would loose track of what he was doing. At the time he was folding large bolts of cloth and loading and unloading truckloads of fabric. We decided that he would begin looking for another job but that he should not quit since he needed the money. Phil chose to save money for contact lenses and a car of his own; he decided these were better investments than wine. When in a few weeks he was fired, he chose to look for another job rather than retreat to his room. He began making pizzas in a local pizza parlor. He viewed this situation as temporary but essential. Having decided to purchase contact lenses and a car of his own, Phil needed money. He became greatly animated at the prospect of job hunting during our conversations about finding more meaningful and satisfying work.

It was clear that Phil was not the "business type," despite his father's advice and good intentions. Phil had suffered greatly in the school setting, and he believed that his own experience had heightened his sensitivity to students and their needs in school. He was intrigued with the world of books, reading, and writing, and while fiction had provided him with an escape from his own painful reality, it also kept alive the world of ideas and adventure.

Phil brought a copy of a futuristic short story he had written. Set in a subsequent millennium, the story featured a young man and his mentor, who discuss a black hole entryway into alternate universes. The plot is replete with government suppression of alternatives, "idiotic wars," escapist and utopian expectations, and deviousness as a means to the ultimate good. The mentor in the story tells the young man about a way to create one's own universe "ranging from starkly simple to extremely baroque." Phil wrote, "Of course, the governments of Earth regarded any attempt to escape from the bland world of the here and now they had created as implied social criticism and classified it as treason." Finding himself in the presence of a force, whether it be "karma" or "higher destiny," the young man in the story chooses to seek a new world called "Novum Virginium." The young man, as represented on Phil's concluding page, "felt maybe something was lacking from his life" and that "people should take more risks in life." Oh well, what do I have to lose, he thought. He hesitated, then moved toward the beam, stepping into nothingness, never to return."

The story was rich with implications for therapy and Phil's own unique life process. Did the mentor in the story represent Phil's father? Perhaps so, when the narrative addressed "the subsequent bitter disappointments he and his friends had suffered." Yet the mentor was more radical than Phil's father: "he saw himself as a catalyst, thinking that the least he could do, given his many and obvious intellectual gifts, would be to stir up doubts within the masses, forcing people to stop acting like sheep and assert themselves again and maybe shake up the too oppressive, too complacent society he unfortunately found himself in." The mentor in the story was probably both the father Phil had, and the father Phil wished he had. Of Phil himself, the story spoke with precision when its youthful character "was so overcome by a bit of hyper-anxiousness that when he started to talk, he couldn't get the words out fast enough and began to verbally stumble all over himself."

I was convinced that Phil had written a metaphor for his own life. At first, it would have been easy for us to accept its meaning as making a statement about being able to escape, to go into "nothingness," even the black hole of suicide. Instead, we held the story up to the light of therapy and turned it a bit, like a prism, so the light came through differently. We saw the story as essentially a journey taken by a young man, guided by a wise but aging mentor. The young man wants a new and better world, and he decides to risk finding it by entering the unknown.

I talked with Phil about the presence and purpose of ambivalence in life, and I assured him that his current situation was normal and developmentally correct. Using Daniel Levinson's *The Seasons of a Man's Life*[1] as a catalyst, Phil and I discussed ambivalent feelings that constitute a paradox within the mentor relationship: respect, admiration, and gratitude for the mentor, but also resentment, inferiority, envy, and even intimidation. In this context, we were able to discuss self-doubt: would Phil ever become all that he and even his father might want him to be? Phil saw himself as inept but, at the same time, having the potential to rise above his father's horizon. We talked about Phil's journey through what Levinson calls "the Novice Phase," and we said that while there may have been a bit of a developmental delay, Phil was nevertheless making many choices that would help him get his life under control and realize his own best potential. We knew that a major task of the novice period would be to differentiate out from his father and his father's pictures of how Phil should live his life and to find his own pictures. A major component of this task was separating out from the family. Externally, this would mean leaving the house, becoming financially less dependent, and entering job tasks and living arrangements in which Phil could exercise more autonomy.

Now he talked about education as his ultimate goal. He had purchased a car and was now driving himself to his sessions. He asked for an extension of his bill because he was now paying for his own therapy. I affirmed his emerging strength, and we continued to discuss the process of assuming adulthood, individuating out from the family, and being one's own person. Since Phil was now much more independent of his parents, at least in his thinking and feeling, he no longer experienced their comments about him as only criticism. He could see that their perceptions of life were simply different from his. His father ranted against the hippie intellectuals, and Phil realized that such a diatribe had perhaps placed a governor on his own iden-

[1]Daniel Levinson, *The Seasons of a Man's Life* (New York: Ballantine Books, 1978).

tity—he wanted to be one of those hippie intellectuals. He wanted to revel in the world of books, and he did not "see a communist under every bed." He still wished he were in that bed with a woman but, alas, that was still not to be despite the enormous improvement in his appearance and demeanor.

He tried reaching out to people in his past and wrote to several old "friends"—his ex-college roommate and a camp counselor (female) with whom he had worked one summer and had felt some rapport. (Unfortunately she had a boyfriend at the time, and Phil never acted on his inclination to ask her out. He had been too terrified.) He did not get much of a response to this "reaching out." While he was understandably disappointed by reaching into his past for affiliation and not finding any, we chose to view this as evidence that the good life we were seeking was in the present and in the future. We acknowledged that affiliation was an ongoing frustration for Phil, and we would have to find other ways to satisfy this need. One of the other ways in which Phil tried to expand his affiliation possibilities was by going to concerts. Now that he had a car and could travel, he went not only to concerts, but also to lectures and films at nearby colleges. But he was still incredibly "shy" and had a difficult time meeting people and maintaining a conversation. His conversational style and manner with me had improved, and our exchanges often had the ring of authenticity now. But I noticed that over time he was still not totally at ease conversationally.

Our sessions were full of his dreams, early recollections, favorite stories, hopes for the future. Since we talked about the possibilities of his teaching English or even philosophy, we thought it important that Phil continue to write. He worked on some more short stories, and I was reassured by their construction and presentation. These writing samples were more indicators that Phil was beginning to see himself as a writer and a "teacher-type." I was convinced that Phil could handle graduate work. He wrote the state certification officer to find out what he would have to do in order to become a teacher. His transcript analysis was discouraging to him since he would have to take at least five or six courses.

One of these courses was student teaching. I told Phil that sometimes a novice teacher can begin in the private-school setting and that work experience is taken in lieu of student teaching. He began looking around again for a job change. When he got the idea in his head that maybe he would like to live and work in Boston, I did not discourage him. I had some concerns that he would be increasingly alienated in a city without some group with which to identify. Phil appeared to me to be a good candidate for communal living. He decided to go to Boston and check out a couple of jobs. Although his father protested, Phil drove to Boston on his own. He had car trouble, managed to get his car fixed, stayed overnight, made and kept his job interviews, and returned home. Quite a feat!

But Phil was reluctant to move to Boston. By the time one of the jobs came through, he had decided to remain nearer home. He applied for two jobs in private-school settings and for a job at a bookstore in a nearby college town. One of the school jobs was offered to him, but Phil figured he could not make enough money to keep his car on the road, live independently, and pay tuition for course work. So he decided to ask the school to keep him on file and let him know when the position became available again. He told them that he needed to earn more money and why. He then took the job at the bookstore and moved away from home.

At first, Phil lived in a boardinghouse and then in an apartment. He had a few dates with a woman also employed at the bookstore and found his bookstore job more satisfying than any previous one, but he still maintained his goals for more education and ultimately teaching and being in an educational atmosphere.

While Phil was more clear on setting his own goals, knowing and valuing himself, and understanding his individual choices, as his therapist I had abiding concerns for him. The form and content of his speech were both excellent. He understood the system of the language and used it well. His grammar and syntax, both in oral and written expression, were much better than the average. He also understood the underpinnings of the function of language. He had good, long-term memory and could formulate concepts well. There were, however, problems in his use of language for effective communication with others. He could be fluent and could recount and elaborate a topic well, but he sometimes rambled tangentially or became once again reticent. At my suggestion, he took a course in "Life Work Planning" taught by a close friend of mine who is an "expert" in communications. I consulted with her about Phil. She said he became the darling of the class and was highly entertaining and a boon to the group. But he had not made any lasting friendships, and she agreed that his social functioning was not smooth.

This tendency, his self-perception of "spaciness," and his lack of comfort and fluidity with his own body movement contributed to our judgment that Phil might be well served by an intelligence assessment. The results indicated WAIS (Weschler Adult Intelligence Scale) scores of verbal 121 and performance 97. His verbal abilities were only average. The examiner believed that there was no brain injury, but that Phil's spectrum of abilities was a lifelong condition to which Phil was showing good adjustment. The examiner said that "the best general feedback one can give Phil is reassurance that many of his intellectual abilities are very fine, that he is less gifted in some spatial-perceptual skills, and that he needs to choose vocational tasks carefully so as to take advantage of his considerable strengths and avoid his relative weaknesses."

This assessment was received by Phil with interest and enthusiasm. It provided some objective affirmation of his decision to be drawn closer to the world of words and books. His arithmetic subscore on the WAIS was 8. (The mean for the test was 10, and Phil's score in vocabulary, for example, was 16. Obviously, mathematics was not a strength.) Putting his father's plan for a career in banking behind him, Phil was very enthusiastic about devoting his goal more to the humanities. He began reading more and more, and even auditioned for a locally produced play in a community theater group. He was a wonderful soda fountain worker in Thornton Wilder's *Our Town*. He wrote to me about this triumph. I attended the play and enjoyed his performance. He was particularly delighted with the notion of being a member of the cast and attending a cast party. It was perhaps the best affiliation he had had in adult life, and he subsequently became a stage manager with the same theater company. Here his differentness was not a liability but an asset on his humanities ledger.

At this point, Phil had gained considerable strength and control in his life. He seemed strong enough for me to begin to make an inquiry on a point he had shared about midway through his therapy: he was adopted. I now asked him whether he would like to know anything more about his biological parents, and he said yes. When he approached his adoptive parents, they told him that he had been a "preemie," and they told him which agency had handled his case. Phil contacted the agency and made an appointment for an interview. Attending the interview necessitated a trip to New York City, which he navigated successfully despite the intricacies of driving his car, leaving it at a garage nearby, and using public transportation within the city itself. During his conversation with the agency officials, Phil learned that his father had been a United States serviceman stationed in Europe and his mother had been a writer employed by a government agency. The record indicated that Phil's mother was very interested in his placement throughout his infancy and that knowing he had been adopted by a loving family had been of utmost importance to her. Her career in writing was seen by Phil as another indicator of his emerging identity as a man of letters.

For nearly two years, Phil remained at the bookstore, lived on his own, learned to cook, and remained active in the theater troupe. Throughout this period, he anticipated a future inclined toward the world of education. He planned to become more financially stable so that he would be seen as a good risk for an educational loan for graduate school. Since he now lived a good distance away, and because of his realization of his strengths, the more structured and formal phase of active therapy ended, although he would occasionally call for a little fine tuning.

Phil had initially presented himself as a client who was experiencing frustration across the spectrum of psychological needs. He was so impoverished at not finding the potency to meet those needs in the real world that he had begun retreating into fantasy and alcohol. He was so desperate about his perceived inability to meet with success that, despite his good intellectual ability and his college university degree, he was suicidal. He was not meeting his needs for bonding and cooperating, his needs for power and significance, his needs for fun, or his needs for freedom.

His attempts at finding effective behaviors had not been successful, and he was indeed becoming "crazy" in an attempt to get some control. In his fantasy and dream world, he often got what he wanted and often got revenge on his father, who seemed to attempt to control Phil and limit his freedom. In order for Phil to do what his father wanted, his father would have had to show Phil how his being in banking and business could be satisfying for Phil. Not convinced of his father's choice for him, Phil was also not able to be strong about pursuing his own, more compatible interests. Instead, he chose to "do nothing," but he did go to work at a menial job because he had "nothing else to do." By addressing first his physical appearance, then his intellectual and emotional creativity, I assisted Phil in getting control of his own life situation and process. While I encouraged his differentiation out from his family, and his father in particular, I also encouraged Phil to share activities with his dad, such as washing their cars together or going to an occasional movie together. During his bookstore days, Phil often purchased books (with his employee's discount) that he believed would be of interest to his father. These he would take when he went home for weekly Sunday dinner.

Phil came to understand that it is impossible to control another person, and he stopped criticizing his father's ultraconservative views. He just accepted them and did not expect his father to change. He used humor as a coping strategy. Understanding and valuing his own views kept him from having to anger and rail against his dad. Phil knew now to spend his energy on pictures he could achieve—his own goals in life. He became much better about getting information and surveying options, and he did not perceive himself anymore as life's victim.

To take control of our lives, all of us must muster the strength to find out what we want and then to follow through by making and keeping plans that help us reach our goals. Life is a constant process, and in a way we never really "arrive," since those goals may change with our own growth and change in circumstances. Learning flexible behaviors and opening our thinking wide is helpful. We have far greater chances for satisfaction in the real world if we nurture ourselves, remain open to the wonderful differences and similarities of others, and go forth with the conviction that we can find what we need for living our own idea of the "good life."

For Phil, the "good life" was graduate school. His "Novum Virginium" was not suicide and death, but choosing life and making concrete, specific plans for living that life in ways congruent with his own personality. Now, nearly three years after Phil's initial therapy session, he is in graduate school working toward a master's degree and certification to teach social studies and English. In a recent letter, Phil wrote, "It feels really good to be going back to school and to be in a classroom setting and in a career path situation." His letter was long. In fifteen pages, Phil brought me up to date with him. He made the decision to leave his bookstore job, and certain aspects of this separation made it easier to move on. He wrote:

> During the last five months, I was in the exploratory stage getting information in the mail and on the phone. Although it had been normal practice at the bookstore to give employees rotating days off, which could have given me time to drive over and visit schools, during my last three or four months there they didn't let me do this (citing computer foul-ups and other excuses), although all other employees continued to get weekdays off. . . . I was definitely "low man on the totem pole." I was there much longer than I should have been.

Phil had been careful to select just the right college setting for himself. He had visited several campuses and gotten all the information he needed in order to make comparisons about requirements, course offerings, and financial cost and assistance. He said he was having to budget, and in this regard he expressed frustration in that his father was helping him with his car. He wrote:

> Although my father does get moody at times and is sometimes hard to deal with (not all the time), he has been helping me a lot with the car and has been putting almost heroic efforts into keeping it on the road. While I'm very grateful for this, I'm still not entirely independent of my parents.

I did write to Phil on this point, telling him that I plan to always support my children in appropriate ways. In a way, the car is a metaphor for Phil's independence: perhaps his dad is helping Phil maintain his good gains in independence.

The letter related other anecdotes that gave me clues about Phil's present level of functioning. For example, he had been clipping news stories about the Middle East, and his landlady went into his apartment and threw them out, thinking they were trash. To Phil, they were a fascinating history in the making that he valued highly. He asserted himself and "made her fish them out of the garbage can." Phil had been reluctant to alienate this woman, since she was related to the man in charge of the community theater group. Actively affiliating with this group was important to Phil, and he hoped that his self-assertion with the landlady would not damage his reputation with the manager. Later, he said he learned that the man had been giving him very good recommendations. In fact, one of them was a boost in his gaining admission to graduate school. He was considerably reassured by this news and affirmation of his worth. In addition to reading more plays, Phil had also read Aldous Huxley, Dietrich Bonhoffer, Theodore Roethke, and Kurt Vonnegut.

In the last paragraph of his letter, Phil wrote, "I like what I am doing right now, and I feel I'm on the right track and I'm very optimistic about the future. . . . I am on a generally upward course." He quoted a thirteenth-century Zen master as saying, "If you want to obtain a certain thing, you must first become a certain man. Once you have become a certain man, obtaining a certain thing will not be a concern of yours any longer." And then Phil said, "I think that is what I am gradually doing."

Always interested in words and their impact, Phil is living a life that now resonates with congruence. Perhaps all of us know about the nature of a paradox. On the road to becoming his own man, a certain man, Phil wants to obtain certification and his professional identity as a teacher. In his prerequisite studies and anticipated teaching position, Phil will have the strength of realizing in the real world his own strengths and purposes. Having his own picture of success in his head and hands, and finding the behaviors that work in the real world, Phil has now made a good start on his own life's journey. As Dr. Glasser tells us, "Once these are solidly within [his] grasp, the rest will follow."[2]

DR. GLASSER'S COMMENTS ON "BECOMING A CERTAIN MAN"

If the counselor detects that her client is destroying his life because of a picture in his all-we-want world, she has to help him to change that picture. Phil had almost destroyed his life because he had a picture in this world of not doing anything that his father wanted him to do. Pictures like this are destructive because they depend on what others do, more than on what we can do ourselves. Despite all the self-destructive things Phil was doing to show his father that he was wrong, Phil still had no guarantee that he could control his father. And if he could not, then all his efforts were in vain.

It was hard for Phil to learn the control theory lesson that the only person he could control was himself, but this is never an easy lesson for anyone. He did not learn it directly: he learned it when Suzy Hallock was able to help him see that he had to replace this destructive picture with another one that did not depend on anyone else. Had she not been able to do this, she would not have helped him. Pictures that depend on others rarely satisfy our needs, and in Phil's case, they were a disaster.

[2]*Control Theory,* p. 236.

Neither Phil nor his father realized it, but they had been fighting a long war over the fact that Phil was dedicated to being anything except what his father wanted. Although unhappy with Phil's behavior, his father had a life outside this relationship. All Phil's energy, however, was being consumed by this struggle, and to any objective observer, he was close to losing at the time he came for counseling. If ever there was a description of a loser, it is Suzy Hallock's description of Phil at the beginning of her narrative.

There is no detailed description of how Phil and his father got into this war, but throughout the case Ms. Hallock alludes to the fact that it had been going on for a long time. Early in the narrative she writes, "He [Phil] was a social isolate and could not envision authentic conversation with his parents, whom he characterized as 'Archie and Edith Bunker.' " A later sentence confirms this struggle: "His father ranted against hippie intellectuals, and Phil realized that such a diatribe had perhaps placed a governor on his own identity—he wanted to be one of those hippie intellectuals." Another example was: "In his fantasy and dream world, he often got what he wanted and often got revenge on his father, who seemed to attempt to control Phil and limit his freedom."

The weapon that Phil used to fight this war was self-destruction. He would win by proving to his father that he could be less than whatever his father wanted him to be, no matter how low his father was willing to set his sights. To do this, Phil made a strong and, from the initial description of him, very successful effort to be a total mess physically as well as mentally. As Ms. Hallock wonders after his father told her that he would have to drive Phil to her office, "Was it possible that a twenty-six-year-old college graduate could not 'find his way' to a destination one hour away?" I am sure that it was not only possible that Phil would not have found his way if his father had let him try.

The world is filled with children who battle their parents and try to win by losing. If they succeed, and Phil was very close to losing enough to "win" when he came for counseling, they lose totally: sometimes they even lose their lives. Ostensibly, most children get into wars with their parents to prove that they are their own people. Our needs for power and freedom push us to try to fulfill our own expectations ("to be one of those hippie intellectuals") and not to fulfill the expectations of parents ("putting his father's plan for a career in banking behind him"). But many children are able to do what they want even if it does not meet their parents expectations and still manage to avoid long wars with parents. They may struggle a little, but they stay off the road to self-destruction.

Phil's reason for fighting the war was not this noble. He engaged in it not so much because he wanted to be his own person as because he did not want to make the effort he felt it might take. In fact, he was so busy destroying himself in the struggle that when he came to counseling, he no longer had much of an idea what he wanted to do. What he was doing was painful, but it was easy: it took almost no effort at all. For example, it was easier to destroy himself and blame it on "Archie Bunker" than to buckle down and do the work that it took to do something for himself.

Although Phil's father did not understand what was going on, by the time he brought Phil to the counselor's office, he was more than willing to concede that Phil was winning in the battle to prove that he was physically and mentally incompetent. Besides, his father correctly feared that suicide was a possibility.

What Ms. Hallock did was persuade Phil to give up the struggle to be totally incompetent. She did this at first just by listening, "And when he talked, all the history of his torment was unleashed, and I wondered whether I might just as well be a computer or a parrot who occasionally nodded and added 'Um' or 'Oh, really.'" Just having a sympathetic ear got him started on the road to competence because by this time he, too, feared tht he was too close to "winning."

Listening, while very important in the beginning, is not enough to help as dedicated an incompetent as Phil was at this time. What Suzy Hallock needed was a key that would unlock his competence, something more than just talking to a sympathetic ear. In this case she found it in the "futuristic short story" that Phil had written and shared with her. The rest of this case built on what was evident in that story. The story proved that Phil had intellectual competence, but to get this small seed to flower took a lot of nurturing. Eventually it did flower, and the end of this case is very heartening. Phil will be a good school teacher. He will also have a spot in his heart for students who need the kind of intellectual support that he and others like him often fail to find in school.

From a control theory standpoint, this case shows how far we are willing to go to get what we think we want. Driven by his needs for power and freedom, Phil had placed a disastrous picture in his all-we-want world, and as he pursued that picture, he almost destroyed himself. What he thought would satisfy his needs was totally negative: don't do what father wants me to do. Whenever we dedicate our lives to a negative or "don't do" picture, the result is almost always disaster.

If we are to lead a satisfactory life, we must put positive or "do it" pictures in our all-we-want worlds. Positive means that we can achieve it through what we can do, and it does not depend on what others do or want us to do. As Ms. Hallock says, "We talked about individuating out of his family, about choosing life and about choosing one's own life." As she did this, Phil began to realize that being positive was the way to go, and his life turned around.

If she had engaged in long discussions with him about how much he did not like his parents and how wrong their conservative ideas were, Phil would have seen therapy as supportive of his negative pictures and continued on the "don't do" road to disaster. When he began to separate his life from them, the pictures of what he wanted became more and more positive. Considering where he started from, therapy was extremely successful.

11

So Good at Acting Bad

A Teenage Girl Who Just Wants to Make Trouble at School Changes Her Image

BARBARA HAMMEL

WHEN I STARTED to work with Yvonne Smith, she was in the eighth grade and on the verge of school expulsion. In our district the expulsion procedure requires the student and parents, together with their legal representation, to appear for an informal hearing before the Board of Education. Yvonne's problems were serious: aggressive acting-out, disruptive behavior, and academic difficulties. She challenged teacher authority by refusing to follow directions. Often Yvonne answered back in a loud voice using foul language. She cut classes and spent the time roaming the halls or hiding in the lavatory. When hall monitors questioned her, she became very nasty, telling them to mind their own business. As the gap widened between academic expectations at the eighth-grade level and her academic performance at a fifth-grade level, her acting-out behavior had begun to replace her former desire to do well academically. I knew that she wanted to learn because she had told me so. Her way, at this point, of dealing with academic frustration was to act "bad" instead of letting her teachers know that she did not understand the work. She chose to fight for power in the classroom by clowning and being disruptive.

Yvonne was aware of her academic deficiencies and was concerned and anxious about her performance in relationship to other classmates. She was an accessible youngster who was motivated to learn, but in order to do that she needed, initially, to relate on a personal rather than a program level. She had a strong need for belonging and identified with teachers and school staff when they took the time to be involved with her. Yvonne is one of a legion of youngsters who do not readily bond and identify with the traditional school system and its values. Her motivation to perform was directly related to how well she perceived adults were treating her.

As is normal for her age group, socialization with her peers was a strong agenda item for Yvonne, but she was choosing to accomplish this through negative rather than positive involvement. She had clearly established herself as a troublemaker and took pride in her ability to do that. In a one-on-one counseling session, she was candid and delightful. When she was with her peer group, she chose to give in to peer pressure and continued to act out in an antisocial manner. During my initial interview with Yvonne, as the middle school social worker, my credibility was established to some extent because I had known and worked successfully with other family members. If I were to work successfully with her, she needed to develop a picture of me as a caring, need-fulfilling person who could be trusted.

During my first interview with students, I always ask, "Do you know what a social worker does?" The answers I get are varied: "taking kids out of the home," "giving welfare," "investigating child abuse," and "helping people with problems." I explain that in the school setting my job is to help students solve problems related to making good choices and getting along with people. I use Dr. Glasser's example of a car stuck in the sand getting in deeper by spinning its wheels. I use this model to describe my job. A tow truck works directly at pulling a stuck vehicle out of the sand, but once the car is out it needs to go in the correct direction to stay out. I compare the tow truck to the first part of reality therapy, the involvement stage, when I will help the student directly by pulling him or her out of the sand one or two times. It is during the direct helping phase that I try to make friends with students like Yvonne. In Yvonne's case, during this direct helping process I offered to speak to her teachers and administrators, but my real job was to help her change direction if the direction she was then choosing was a trouble road. My job was to help her develop behaviors to talk to authority figures and solve her problems in a socially acceptable manner. Yvonne giggled frequently during my explanation, but nodded her head several times in agreement.

During this initial interview, I give the students a choice about working with me. I ask if they know why they are there to see me. Frequently, they reply, "No." They have no problems. It is the teachers, other kids, or parents who have the problems. I call this "spotlighting." By focusing blame on other people, students deny their own problems. When they do this, I tell them directly what has been presented to me as the perceived problem by the referring person. Yvonne knew that I was familiar with her problems, as I had witnessed and even intervened in several of her aggressive actions toward her peers in the hallways. I had also observed her challenging, hostile stance in a street-smart manner with authority figures.

It is my job to create a comfortable nonthreatening climate in my office for students like Yvonne in the hope that they will be able to create more positive pictures about school, develop positive self-esteeming, and eventually develop acceptable social behaviors in school. I explained to Yvonne that she did have a choice in working with me. If she decided to say yes, we would have a lot of hard work to do together. I told her the approach I used in working with people was called reality therapy. She asked me what that meant. I explained that our job is to help people focus on developing responsible behavior in everyday life. We usually let the people we are working with evaluate what they want to change to get more satisfaction from school, home, or work and how they will accomplish the changes. In her case, her teachers, guidance counselor, and principal had already evaluated what she needed to change. Some goals I thought we could work on would be to help her examine how her behavior matched the expectations of the school staff. She was to let me know the following day what her decision was.

At the appointment time the next day, Yvonne stopped by and told me she would like to try working with me. Giving the students an option seems to work well for both of us. They maintain their power if the choice is theirs. They also feel a sense of freedom in not being "forced." Coming for counseling is hard work for the students, but it is also a lot of fun.

During our second session, we filled out an interview sheet that I created and call "The Pictures in the Student's Head." I use this to get to know the student more quickly. I explained to Yvonne that I knew some of her conflict areas, but I wanted to know other things about her as a person that did not relate to conflict. She seemed surprised that I was not going to launch off into problems and advice giving, but she liked the idea of an interview. Most students are familiar with talk shows on television and can tell me who their favorite interviewer is. I ask them to pretend, if they want, that this is a television talk show interview. Sometimes we tape record the answers, sometimes I write them out, and sometimes the student does.

Yvonne told me that she was a fourteen-year-old eighth grade student who had been attending Long Branch schools since kindergarten. Her picture, or idea of what school was for, was to learn reading and spelling. Her job in school was to work and study, but she slipped in, "This doesn't include the rules." Her favorite school subject was math because it was easy and she liked the teacher. Social studies was difficult because often she did not understand the reading. I asked her if she ever sought help: she said she had not because she was too embarrassed. In elementary school, it had not been as difficult for her to read, but the work was more difficult now. She felt that she learned best in the afternoon in a quiet environment and better with a group than independently or with teacher supervision. Her favorite teacher since starting school was Mrs. Brown because "she didn't holler except when she had a headache, but she really cared about kids." When I asked her how she got along with authority figures, she grinned and firmly replied, "I am loud and get in trouble."

She seemed to be watching for my reaction, but I didn't give one. Instead, I tucked this information away for a future session. Throughout the interview, Yvonne threw in answers for shock effect; she also seemed to be testing me. Yvonne felt a sense of importance in school when she was with her friends making trouble (again I underacted). I asked her if she ever had fun in school, and she quickly replied, "When I make my friends laugh and annoy the teacher." I restated my question: "Yvonne, I meant do you have fun in school in a learning situation?" She thought this over for a moment and said, "Yes, I suppose I do in math class." She felt there was no place in school where she experienced freedom or decision making.

I asked her, "If you could create a school where most kids would be happy and get their needs met in a reasonable way, what would that school be like?" She looked serious and answered, "The teachers would care about the kids and listen to their ideas and problems." Something she liked about herself was her sense of humor. I told her that I, too, enjoyed her humor.

Yvonne told me that she lived at home with her mother, father, three brothers, and two sisters. We talked a little bit about her two brothers with whom I had worked in middle school. One had now graduated and was working at a race track in Florida. Yvonne shared a room with her sister. Her jobs at home were to wash the dishes and clean her room and the kitchen. She felt she did her chores without prodding and that she definitely was a self-directed person. We talked about what a positive characteristic this could be. During my interviews with the student, I am looking for strength areas on which to build. Yvonne felt that she was a good family member when at home, but she was out most of the time and she liked to "party." When asked if she had a hero, she said it was her older sister who worked in New York as a secretary. She had a best friend with whom she shared her worries and secrets. At times she viewed herself as a leader, at other times as a follower. Yvonne really enjoyed the interview, and we had quite a few laughs during the process. She did not seem to understand the question, "What are some important rules you live by?" When I explained it, she thought a few minutes and with a solemn look on her face said, "I guess to be a good friend." Her favorite music was by Run DMC, a rap group. She enjoyed horror movies, and we shared some of our favorites. She did not particularly like television. She liked reading mystery books, going to football games, and eating hamburgers. She looked puzzled when I asked if she had any talents, but then smiled shyly and said she was a good singer. If she won the New Jersey lottery, she would buy her family a new home and then move out on her own. She would like people to remember that she was fun to be with and was a good friend.

Using this interview helps both me and the students. Obviously, I get a lot of pictures quickly about the students, but it also gives them the opportunity to share their perceptions about school, their likes, talents, hobbies. Even though we touch on conflicted areas, we do not focus on them. We frequently stop after an answer, process it, and explore it further.

When we finished the interview, I asked Yvonne what her day was going to be like in school. She said she could not promise anything. I told her that I appreciated her honesty, but it would make me feel better if she could try for some improvement that day. It would also help me feel that I earned my salary. She smiled and said, "I like the idea of helping you get paid." She agreed that she would not fight or be disruptive in the hallways and cafeteria for two days. We made our next appointment for two days later.

In the beginning of counseling, I try to see students a few times a week for brief sessions to establish the involvement. During our next interview, Yvonne stated that she enjoyed making trouble and wanted to continue doing so. I told her that I admired the strength she had in "making trouble," but I wished that she would direct this strength in a different direction. I also pointed out that legally she had to remain in school until she was sixteen. What she did about her behavior in school until then was her choice.

During this session, I taught Yvonne a little more about

reality therapy and control theory, internal motivation, internal worlds, and the basic needs. On the bulletin board in my office I have several teacher-made projects that visually represent the basic physiological and psychological needs for belonging, power, fun, and freedom.

I asked Yvonne what would happen to her if she had no water or food over a long period of time. She responded that eventually she would dehydrate and die if she had no liquids and that if she had no food, she would eventually die of malnutrition. We talked about the need for all people to have their survival and security needs met. We also talked about a healthy physiology. I taught her about the basic psychological needs for belonging, power, fun, and freedom. I explained that belonging is a cooperative need, and power could be a competitive one with ourselves or other people. I taught her that there could be a conflict in needs, for example, freedom versus belonging. Yvonne liked the idea of the basic psychological needs. I explained that the basic needs are common to all regardless of race, religion, or socioeconomic condition, but how individual people get their needs met is specific and different. I asked her if she would go "funning" with me. She laughed and said, "What do you do for fun?" I replied, "How about a helicopter ride?" "Not me," she said, "I am not getting off the ground." Using examples helps the students to understand about individual pictures. We spent this interview discussing different kinds of belonging (family, friendship, romance), fun, power, and freedom. We especially talked about how students get these needs met in a school setting, in a social setting, and at home.

Yvonne responded in a most positive way and understood the basic needs. She especially liked talking about power. Her homework assignment was to figure out how she was currently choosing to get these needs met in school and what she would be doing if she were attempting to achieve these needs in a positive manner.

Yvonne began working with me in early September, and by November she did tell me some of the things she wanted from school. It was not until mid-December and our eleventh meeting that we reexamined together what she really wanted. It was to develop a more positive school image and get help with reading. She admitted that she had been moving in the wrong direction. She further admitted that she had been "spinning her wheels" for so long that she needed help in changing behaviors to get what she said she wanted.

At this point we looked again at the earlier assignment I had given her on what her basic needs would be like if she were achieving them in a positive manner. For belonging, she wrote that she would be with her friends in the cafeteria trying to select a school activity to join. For power, she saw herself as a member of the cheering squad at the football games and working in math class. For freedom, she wrote that she would understand school material and pass. For fun, she would join the Choral Club. I also asked her what her picture of a positive school image would look like. She told me that she would stop being disrespectful and getting into fights. I told her that was good, but I wanted her to be even more specific. What positive things would she be doing? I wanted her to put an exact word picture on my desk. She thought it over and replied, "I would be cooperating with the teacher in a quiet manner, I would not use street language, I would be a good reader, I would be in cheerleading and chorus, and I would give up making trouble." We laughed together as she painted this picture of every teacher's dream student.

At this point, Yvonne was very powerful with her friends, and they still expected her to make trouble. She also had a lot of power over her teachers, whose lives she was disrupting. Yvonne had a wonderful sense of humor that she was using to her disadvantage. She admitted that she was using her humor as a weapon. She had the ability to make people laugh by creating funny facial expressions and body motions, and she acted silly during serious times. It was very disconcerting to teachers when she would suddenly appear to be falling out of her seat and draw the attention of the class from the lesson to herself. She also poked fun at people's shortcomings with sarcastic remarks. She admitted to me that she really enjoyed the Bill Cosby show. We talked about how the Cosby kids used humor in a way that was not hurtful to other people. We began, in this manner, to have her work on using her humor as a creative tool at appropriate times, not class time, to get her positive attention. One avenue we explored was the Drama Club.

I assigned Yvonne to watch television and to look at comic strips or jokes to find humor that was fun and included people. She was also to pick out "put-down" humor, and during our sessions we explored the differences. Trouble was Yvonne's status symbol, and acting out, disruptive behavior, and ill-timed, put-down humor were the tools she used to maintain that image.

It was not until several more sessions that she admitted she wanted to change. Now some hard work was ahead of us.

I have developed various forms to work with students. They are like skeletons on which we build the flesh from their internal worlds, self-evaluations, and plans for change. We spend a great deal of time processing the information from these forms, stopping at difficult points, and enjoying the counseling sessions.

By our next session, Yvonne was ready to evaluate her behavior, using the "Student Self-Evaluation Scale for Those Who Admit They Want an 'Attitudinal Adjustment' and Better Academic Performance," one of the forms I have developed. With this self-evaluation form, I went through Yvonne's day period by period. She told me what grade she was getting currently and what grade she could be getting if she did her best. We also looked at her behavior and rated it 1 for poor and 10 if she did her best.

Yvonne identified the behaviors she wanted to change: "I want to be a better reader. I want to develop a more positive school image. I want to stop being a 'trouble maker.'" The changes she needed to make to accomplish these changes were to stop being disrespectful, loud, and rude and to stop using street language. She needed to stop fighting with teachers and students. I asked her if making the change was worth the time and energy it would require. If so, what made it worth it? Yvonne thought she would get to like school better, get better grades, and get her parents off her back. I asked what supports she would need to make the plan work. She thought she could

---

Long Branch Middle School—Student Interview Based on the Pictures in Their Internal Worlds, Not Others' Expectations

The reality therapy process—making friends, finding out who they are and what they want.

Name: _____ Age: _____ Grade: _____ Repeated: _____
School data: _____ Schools attended: _____
What is your idea (picture) of what school is for? _____
_____

Describe your job (role) as a student in this school _____
_____

What is your favorite subject? _____ What do you like about it? _____
_____

What subject/s are difficult for you? _____
What is difficult? _____
What time of day do you learn best? _____ What kind of place do you learn best in?
_____

Do you work best: Independently? ____ With a buddy? ____ In a group? ____ Teacher? ____
Who is or was your favorite teacher since you started school? _____
What makes that person a good teacher? _____
What books do you own? _____
_____

Meeting the basic psychological needs for belonging, power, fun and freedom in school.

Where in school do you feel a sense of belonging? Who do you identify and relate with?
_____

Where in school do you feel important? (Feeling good about yourself—a sense of power and worth.) _____

Where in school do you have fun? _____
Where in school do you experience freedom—making decisions and choices? _____

If you could create a school where most students would be happy and learning and have the above needs met in a reasonable way, what would that school be like? _____

Do you belong to any school activities, i.e., sports, newspaper, art club, band, glee club?

---

speak to two of her teachers about her plan to try to behave better, and she asked me to speak to her guidance counselor and other teachers to let them know about her plan and to ask them to give her a chance to change. We explored possible blocks, problem areas, or negative forces to be considered against the

Personal and Family Data: _____

Family Picture: Who lives with you? _____

_____

Do you share a room?_____ What jobs do you have?_____

Are you: Self directed?_____ Need to be prodded?_____ Other directed?____

What kind of a family member are you?_____

Who is your hero (someone you admire)?_____

Do you have a best friend?_____Who do you share secrets with?_____

Are you a leader or follower?_____Do you have a special place?_____

What do you do in your free time?_____

Do you like to spend time alone?_____

What is your favorite music?_____ Movies?_____

TV programs?_____ Books?_____Color?_____

Food?_____Hobby?_____Talent?_____

Do you think reading is: Fun_____ Hard work_____ Boring_____Other_____

What would you do if you won the lottery?_____

_____

What do you want people to remember most about you as a person?_____

_____

What are some important rules or values you live by? _____

_____

What do you like about yourself?_____

_____

What do other people like about you?_____

_____

What direction are you going in school right now?   (Behavior and performance)_____

_____

What direction do you really want to go?_____

What kind of school image do you want to project?_____

_____

How do you picture your future?_____

Created by Barbara Hammel

plan being successful. Yvonne thought her friends might not believe that she was giving up making trouble. She also thought the teachers might not believe her, but the main issue for her was her own attitude. She was going to record her progress in weekly meetings with me, and she would evaluate her progress

Student Self-evaluation Assessment for Those Who Choose to Make an "Attitudinal Adjustment" and/or Better Academic Performance

What direction are you going right now?

Period	Subject	Teacher	Current Grade	If I did my best	Attitude Measurement									
					current if I did my best									
					1	2	3	4	5	6	7	8	9	10
1														
2														
3														
4														
5														
6														
7														
8														

Is the direction you are going getting you what you said you wanted? Getting you what you need? Helping you? Helping others? Is it against the rules?

See attached plan for student self-evaluation plan for change.

How is commitment to the plan made?

Did the student make excuses? Don't accept excuses, re-cycle plan.

Don't punish, but don't interfere with the natural or reasonable consequences, school rules, and what happens when they are broken. Student should know the rules and understand consequences for infraction.

Student must experience something different than s/he has in the past.

Accept the person—reject the poor behavior and separate the two—don't criticize or control.

Do not give up—do not confirm the failure identity—either the acting-out behavior, withdrawing or academic impotency.

Does the direction you are going have a reasonable chance of getting you what you want down the road?

Created by Barbara Hammel

by gauging her own attitude change and behavior and reports from teachers on her behavior. The plan would start on December 14 and she would try it for a week.

Sequence of Steps
1. Ms. Hammel will speak to the guidance counselor and teachers.
2. I will speak to two teachers by making an appointment with them.
3. I will tell my friends, "I can't afford to make any more trouble."
4. My guidance counselor will get me an additional period of Resource Room during English period.
5. Target Date to Complete the Plan: June 1986

Yvonne further agreed to try this plan a day at a time. She and I agreed to do some role playing to help her handle conflict situations and reverse her pattern of making trouble. The contract was signed by both of us.

She began to understand that I cared enough about her to expect only her best self. I also explained that my job was to help her exhibit the good behaviors that she used with me in a group and classroom situation as well. We also worked on coping with personalities she didn't like. I gave Yvonne several assignments to build self-esteem and a sense of importance. She "hired" an advertising agency to write a television commercial selling her positive characteristics. She also wrote a "Super Student" ad for a Want Ad column read by teachers who select students for their classes on the basis of these ads. Yvonne's ad read:

Super student available: Yvonne Smith, a friendly, humorous student will bring a lot of laughter to your class. She enjoys learning new things and will work hard to get good grades. She has a good memory, is neat and organized. A good student for teachers who believe that learning can be fun.

Yvonne was to watch television commercials to see how advertisers got their products across to the public and then to think of ways to get herself across as a positive person to her teachers. These activities were very enjoyable for her. I told her that she impressed me as a youngster who often showed her "first" side to the staff, and they all needed to see the softer "palm" side she shared with me.

During our sessions, we discussed the responsibilities that go with being a woman. When Yvonne acted in a positive, dignified way (as dignified as teenagers can get), she was a credit to all women. When she was choosing to make trouble, she diminished all of us. We explored the "use of making trouble" in a positive way. For one assignment she made a list of leaders who had made trouble for social change: Dr. Martin Luther King, Jr., Susan B. Anthony, Mary Bethune. We explored careers such as a paralegal and human resource personnel for fighting social injustice. She liked the concept of being able to make a positive contribution for all women. She also liked the idea of using her personal strengths in a future career and was pleased with the thought of reversing "trouble making" into positive energy.

There was constant review of her initial evaluation of wanting a more positive school image and meeting her basic needs for belonging, power, fun, and freedom in a positive way. We assessed if the direction she was going was getting her what she said she wanted both today and in the future.

We did a lot of role playing. I would be the teacher who did not believe she was sincere in her desire to change, and she had to convince me otherwise. It was hard work getting Yvonne to give up her street-smart answers. She tried to find excuses by claiming that the teachers would not give her a fair chance. I would play the role of a student hassling her.

BARBARA: C'mon, Yvonne. What's wrong with you, girl? You sick or something? Sally Sue got up in your face. You gonna take that?

YVONNE: [Giggles]

BARBARA: Yvonne, you are acting real "un-cool" lately. What are you afraid of, her static? Sally Sue said you're scared of her. Are you, girl?

YVONNE: What do you mean, man. I am not worried about her static. I'll shut her face down.

BARBARA: [Out of role play.] Is that kind of answer keeping you out of trouble?

YVONNE: No.

BARBARA: Do you really want what you said you wanted? A better school image?

YVONNE: Yes, I really do.

BARBARA: Try to respond to the student with, "I just can't afford to be in trouble anymore. My parents are on my case."

BARBARA: [Back in role play.] Hey, Yvonne, you're no fun any more!

YVONNE: I just can't afford to be in trouble anymore. My parents are on my case!

BARBARA: [Out of role play] Say it louder and like you mean it.

YVONNE: [Louder, firmer.] I just can't afford to make trouble. My parents are on my case!

At first she would giggle a lot. I was tough on her and made her practice saying, "I can't afford any more trouble" firmly in a loud, clear voice. She knew that I would not let her off the hook.

Bright, quick, and street-smart, with a marvelous sense of humor, Yvonne was a challenge to work with all year. We had to constantly re-plan and recycle, increasing her strong areas and building up her weak ones. She admitted that she did not want to give up all the trouble making at once because of peer pressure, but she did stop making trouble in two classes immediately. If Yvonne's plan for change was to be successful, staff members needed to accept the fact that total change would not take place overnight. It took a lot of convincing and trading on good staff relationships to persuade some of the staff to give Yvonne a chance to prove that she wanted to change her behavior and do better in school. We changed one of her directions completely by removing her from one particularly problematic class and giving her some additional remedial reading work.

In May, Yvonne and I established a Real Women Don't Fight Club at school, and several of her peers joined. This has become a self-referral group of young women who like the idea of having something positive to contribute to school. I encourage them to join school activities and do volunteer community service.

Yvonne graduated with her eighth-grade class that June. She was proud of herself, and her parents were equally proud. So was I. I know the guidance counselor at the high school, and I alerted him about Yvonne's arrival there. Most students have some regression at transition points, and I wanted him to know that Yvonne was a student who needed some personal involvement and support to keep moving in the right direction.

What I have learned in working with Yvonne and many other students is that most of them want to be positive about school and meet their basic needs in a good way, but they often act in a negative fashion if they perceive that their lives are not in effective control in school. They become so good at "acting bad" that the act becomes their security blanket. This is exacerbated if they have some learning difficulties.

I see Yvonne frequently as I walk through the high school on my way to the middle school. She is in the tenth grade this year and has a job at a local shopping mall. She mischievously admits some minor relapses, but so far is keeping her plan to give up "just wanting to make trouble." I will be working in the high school next year and will have a better opportunity to give her more personal support as she moves toward graduation. She has come a long way from the expulsion hearing where I first met her, when she was "so good at acting bad."

DR. GLASSER'S COMMENTS ON "SO GOOD AT ACTING BAD"

Teachers who work in urban school districts are very familiar with students like Yvonne, who at age fourteen was on the verge of expulsion from school. Without intervention by someone like Barbara Hammel, it is almost certain that Yvonne would not have come close to finishing high school. As a dropout or pushout, she would hate whatever life she would be able to make for herself. Whatever she was enjoying at the time she was seen in counseling was probably the best she would have for a long time, maybe for the rest of her life. She was fortunate to get help when she did because her chance for a good life was already almost over, although she did not know this and would not have believed it if she were told.

But Barbara Hammel knows this sad fact. Every teacher and counselor who works with girls like her knows this, and books, articles, and research confirm it. Little is being done to solve this problem, however. Yvonne and her children (statistics indicate that she is likely to have several by the time she is twenty years old) will have to be cared for, maybe for their whole lives. Neither she nor they have any reasonable chance for a better life.

Was the problem so bad because Yvonne came from a bad home? No, she came from a good home; her parents cared about her but did not know what to do. Was it because she was mentally retarded or learning disabled? This is rarely the case, and it was not the case with her. Is it because no one knew what to do? No, Ms. Hammel knew exactly what to do, as do the other counselors in this book who work in or with the schools. Is it because our schools do not have enough people like Barbara Hammel? Yes, we need more counselors and social workers. Is it because the ones we have are not given enough support and time to work with students like Yvonne? Yes, they need more support and more time. Do we as a society really care about students like Yvonne? A little, but not nearly enough.

Can this be changed? Only if the taxpayers who support the schools can get a clear picture of how a girl like Yvonne can be helped. Right now most people, including many teachers and administrators, do not believe that a hostile, low-performing student like Yvonne can be helped. They not only don't know what Ms. Hammel does, but they don't realize that they could do much of the same themselves if they would learn and use control theory. Even Yvonne learned when it was taught to her.

There is no mystery to what Barbara Hammel did. Using the techniques of reality therapy, she taught Yvonne how to satisfy her needs in school. If this had been a concern of all her teachers and administrators, and if they had known better how to do it, Ms. Hammel would have had an easier job. (And yet Barbara Hammel's school is much more concerned than schools that have not been introduced to these ideas.) What we need is more school and public awareness of the fact that the best part of the lives of girls like Yvonne need not be over at age fourteen. It is this awareness, plus publicizing many more examples of what was done with Yvonne, that may move us to begin to do something more about this problem than wail about its magnitude.

Extensive research has shown that the uniform complaint of almost all the many "Yvonnes" in our schools is that "Teachers don't care." When they say teachers, they mean the adults who work in the schools. As Barbara Hammel says, "Her motivation to perform was directly related to how well she perceived adults were treating her." But to be fair, from the teachers' standpoint, Yvonne was a terror. The teachers had to deal with her foul language, disruptive behavior, clowning, hiding in the lavatory, and low academic performance while struggling to teach 150 other students, few of whom were easy to get along with. Still the only answer is in expanding what Ms. Hammel was doing and making our classrooms more need satisfying. Nothing less will have any effect.

To learn the basics of good counseling using reality therapy and control theory is not hard. We teach this to many people each year. What is hard is moving beyond the basics and figuring out techniques that reach out and grab the client's attention. Barbara's technique of interviewing the student to find out what is in her all-we-want world is a wonderful one that I hope any of you who work with young people will try. It encourages them to open up when many of them, because they have been in trouble, don't want to talk. They fear, from previous experience, that they are going to receive a lecture or that what they say will be held against them. As Barbara Hammel says, "She seemed surprised that I was not going to launch off into problems and advice giving, but she liked the idea of an interview."

The other thing that Barbara Hammel did was teach Yvonne some basic control theory. It is Ms. Hammel's experience, and I have heard this from many others I work with, that young people, even as young as first grade, are easily able to learn control theory if it is taught to them using visual aids and many examples they can relate to their lives. Ms. Hammel used the question, "What would happen to you if you had no water or food for a long time?" to introduce the need to survive. Yvonne had no difficulty relating to this question and then going on the psychological needs from this clear beginning.

My hope is that we will make an effort to teach all children the concepts of control theory so that they realize what motivates them, and even more important, that they have a choice as to what to do to satisfy this motivation. When Yvonne came to Barbara, she had not thought at all about her choices: what she thought about was what most kids like her think about when they come for counseling, "No. I don't have problems. It's the teachers, other kids, or parents who have problems." When control theory introduces them to the idea that they have choices, they begin to accept that they have problems. This is because once they see that they have choices, they also see that they have some control and with it a chance to solve their problems.

Another technique that Barbara Hammel used extensively in counseling with Yvonne was role playing. Most kids have a natural flair for drama, and once they get over the initial shyness, they love to role play. In role plays it is possible for a counselor to introduce ideas and make points that are awkward to make in straight counseling. When Barbara played a tough student hassling Yvonne, she was able in only minutes to get to the core of her defensiveness by using language that she could not have used otherwise.

Done the way Ms. Hammel does it, counseling is a lot of fun. And it should be fun. If it is seen as a drag, it cannot be done well. Doing the "Super Student" classified ad with Yvonne must have been very enjoyable. This is another technique that I think will pay off for teachers and counselors who get off to a good start with a difficult student and then get stuck, not knowing where to go. Getting the students to write their own ads is a great way to involve them actively in carrying on what you are encouraging them to do. It keeps them involved with you, and as long as they enjoy this involvement, they will be open to changing what they do so that they can increase what they enjoy in other parts of school. This is exactly what Barbara Hammel and Yvonne did, as this case study illustrates so well.

12

Father and Son Learn Together

A Father Gives Up Depressing and Criticizing as a Son Struggles to Develop Responsible Behaviors

GEORGELLEN HOFHINE

THERE WAS AN URGENCY in Rob's voice when he called for a first appointment, and I decided to see him immediately. He had been referred to me by his wife, Marion, who had recently completed a Life Redirection and Management course that I teach.

I was not surprised to greet a handsome, well-groomed man in his early forties with a courteous but restrained professional manner. Marion had spoken with great pride of her estranged husband as a "brilliant surgeon." But I was not prepared for his deep depression. His demeanor was one of hopelessness. His voice and facial expression were flat. There was no bounce in his step and, I suspected, little spark in his life.

Rob made it clear that he expected me to do something to him or for him to ameliorate his depression—to "cure" him. His desperation was obvious, and I wondered if, as a physician, he viewed counseling as a last resort. We exchanged a few tentative attempts to get acquainted. I knew that we had to establish a warm and honest environment in order to find what he sought, a change in the way he was feeling. Although courteous, he showed little understanding of how we would proceed. I explained that my approach could only be to guide and help him learn to choose more effective behaviors to meet his needs. Then I asked questions to learn about the pictures in his inner world and how well he was fulfilling the wants they represented. Knowing that he was successful in his career, I explored those daily activities. It was soon obvious that he was totally committed to excellence and dedicated to his patients and medical practice. This commitment played a major role in his present distress. He had been diagnosed as being in the early stages of Parkinson's disease, of which one of the first manifestations is a hand tremor, and he envisioned himself as a victim of a relentless illness. His physician's knowledge of the ramifications of this debilitating, progressive disease did not serve him well. He was, of course, deeply concerned about how long his career could continue.

While we talked, I was gathering additional information about how he was meeting his basic needs. When I inquired about personal relationships, I was surprised to learn that this highly successful doctor could be so ineffectual in his personal life. Rob and Marion had recently separated after twenty years of marriage. He had been forced to move from his comfortable home into a small apartment. As often occurs in marriages, Marion had attended to all social activities, at the same time managing the household and taking responsibility for the two children. This quiet gentleman had assumed a passive role in all but his medical practice. As we explored relationships, it seemed that he had not been deeply involved personally with people at any time in his life. Pursuit of his career had consumed him: I was beginning to think he met all of his needs through his medical practice. Now, suddenly and unexpectedly, when his career was threatened by physical problems, he no longer had the support and comfort of a loving wife, children, home, or, in fact, any support group. He was reluctant to socialize with colleagues and friends who might become aware of the slight tremor in his hand. His partner, in whom he had confided, accompanied him in surgery. He greatly valued the loyal support of his friend and colleague in protecting the welfare of his patients. Rob, medically sophisticated, discussed an array of symptoms of depression. He cited early waking, lack of interest in anything, no appetite, and a feeling of hopelessness. Then, rooted as he was in the medical model in which he saw depression as a disease, he waited for my prescription.

What Rob had to do was figure out some need-satisfying behaviors, and my job was to help him do this. We made progress quickly over the next six months. He began to gain enough strength to function without his wife and embark upon some new, more need-satisfying directions to regain better control of his life. As we worked together in the following weeks, Rob seemed to appreciate our interaction and made every effort to comply with suggestions and be a "good patient." With his medical training, however, it was difficult for him to make the transition to depend on selection of behavior rather than on medical treatment. He continued to research new approaches to controlling the progress of Parkinson's, conferring with a major medical research hospital. Although this was a necessary and important step for him, he continued to come for counseling, and we discussed many things: life, books, furniture, music, eating, but seldom his depressing. He knew how to depress: he needed to learn more skill in interaction.

Rob seemed interested in the variety of my activities and interests, so I used this as a way to talk about needs and how we fulfill them. He was eager to learn more about behaviors. His intelligent questions often directed the counseling. He would anticipate my direction. Each time I explored his present behavior to meet his needs, he quickly evaluated its effectiveness and shared his plan to select more useful behaviors. Just sitting back while a client used what were once called the "responsibility steps" of reality therapy was fun for me. For example, he would acknowledge that he presently had difficulty meeting his need for love and belonging, but that meeting his need for power was easy. Then he would quickly summarize his recent unsuccessful attempts to find a loving companion, evaluate them as ineffec-

Father and Son Learn Together   227

tive, and explore several possible behaviors to meet the "right one." We would then discuss his plans and his perceptions of an appropriate mate before he made a concrete plan. We also examined his perceptions of how to meet his power need if the time came when he could not practice medicine. He would not consider teaching, research, nor any other alternatives. Rob felt greatest power when performing delicate surgery successfully. He enjoyed prestige and other accoutrements of success through his reputation as a superior surgeon and as an effective chief of staff of a hospital in a neighboring county. Having achieved the goals of his career, he now saw many of his choices slipping away. Depressing was the total behavior he elicited as his best choice at the time to regain control of his life.

When Rob began to bring in accounts of changed behavior following his own use of evaluation, I knew we were making progress. His new behaviors included activities that he initiated with others. He met with a few colleagues at lunch and continued to date. He even renewed a friendship that he had neglected. He was learning to meet his belonging needs in different ways.

At my suggestion, Rob read Dr. Glasser's *Control Theory,* made notes, and came in with questions about the section on criticism. "Please explain Dr. Glasser's views on criticism," he asked. He seemed most interested when I quoted Dr. Glasser: "It is harder to gain control when we are criticized than in any other situation. . . . It is by far the single most destructive behavior we use as we attempt to control our lives." I was to understand the significance of this later when I met his son.

As we discussed internal motivation as developed by Dr. Glasser, Rob announced that his only unmet need was for a loving companion. We spoke of other pathways to meeting his need for belonging. We explored other needs as he understood them from his reading. I asked when he felt most alive. "When I am able to perform successful surgery." Knowing his need for power was met exceedingly well through his work, and recognizing the threat his illness was to this pathway of fulfillment, I probed further to understand how he functioned outside his profession. He owned a small plane and enjoyed working on another one he was building. His developing illness and depressing had temporarily closed off this path to feeling able and important. His one activity outside his medical practice had ceased, and the seriousness of this client's demeanor had me wondering if he had ever met his need for fun. He insisted that the pursuit of medicine when a student had been fun, but his lackluster presentation of himself led me to believe that I had to lighten our sessions with as much humor as possible. When I was able to elicit only a gentle smile, I thought perhaps this was a commentary on my humor. But at the same time, I could only hope that if I ever needed surgery, there might be some measure of Rob's need for seriousness and perfection in my own doctor.

Having now become familiar enough to feel that I understood Rob, I decided that what he needed most was to find a way to become more involved with people not in his professional life. What he wanted was eventually to find a new mate.

At my urging, Rob set out methodically to become involved with people and find companions and a new wife. Each week he was prompt and attentive. He reported results of his weekly plans, which were activities to attempt to become involved, but his focus was on dating. Just as I do not see my role as problem solving, it certainly is not providing a dating service. But I chose to deal with the pictures in my client's head. Still, I persisted in trying to help him see the connection between his choices of behavior, especially depressing. We investigated the pictures in his head and matched them to what he was doing. The stimulus-response way of looking at everything was strong in Rob. He insisted that if one particular young woman of whom he was enamored would return his ardor, he would not depress. We then began to look at despondent feelings as the feeling component of the total behavior of "depressing." When I inquired about the acting and thinking components, it was difficult for Rob to focus on anything but feeling. I persisted. He did admit that he was not taking any action of a positive direction, and certainly he was thinking only in negative terms.

At the same time, I began to see changes. Rob was learning to reach out beyond his medical practice for involvement and pleasurable activities. He continued to present himself to me as someone who, he thought, could "fix his life," while I continued to try to teach him to examine his behavior in relation to meeting his needs. As he came to understand that his depressing was his way to deal with the difference between what he wanted and what he had, Rob concentrated on changing more behaviors. We had traveled a long road. Through friendly noncritical examination, we repeatedly focused on what he wanted and on what he was doing to get it. The pictures in his head changed very little in those months of a hopscotch of behaviors he tried. He began to jog in the mornings with his son, Tom, who was with him now. Both frequent meetings with Marion to figure out ways to deal with two unhappy teens and finding some new friends kept him involved in activities besides his career. A busy social life with lunch, dinner, and weekend dates became the school in which he learned. As he expanded his activities, his need to depress reduced. Also, his intense searching for a new approach to Parkinson's provided some satisfaction and a sense of gaining control. As father and son shared an interest in flying, he started taking Tom on short flights. They took another teen to an air show in the Midwest, where they also visited Rob's mother.

When Dr. Glasser and Norman Cousins presented a workshop at UCLA entitled, "Your Health Is the Way You Are Choosing to Live Your Life," Rob was quick to buy tickets for himself and the woman then in his life. He was a man of few words, not comfortable with sharing: he had little comment. The word *parsimony* often came to mind when we talked, but I was undaunted. I continued to work to involve Rob in conversation, but usually it was I who talked: he listened.

We continued to speak of things unrelated to his depressing as we deepened our respect for one another. It was my belief that our friendship might become a model for Rob as he learned to become involved with others. I was invited to lunch to meet a young woman who had become important in his life. After casually dating several others, he had decided Pam was "special."

Marion, in the meantime, was choosing behaviors to move

her life in a better direction. She, too, had learned control theory, and I heard from her occasionally as she pursued an advanced degree at UCLA. Perfection, orderliness, and doing what they thought was appropriate must have characterized their marriage. Never once did I hear Rob criticize Marion. They continued to work to maintain a friendly relationship as they dealt with their two unhappy teenagers. Rob often made comments about discipline and responsibility. We discussed responsibility as meeting one's needs without interfering with others meeting their needs or breaking laws. Rob had made progress in enlarging his world and filling it with need-satisfying friends and activities. I suggested that we taper off the counseling sessions.

One evening several months after Rob had terminated counseling, I was alerted by phone that his seventeen-year-old son had disappeared and would be in need of an appointment on short notice. This was fifteen months after Rob had first come for counseling.

It was several weeks later that Rob and Tom appeared. Even though I did not yet know that they had not even spoken on the long drive, the tension between father and son when they arrived was obvious.

Tom was in some ways a younger clone of his handsome father: quick and intelligent, but different in that he was outspoken. It was easy to communicate with him, and I liked his directness. His hands and face were clean, but his clothes were not. Tom wasted no time in telling me why he had come. "I need a place to sleep," was his clear statement, and the problem was that Rob was just as clear with his refusal to give him that.

Since I am not fond of refereeing, I chose to determine a little more of what was going on. I had been told what each wanted. Then I listened to Rob's account of Tom's many ineffectual behaviors and what he considered his total irresponsibility. Tom had been living with his father in the apartment when, after several traffic tickets and fines, his driver's license was revoked. Although he had superior ability, he was failing his senior year of high school and had been "kicked out." Not able to satisfactorily meet his needs, he had chosen alcohol and drugs as his way to deal with frustrations.

Tom and his mother had suffered a poor relationship. She had in fact asked him to leave the home he had always known because of his abusive language. Several weeks later, he borrowed her car without permission and drove it about 350 miles. In reviewing a couple of years of entries of behaviors in a diary she kept, Marion realized that none of her actions had worked to correct the direction of her son's life. With the help of a parent support group, she decided, as his punishment, to have all his belongings except clothing removed from his room. In a protest of rage, he left. Until this evening, several weeks had passed without any word from him. When this situation arose, Rob brought Tom to me to "be corrected." We did not discuss our previous sessions nor Rob's personal life.

I tried to start the process of change by encouraging them to negotiate. Throughout this stormy session, father and son communicated only to demand or criticize. Rob had always used few words, but now he said even less. He frequently just shook his head to indicate "No." I asked each of them to state a position so that we could begin negotiating. In essence, Tom's was "Help me," and Rob's was "No," peppering the refusal with explicit criticisms.

Each was alone and in pain: neither father nor son saw the other as need-fulfilling. That first evening they sat at opposite ends of a couch, worlds apart. It was apparent that each had isolated himself and was focusing only on the pictures in his own inner world. Rob made it clear that he wanted nothing to do with Tom. He saw his son as a nuisance: messy, rude, and unrealistic. He viewed Tom as totally irresponsible because he did not behave as Rob wanted. Tom, in fact, was not succeeding in any area of his life. I, too, perceived Tom as irresponsible because he was not meeting his needs effectively. Tom felt that no one cared about him, and his choices were few. He was quite direct and abusive in telling his father that he did not feel loved, that he would never be in the same room with his mother again, and that even school had rejected him.

Negotiation was the immediate task at hand. We began. Rob critically listed claims of Tom's incorrigible behavior, while the youth, struggling for a place to sleep, turned each accusation into a plea for help. We began again with what each wanted immediately. Rob had almost nothing to say to his son, while Tom engulfed him with requests, complaints, and demands. "It isn't fair. I haven't any place to go, no license or car. School doesn't want me. It just isn't fair," he cried. "You have everything. Where can I sleep and bathe? I need a place to sleep. Why can't I go home with you? I won't take up much room; you are never there anyway. I'll sleep on the couch, and I'll clean up after myself. You don't care; you're not at home. This time I'll keep up my share." Tom made his attempt to compromise to get what he wanted. Rob was deaf to him. These two, alike in many ways, held tenaciously to such differing perceptions of how their lives had been under one roof. Each blamed the other, and each was adamant. Accusations and criticisms were all they could offer.

For about two hours, I asked questions to allow for clarification of perceptions and wants. A pattern emerged: first an accusation, then questions by me for clarification and verification of the accuracy of perceptions and focus on what each wanted, then assessment of how realistic the request was. It was always the same. Rob did not want him to return, and Tom demanded a place to sleep. At this point, I directed my question to Rob, "Are there any circumstances under which you would allow Tom to stay with you for a while?" Finally, we agreed on a tentative arrangement. Rob reluctantly made the first concession—Tom could sleep on the couch in exchange for paying his traffic tickets and attending to various restrictions and duties. Tom made promises of improved behavior and attitude. Each had made concessions, finally.

As they left, Rob commented to me, "You should be negotiating for General Motors. I came here tonight determined that Tom would never return to me." That first step was a giant one, but the road ahead was long.

The next week we embarked upon that bumpy road. Tom was a little less frantic and Rob less hostile. But frantic or hostile, they had not agreed to communicate, making progress difficult. Each was courteous to me, responded until the other spoke, and then we had silence. We all hung in. Every utterance from Rob was a criticism of Tom. The youth, so much in need of better control, lost a little with each criticism. Knowing that Tom had been using drugs, the potential for his violent behavior through reorganization was a constant concern to me. I had developed a relationship of trust with Rob through our previous sessions. However, Tom was not anxious to trust anyone. The best I could hope for was that he would see me as fair. I tried to guide them to examine what was working for each and help them learn how to make it a little better for both.

Although Rob and Tom sought to air differences and exchange accusations, when they finally spoke at sessions each week, I chose to help each look at the positive changes in their lives. For example, Tom did make some improvement toward the behaviors and attitude that Rob wanted, but Rob would not acknowledge these changes. When I pointed out this progress, Rob would then counter with what he was contributing to the improved situation. Then they would evaluate what was working for both. We dealt here not only with looking at one's choice of behavior, but with perceptions. Despite the fact that Rob and Tom were living together more harmoniously through attention to behavior choices, each still harbored old pictures of the other. For example, as Tom learned to complete chores and to be less messy at home, Rob still saw him as inconsiderate. I challenged this perception by asking Rob to evaluate the degree of consideration in several of Tom's present behavior choices. In the same manner, it was necessary to help Tom examine his image of his father as unloving. He began to see that Rob had made many difficult and caring concessions in order to give his son another chance to make his life a little better. Tom became less demanding of adult privileges as he assumed more adult responsibilities. Change occurs in very small increments, indeed.

During the next few weeks, always friendly and listening intently to these two, I was delighted as I watched them learning to communicate. The way was difficult as Rob still held the picture that a "good father" corrects and criticizes his son to make him perform as he "should." To a healthy teenager seeking independence, this was totally unfair. Tom demanded the privileges his father enjoyed. Rob, thinking he had worked hard all his life, had met his obligations, and did not break the law, felt that he had earned his privileges. I continued to work for clarification and examination of perceptions as well as behaviors. "How do you see it?" "Is it working?" "Is that what you want?" "Is it against the rules?" "How does that help?" These questions became so familiar that they were anticipated by these two clients. I became increasingly appreciative of the superior intelligence of father and son. They became friendly to me and attentive, recognizing that we were all working to try to make them feel better.

I focused at this time on helping Tom find better ways to meet his needs. We had explored relationships with family and friends; now I decided that he could gain some more effective control through achievements. We examined ways for him to do this. Since a jail sentence was imminent if he did not pay his fines, we calculated earnings against time allotted. Minimum wage at twenty hours per week would not cover the several hundred dollars required. Rob would not pay Tom's fines. Tom spoke unrealistically of getting a full-time job that paid an enormous sum. But when I asked questions, he admitted that he had no job skills, no diploma, no transportation, and no idea of where to begin. Rob commented that Tom was still unrealistic as we made plans for job hunting.

Several weeks passed, with Tom always requesting the next appointment. With no warning, he was fired from his service station job about the time of his eighteenth birthday. This was a setback, as Rob announced that he was no longer legally responsible for this young adult. Rob's solution was simple and clear—military enlistment. It did not matter that this was not the picture in Tom's head. As they left, Tom commented that at least they spoke to one another during these sessions, if not at other times. They arrived and left in a four-wheel drive vehicle and always in silence.

I continued to urge father and son to find some mutually satisfying activities. I suggested jogging, which they had once enjoyed, flying or working on the airplane as they had at one time, or perhaps just having dinner together as Tom had requested. After a few attempts to find a job and attempts to offer excuses to me that I would not accept, Tom turned his attention to community college. Surprisingly, Rob supported this pursuit. They traveled together to another city to investigate an aeronautics program and housing.

I recall one particularly difficult session. Tom had requested additional considerations at home, citing his improved behavior as justification. He asked for a greater selection of food. Rob indeed provided only a very limited variety. But Rob found it almost impossible to admit to changes in his son's behavior. He still clung to his earlier perceptions. We spent much of that session examining perceptions and verifying accuracy. Begrudgingly, Rob did admit to some positive growth in Tom. The response from Tom was unconcealed delight. Finally, some progress.

Father and son resumed flying together. They shared interest and excitement in this, and, I suspect, companionship. Also, I believe that there was some mutual dependency. We were seeing more progress.

There was a court hearing at which Rob appeared with his son, having taken time from his practice. (Although about half the fines had been paid, jail was still a distinct possibility.) Later, when we looked at what Tom wanted to have happen, it was he who evaluated his own behavior as ineffectual. Tom had begun to pay attention to the relationship between the pictures in his head and his choices of behavior to achieve them. I had frequently asked, "Is this the way you want your life to be?" In the courtroom, he had examined his present situation in relation to how he had wanted it. He definitely did not want to go either to jail or into military service. He had been asked in counseling many times if what he was doing was working. His behavior was certainly not getting him what he wanted.

About three months after that first stormy session, it was Tom who made a dramatic change. This articulate young man actually convinced the school authorities that, although he was over-age, he should be allowed to gain admission to high school to complete requirements for graduation. He lacked six classes and was allowed to enroll in five. The sixth he took as an adult night class. Tom had decided what he wanted and made his own plan. He had assumed a major responsibility.

They returned for a few sessions before Tom served several weeks in jail with release time for school attendance. Natural consequences of breaking the law are not seen as punishment by a reality therapist, but as assumption of responsibility. I have not seen Tom since he accomplished this and completed his classes, but I hear from his parents that he is succeeding. For example, he has a driver's license, has earned a pilot's license, and is winning motorcycle competitions. He has just completed his first year in a local college. Also, Marion tells me that her relationship with him is much improved. These are realistic achievements by a young man who has learned to assume responsibility. He is quite self-reliant and is moving in a positive direction in his life.

I received an announcement of Rob's marriage to the lovely young woman with whom we had had lunch almost two years after our first counseling session. I have not seen him since then, but over the phone a lilt in his voice reveals a new joy in living. He tells me that he is functioning well and that the tremor in his hand has lessened, which is evidence that the Parkinson's has not progressed. He leads an active social life. He and Pam are building a new home for his expanded family. Tom now has two stepbrothers about his age and is learning to be part of a caring family. Father and son are making more effective behavior choices, living more responsibly, and feeling better.

DR. GLASSER'S COMMENTS ON "FATHER AND SON LEARN TOGETHER"

The hardest part of counseling is to resist the client's request for a "cure." I remember my first client, a dowager about sixty-five years old who was accustomed to getting her own way. Because she had been very frustrated when she could not get something she wanted, she had created some delusions of persecution and was sent to me. She came in, sat down, and said to me, "I'm here, Doctor. Do psychiatry!" In a sense, she was right: it is my job, not hers, to do the counseling. But in the sense that she would sit there and wait to be cured, as if I could give her a shot of psychiatric penicillin, she did not understand the process at all.

It is, however, not the client's responsibility to understand the process. As my teacher, Dr. Harrington, told me on several occasions when I expressed my frustration with a client who did not understand what he "should" be doing, the only responsibility that the client has is to come for the session. Anything above that, you have to teach. If the client does not learn it well enough to help himself, you have to teach it better.

As you read this case, it is apparent that Georgellen Hofhine resisted the temptation to tell Rob what to do and, instead, did a lot of teaching. In a sense, he was very much like my first client. She says, "Rooted as he was in the medical model in which he saw depression as a disease, he waited for my prescription." She taught him, she taught his ex-wife, Marion, and she taught their son, Tom. She taught them all that they had choices, but mostly she taught Rob.

She asked him to evaluate the choices that he had been making, and to his surprise he found out that depressing was a choice, too. He caught on to control theory quickly. He learned about the needs, and he soon learned to evaluate the behaviors he was choosing to meet them and to make plans to change when he saw that what he was doing was not responsible.

Rob's progress was systematic and quick. He was a capable person who very quickly became able to put control theory to work in his personal life. In about a year, he terminated counseling, his life in much more effective control than when he began. What was much more difficult happened three months later when he had to deal with his son, Tom, who was homeless and begging Rob to let him come live with him.

One of the most serious tests of counseling is not when one person comes for help. It is helping two people who do not want to be together, but for some reason (in this case, parent and child) cannot or will not separate, to learn to get along with each other. Tom was desperate, and Marion felt that it was now up to Rob (she had had enough). Rob wanted no part of the whole situation, but he was stuck with it. So, in Georgellen Hofhine's words, Rob brought Tom in to be "corrected." As much as Rob was able to put control theory to work in his own life, he was not then able to make the connection that he also had to put it to work in the relationship with his son.

Ms. Hofhine had to refrain from doing anything different with both of them from what she had done with Rob. This seems easy, but it was not. The child, Tom, could take advantage of the situation and communicate to the counselor in many ways, "Come on, I'm a child. This old man is a brute. Help me. You are a counselor. Don't you see how unfair he is to me?" And Tom had a point; Rob was tough. But it was this toughness and Ms. Hofhine's ability to avoid taking sides that made the results of counseling possible.

Again, as in an earlier case, it was what the counselor did not do, as much or more than what she did, that made the difference. But with both father and counselor holding firm, Tom took charge of his own life and worked out his schooling. I doubt if the school would have made these concessions if Rob or Marion had intervened, but when the school authorities saw that it was Tom himself who was asking for help, they were impressed by his motivation and allowed him to return.

Another lesson to learn in this case is that it is much more difficult to do nothing than to do something when people beg for help. But we who counsel should keep in mind that nothing is an important part of the something that allows them to help themselves, and the core of reality therapy is to learn to help yourself.

13

Pictures in Conflict

A Family Deals with the Unrealistic Wants of Elderly Aunts

ROBERT E. WUBBOLDING

Introduction

This is the story of a twofold conflict in wants and its resolution. Aunt Agnes had a clear picture of what she wanted for herself. Her family, nieces, and nephews had conflicting pictures: on the one hand, they wanted what she wanted. But they gradually came to see other pictures as higher priorities—wants that then conflicted with their own first set of pictures and also with that very clear, high-priority picture held by Aunt Agnes, the focus of this study.

Background

All their lives Agnes and Louise, blood sisters, had lived together. Now in their eighties, both had remained unmarried. Their brother had lived with them until his death twenty-five

239

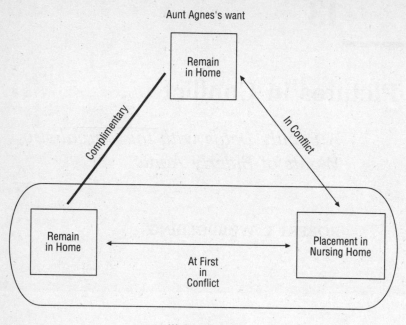

Aunt Agnes's want

Remain in Home

Complimentary

In Conflict

Remain in Home

Placement in Nursing Home

At First in Conflict

Wants of Family
(Nieces & Nephews)

years previously, and they had not yet placed him at the back of their picture albums. They still referred to his bedroom as "Bernie's room" and kept it intact. They had given away his clothes and eventually had removed some of his memorabilia and replaced them with more current ones of their own. They did not, however, depress about his no longer being with them. Nevertheless, the house in which they resided had been *his* selection and to move to a smaller, more manageable unit was, for them, unthinkable.

To live in the spacious house with more yard than they could comfortably care for might at first glance appear to be an irrational clinging to the past. Their unbending attachment to this picture resulted in excessive physical exertion on their part, accompanied by continual worry and endless bemoaning about the difficulties of house cleaning, lawn care, gutter maintenance, painting, snow removal, and so on. In short, regardless of all obstacles, the picture of remaining in the present environment seemed to be irremovably implanted in their mental picture albums. When some mild attempts were *occasionally* made by the family (nieces and nephews) to *imply* by way of a *suggestive hint* that a smaller place *might* be more agreeable, it was made clear that surrendering the picture and changing the total life-style behaviors was definitely not need-fulfilling for Aunts Agnes and Louise. Of course, they did not use the nomenclature of control theory. Rather, they said that they were there to stay until they could no longer breathe or manage by themselves. The family chose at this time not to try to impose their own pictures. For they, too, believed that if the living arrangement was working, if Aunts Agnes and Louise derived freedom and power (effective control) by living on their own, in what might seem to others less than an ideal situation, then they should be able to do so without being victimized by the family's tendency to be what I call picture-imperialists. After all, Agnes and Louise were bright, insightful, willing to give advice to their nieces and nephews on many topics, and on the surface appeared fiercely independent. To disrupt this family system would be most unhelpful and destructive to their need-fulfillment as perceived by them, and, for the most part, by the family.

Gradual Changes

Over a period of about ten years, Aunt Agnes had developed arthritis. She walked slowly and painfully. She eventually used a cane, then a walker, and finally was confined to the house, able to move within it only with great pain and with assistance from her sister, Aunt Louise.

Aunt Louise had to perform more and more of the household duties and eventually all of them. In addition, she had to give Aunt Agnes increasingly more attention. Both were able to call upon extremely altruistic neighbors for help when nieces and nephews were unavailable—for lifting heavy objects and household repairs. The demands resulting from the single-minded determination and persistence of both aunts to function independently, as they thought they did, were not yet excessively burdensome to neighbors or relatives. This single-mindedness of purpose and focused energy enabled the aunts to remain in control of their living arrangements and fulfill the needs for power and freedom. Any attempt to exhort them to change their place of residence and to live with the family, or at least nearer to them, fell on deaf ears. It is noteworthy that the family perceived themselves as monitors rather than mentors, as facilitators or at most advisors, but not as manipulators or directors. Furthermore, attempts to assist the aunts with shopping were welcomed, but the limits were clearly drawn and overstepping them was met with protestations such as "I can do it," "Oh no, we'll manage," and "We'll wait and see." It was permissible to drive Aunt Louise to town, but she insisted on returning by bus. It was permissible to take both (and eventually only Aunt Louise) to visit the cemetery or relatives, but they (she) would attempt to pay for the gasoline. (The family drew the line here and adamantly refused to accept payment. Fortunately, the aunts did not continue to want *that* much effective control over their situations.)

As the health of Aunts Agnes and Louise deteriorated, the family seemed to experience both increased and decreased "family belonging." When Aunt Agnes's arthritis continued to worsen and when Aunt Louise's eyesight waned and she experienced an increase in generalized aches and pains, the family experienced "out-of-balance scales" and emotional paining. Conversely, they felt a greater sense of closeness owing to the satisfaction of having the opportunity to do something for the persons who had served as friends, benefactors, teachers, and confidantes in the nieces' and nephews' formative years.

Throughout this process, each member of the family (that is, the nieces and nephews) played a slightly different but important role. The oldest, Nephew George, served as financial advisor to the aunts and was the reliable support for other nieces and nephews. The second oldest, Niece Betty, served as companion, shopper, and chauffeur until sickness and finally, death, claimed her. The third oldest, Nephew Gordon, had returned to the city of his birth after taking early retirement from his company. He became chauffeur, plumber, carpenter, plasterer, heating and air conditioning specialist, and the person with power of attorney. The fourth oldest, Niece JoAnne, functioned in the same roles as Betty with the additional responsibilities of practical nurse and laundress. The youngest, Robert, the author of this case, served as counselor to the aunts as well as to the other nieces and nephews. He listened for many hours to the aunts, who wanted to reminisce about their own youth and about the nieces' and nephews' childhoods. He still cherishes these hours as time well spent in the service of others. He also helped the other nieces and nephews to maintain a sense of humor by seeing the aunts' idiosyncrasies as exaggerated reflections of their own behavior. In other words, he helped the family to learn to laugh at themselves in a gentle, humane, and liberating manner.

Finally, the roles of the spouses of the nieces and nephews can hardly be underestimated. They provided services similar to those of the nieces and nephews but also were listeners to the many complaints, frustrations, and hurts felt by George, Betty, Gordon, JoAnne, and Robert. In summary, each person in the support system seemed to be an integral part of the whole, and each played a unique role.

Sudden, Unexpected Illness

For many years, the family constellation functioned with a fair amount of consistency and need-fulfillment for all. The execution of their responsibilities did not require a full-time commitment by the nieces and nephews. A total of one or two personal visits a week from one of the nieces or nephews, in addition to telephone checks, were sufficient to ensure the safety and independence of Aunts Agnes and Louise. Then one summer Aunt Louise was diagnosed as having inoperable and untreatable cancer. She and the family were told that her time would be short and that her strength would gradually ebb to the point where she would require continuous care. This, indeed, occurred. From being the able one who cared for her sister, she became the primary care-receiver. As Aunts Agnes and Louise gradually exhausted their own storehouse of power and freedom-fulfilling behaviors, the neighbors as well as nieces and nephews assumed more and more of the responsibilities. The neighbors brought in meals occasionally and ran errands. Because of the neighbors' fondness for Aunts Agnes and Louise and because of the clear pictures related to independence and power in the aunts' mental picture albums, the extent of this service was not fully revealed for several months after the diagnosis of Aunt Louise's cancer and the consequent diminution of her physical strength. For example, when nieces and nephews visited Aunt Louise, she attempted to act healthy and strong—serving drinks, talking about current events, and showing photographs. The degree of effort exerted to maintain the image of control became evident only later: these few minutes or hour of such behaviors required an amount of energy that sapped all strength until the next day, when even less energy would be available for igniting Aunt Louise's behavioral system.

The increasing degree of care required by Aunt Louise and the already small number of physiological behaviors available to Aunt Agnes led the nieces and nephews to maintain close observance and even supervision. Although Nephew Gordon was on call virtually twenty-four hours a day, at no time did the aunts surrender any of their idiosyncratic thinking behaviors. They insisted, for example, that food be fixed only a particular way and that specific utensils be used. Some of these behaviors were honored, but some were so need-unfulfilling for the nieces and nephews that they could not be met. For example, the gas, electric, and phone bills would now be mailed rather than delivered in person by Gordon.

Death of Aunt Louise

In December, Aunt Louise became so weak that she recognized that she would need more assistance than could reasonably be provided by the family. The family also recognized that their needs must be met, that their own employment behaviors could not be put aside for any protracted period of time, and that hospice services were needed. These "facts" as perceived by the family were presented to the aunts, and they reluctantly agreed that such a placement was imperative. Aunt Louise was then transferred from her beloved home to a hospice. She remained there for several weeks and was visited three times by her sister, who herself required three men to help with her transportation. At the end of December, Aunt Louise unwillingly died. She fought for her life until the end; her new brain maintained the clear picture of living, while her old brain could no longer sustain her.

Aunt Agnes's Attempt at Power and Freedom

Aunt Agnes was now alone and felt that she could maintain her house with "some help from all of you." The chasm between her perception of the meaning of "some help" and the perception of the nieces and nephews was nearly infinite. Her sister had repeatedly told her, "We need to think about the future, about going into a nursing home some day." Aunt Agnes had refused to comment on such admonitions and predictions. Now she would be faced with the undesirable probability of placement out of her home. And yet she continued to believe that she could maintain her house. What was perceived by others to be overwhelming evidence to the contrary was not yet perceived by her:

1. In the last four years, she had been out of the house only to visit her dying sister and to go to her funeral.
2. She had not been able to ascend or descend the stairs for an even longer period of time.
3. The time required for her to get dressed and washed in the morning was two hours.
4. She could barely move about the house. It took fifteen minutes to travel from the living room to the bathroom. (A wheelchair was out of the question because of the configuration of halls and doorways.)
5. She attempted to fix her own meals, but this required that she stand shakily at the kitchen sink and eat what

had been prepared for her by someone else and placed in the front part of the refrigerator where she could reach it.

6. She had slid off the edge of the bed onto the floor several times and could not get up again because of her arthritic condition. After a while, she was able to reach the telephone and contact a neighbor, who enlisted the aid of others to lift her onto the bed. She absolutely refused to wear an emergency paging mechanism, which would have lessened this problem considerably.

7. She could do little other than sit in a chair, watch television, eat, and take care of her physical needs in an ineffective manner.

Although Aunt Agnes's perception of these "facts" was vastly different from that of the nieces and nephews, her thinking behaviors were as lucid and explicit as those of a twenty-five-year-old person. When she spoke of her sister, her memories, and her possessions, she was accurate, precise, and convincing. Moreover, though her pictures appeared to be rigid and niggling at times, they were unblurred, clear, and earnest. Furthermore, the picture of remaining in her home was paramount.

Her attempt to fulfill the picture of remaining in her home was also one sacred to her nieces and nephews. They did not, however, rigidly cling to it to the point of neglecting their picture of her being physically safe. Because of this desire to help her remain free and in control, the nieces and nephews attempted to facilitate the necessary plans for her to remain at home, at least for a while. Because of the neighbors' affection for Aunt Agnes, they were willing to visit her and provide assistance so that she could remain in her residence. When all things were considered, this course of action seemed to be worth trying.

Changing Perceptions

After several months, it became clear that this program could not continue. Aunt Agnes's health had deteriorated even further. She could not travel from room to room with even a minimal degree of efficiency. The neighbors were being called by her more frequently for assistance. Although all of the nephews and nieces sustained her, Gordon became the "first-line supervisor," presiding over the multitude of tasks that required attention after Aunt Louise's death as well as caring for Aunt Agnes's many requests and increasingly frequent demands.

Consequently, the nieces and nephews chose to act on their second set of pictures (see Figure 7). And so they delivered another message to Aunt Agnes in increasing frequency and clarification: "The present program is not working. We will not be able to provide the present degree of assistance indefinitely. We would like you to think about a nursing home." Aunt Agnes at first rejected and resisted these injunctions for her to examine her total physiological behaviors and her picture of remaining in her home. The family avoided *asking* her what she thought about entering a nursing home. Rather they *shared* their own perceptions straightforwardly, without expecting immediate replies. It was necessary for her to ruminate about her options and plans. Similarly, the nieces and nephews were loathe to pressure her into surrendering her power and freedom-fulfilling picture of remaining in her home. But it had become clear that the facilitators of the status quo would no longer choose behaviors supporting it.

A Choice Is Made

In conferences with several neighbors, it became obvious that Aunt Agnes was making more demands on them than she was telling the family members. And although the neighbors stated that they were willing to look in on her occasionally, they also revealed that they were being asked to respond to her wants too frequently and for longer periods of time than they chose to endure. On one occasion, Aunt Agnes had fallen in her hallway and remained there immobilized for several hours until a neighbor found her. To Nephew Bob, this appeared to be the indisputable data necessary for an effective intervention by the family. He asked the nieces and nephews to gather to discuss and rehearse an intervention similar to interventions used by alcoholism therapists. It was decided that the oldest Nephew George, the family advisor, and the youngest, Nephew Bob, the counselor, would make the diagnostic presentation.

And so, on a Sunday afternoon, George and Bob presented the data described above to Aunt Agnes in a firm and matter-of-fact manner. Her condition was summarized, with recent falls and insufficient meals being emphasized. This was done gently and firmly and with much heartache for George and Bob. George at one point stated, "Aunt Agnes, your mind is in great shape, but your body has given out. We cannot tolerate your falling and having neighbors find you. If you get hurt in a fall, it will require hospitalization, and you know how hateful that possibility is for you. On the other hand, we don't want, on our part, to find you dead from a fall on the floor. Also, the neighbors cannot continue to do what they are doing. In fact, we have ordered them to cease and desist coming over here. There is only one realistic choice." After some resistance, Bob stated that there was a bed available at an excellent nearby nursing home, and she could occupy it immediately. She remarked, "If I do decide to do this, how will I get ready?" Bob replied, with an apparent non-sequitur, "It's not *if* but *when.* They'll hold the bed for a few days. Will you go Tuesday or Wednesday?" There followed the longest silence on record, and mentally Bob pleaded with George not to break the silence, but to remain quiet so as to allow Aunt Agnes to assume total responsibility for her next statement, which was, "I'll go on Thursday." In view of the fact that George was a skilled salesman and Bob an experienced counselor, both proceeded with the next extremely necessary steps—what to take, how to get to the nursing home, and who would look after the house. The basic arrangements were made within a half hour. No attempt was made to oversell the wisdom of her choice, to "reinforce" it, or to validate it in any manner. Aunt Agnes needed time to grieve for the loss resulting from this most important decision. Any attempt to provide a commentary for her would have been shallow and superfluous. Conversely, it was more effective to lock in the commitment so that she would see it as irreversible. It was now a matter of what to take with her, who would help her pack, and when the ambulance would come to transport her.

The purpose of this case study is to describe events leading to placement in a nursing home. No attempt is made to report in detail what happened after placement. Nevertheless, it is useful to know that Aunt Agnes made a fair adjustment to the nursing home. She was always cheerful, alert, and talkative when visitors came. Yet she was only moderately willing to participate in the social activities of the home. She attended some parties but preferred to eat by herself in her room and to listen to baseball games alone.

Commitment to Power and Freedom

One way of perceiving this case and others like it might be to wonder why a person opposes such an obvious course of events. Another perception focuses on the person's refusal as mere resistance or obstinance. And yet a review of control theory clarifies the entire process. Aunt Agnes generated every behavior at her disposal to fulfill the picture of remaining in her home. This picture would provide her with a sense of power and freedom. She could perceive herself as the competent person she had been for many years if she could remain in her own home. And, as is normal, she did not perceive the multitude of others' behaviors required to assist her to fulfill her needs. Consequently, her "resistance" or "resisting total behaviors" should be seen as healthy, positive symptoms. As Nephew Bob stated after her successful placement in the nursing home, "When my turn comes for such a placement, I will follow Aunt Agnes's example. You'll have to drag me feet first, squirming, arguing, resisting, protesting, rebelling, clinging to my door post. No way will I easily give up the competence and power-fulfilling pictures and behaviors that have served me so well for so long. I'll have healthy total doing, thinking, and feeling behaviors even after the physiological ones are nearly gone."

Generalized Principles

The case of Aunt Agnes serves to highlight several principles useful for people with parents or other relatives whose physiological behaviors have been depleted and who require placement in a nursing home.

1. Define family roles: Various roles will evolve regardless of whether or not there is a plan. Yet a discussion of responsibilities with flexible boundaries for each family member can be useful and need-fulfilling for everyone.
2. Recognize and accept the fact of conflict: There will be conflict between the older person and the younger ones. Also, each person will have contrary wants and accompanying "guilting behaviors." These are natural and can be expected for some family members. There will also be conflict among younger family members regarding the best course of action and the division of responsibilities. A frank, open discussion will help to clarify and reconcile the conflicting pictures.
3. Speak straightforwardly but tactfully: Although open discussion is important, tact and empathy are crucial. All involved have a right to their pictures, perceptions, and behaviors. Each should try to see the others' control systems with acceptance and without judging and condemnation.
4. All should fulfill their needs: It is crucial for caregivers to fulfill their own needs, especially fun. Enjoyment is the need most often neglected when there is a serious illness in a family. Family members who maintain a sense of humor will be more effective in caregiving. And so they need time away from the family in crisis, even though they might choose "guilting behavior" along with the time away.
5. Accept the fact of resistance: The older person will sometimes see the placement as an invasion or perhaps a rejection and will often try to fend off attempts to provide help. This resistance need not be seen by family

members as unhealthy behavior. Rather, it can be perceived as an effort to maintain effective control. At the same time, healthy fighting spirits need not deter the family members from intervening to help the older persons fulfill their physical needs.

6. Make a diagnostic presentation: The older person should be confronted with data indicating that placement is necessary. The data should be specific and exact, with precise instances illustrating the person's lack of physiological behaviors described. Unsubstantiated generalizations should be avoided. Timing is crucial in that the effective diagnostic presentation should be tied to a specific major or minor incident.

7. Recognize the difference between perception and thinking behaviors: This difference is hard to define in many instances. The goal of any diagnostic presentation is to help the person in question view the behavior and wants differently than before. Another goal is to help the person put a negative value on his or her perception of staying in the home in order that he or she will think differently, that is, make a decision to enter the nursing home. This point is rather theoretical but has a practical implication. The data is presented without "arm twisting" or pressure to persuade the person to accept different wants.

8. The placement is a last resort or nearly last resort: Placement out of the home often represents a loss of freedom and power. It might ultimately result in a pleasant adjustment, increased social life, enhanced friendship, and feelings of security. But in the transition and afterward, the older person often feels a loss of purpose and control. Consequently, placement out of the home should be done deliberatively, unhurriedly, and collaboratively with family members.

In summary, this case illustrates how one family used control theory in the placement of an older relative in a nursing home. It is not meant to represent the *only* way to use the principles of control theory in similar situations. Rather, the ideas have been applied in one effective way to one family. The concluding generalized principles are presented as guidelines, not dogmas. And the choice to remove oneself from home under these circumstances is seen as undesirable but necessary.

DR. GLASSER COMMENTS ON "PICTURES IN CONFLICT"

Dr. Wubbolding has provided an excellent description and discussion of this case, which I would like to use as a starting point for a few general thoughts on control theory, especially on the control aspects of this theory. The behavior of these two elderly aunts shows clearly that control theory is called that because its main purpose is control. As control systems, we struggle to control as much as we can because the more we can control, the better we can satisfy our needs. To us, control means that the people and things that we believe are necessary for us to satisfy our needs do what we want them to do.

What is called history is little more than a description of how very powerful people won and lost in that same struggle. Each case in this book, and actually each of our lives, is a small personal history about winning and losing that struggle. Winning, however, does not necessarily mean that we are able to satisfy our needs as much as we would like, and losing does not mean that there is no satisfaction at all. Certainly both aunts could be considered winners as they kept their house and life style long after many others less resolute would have given up. That they were not aware of how much others helped them in no way detracts from what they believed they accomplished. Besides, it was their tenacity that involved the others; not to help would have been a loss for them, too.

Control systems are powerful, much more powerful than most of us realize. Aunt Agnes was willing to lie on the floor unable to move for hours rather than admit that she was not in control. Like Aunt Agnes, we are more than willing to choose to suffer if the suffering helps us to gain control over the people that we need to help us satisfy our needs. All the miserable behaviors that we choose, especially depressing, sicking, paining, crazying, and even suiciding, are ways we struggle for the control we want. Aunt Agnes chose not to involve herself in the nursing home program, which she might have enjoyed, because to do so would be to admit that she accepted being placed in the home. To admit this would be to lose more control than she was willing to give up.

If you review this case and all the others in the book, you will see that the role of the therapists was to help the clients come to terms with their desire to have more control than it was possible for them to achieve, I pointed out several times that clients had to learn to accept that they could control only their own lives: as much as they wanted others to do what they wanted, they could not make them do this. You cannot make abusive parents treat you better, but eventually you can move away. You cannot make a child go to school, but you can stop supporting the child if he does not go to school. You cannot make Aunt Agnes go to the nursing home on Tuesday or Wednesday, but if you give her some choice (control), she might go on Thursday.

When people are helped through the concepts of reality therapy, they learn to accept that they can control only their own lives, but that they can do it well enough so that they can satisfy their needs. They are, however, rarely helped to gain enough control of their lives to satisfy their needs as much as they want. Therapy is a negotiation between what the client wants and what is enough. The difference between happiness and misery is that happiness is the feeling component of what we choose to do that enables us to say, "I have enough," and misery is the feeling component of all the total behaviors we choose when we say, "I haven't enough."

For the purpose of explanation, I will endow the control system with personal attributes that it does not have: it is never satisfied. Left to its own devices, it always wants more than it has. But our job as a human, living in a society of humans with the same needs, is to settle for less than we want and call that enough. Therapy is the negotiation that helps to determine how much less clients will settle for, as the Wubbolding family demonstrated in this case. In all the other cases in this book, the counselors did a very good job of this essential negotiation.

The final question is, how much is enough? I can only answer that with another question: how hard are you willing to work? In this context, misery is wanting more than you are willing to work for. Even taking into account all the inequalities and the lack of opportunities that exist in this imperfect world, which we should all work to correct, there is such a thing as laziness, and many people are lazy. It is one thing to be lazy if you do not want very much, but if you want a great deal and are not willing to work for it, you will never be happy. If a client is truly lazy, as some are, counseling will fail.

The counselor's task is to find out if what seems to be laziness is not. For example, people will not work when they do not see any opportunity, so part of the job of the counselor is to try to teach people that if they are willing to work, there is much more opportunity than they have been able to see so far. This means that the counselor has to be aware of what is going on in the world and use that awareness to alert clients to opportunities that they do not see themselves.

Central to reality therapy is the fact that the client should find warmth and acceptance in the counseling situation, and there was no shortage of this in any of the cases. Warm involvement teaches people that it is possible to experience need satisfaction, and from this small start many begin to believe that there is the opportunity for more. People who believe that no one cares for them have a hard time seeing any opportunity at all in their situations.

There is an old saying: when we are born, we are all sentenced to life, and we have to serve every hour of that sentence. We are not, however, told how this life works, and without this knowledge many of us fail miserably in our attempt to live it reasonably well. Control theory provides a large chunk of what we need to know to live a good life. Most of these cases are living proof of this claim.

14

Starved for Affection

The Use and Treatment of Eating Disorders

LINDA SHIMKO GERONILLA

Session One

To gather information and encourage my clients to talk freely, I ask them questions about their families.[1] I then put this information on a genogram form, where it is readily available to refresh my memory as clients mention various people. I used this form (see page 256) with Gloria at our first meeting.

Gloria was thirty-two, single, and lived in her own apartment. Her father was a disabled coal miner, and her mother a school aide. Her brother was a construction worker.

Gloria had a bachelor's degree in English and had worked as a journalist before taking her current position in state govern-

---

[1]Editor's note: This case study was written differently from the others in the book. Dr. Geronilla chose to write a session-by-session account of exactly how therapy progressed. Although it is much longer than any of the other case studies, I believe this verbatim material has great value.

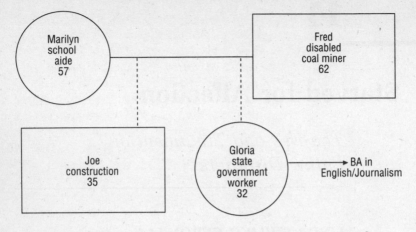

ment, which consisted of keeping a senator's calendar and preparing reports.

LINDA: How do you feel about your current job?

GLORIA: I would like my work if there would be some minor adjustment. If I got respect four weeks in the month, instead of just the one week that the senator is here, I'd really like it. I get respect through the association with the senator. I don't get much respect from my immediate supervisor, Mr. Lee. I think he is threatened by me. He really isn't qualified for the job. He won't admit when he makes a mistake, like hiring some real jerk. I do get recognition from the senator, but he is only in town one week a month.

LINDA: Sounds like your job might be something you'd like to talk about.

GLORIA: Yes, but my major problem is my personal life, or lack of a social life. I think things would balance out if I had an emotional interest. If I had a personal life that was more satisfying, I could probably overlook a lot of things at work. But right now my whole focus is my work, and when that doesn't go well, everything goes wrong. Work shouldn't be that important.

LINDA: Tell me about your personal life.

GLORIA: I've come to the conclusion that I'm afraid of men. That is funny because now that I'm thirty-two, I've come to the conclusion that I would like to be married and maybe have children. And the old biological clock is ticking away. And I look at my life and think that unless some change takes place in my life, I'm never going to get married. I'm headed directly down the road to "old-maidhood." When I used to work for the newspaper, I had no trouble meeting people. When someone new came to town I wanted to meet, I would just go interview them for the newspaper. When I went to work for the state government, I became isolated. I do work in a big office, but I got this idea that there is a certain way to act that is acceptable. But then I gradually became an isolate. Most of my old friends are now married. There is no one at work I have anything in common with. I have only one friend at work, and I know that is a destructive relationship. She's pissed off because she is forty-seven and I'm only thirty-two. It comes out as little digs, and she rarely has my best interest in mind. Without any friends or connections, it is tough to meet men. I haven't dated anyone in two years. It's like riding a bicycle; when you are off it for two years, it's scary getting back on. A guy called me yesterday and asked me to go out for a drink. I said, "Yes, but I have a lot of things going on right now," and I asked if he could call me back in a couple of weeks. It is a major thing to go out with someone. I know it has gotten blown out of proportion. I am having a rough time having eye contact with people, but men especially.

LINDA: Will you see that guy again?

GLORIA: Yes, he comes in the office periodically. And this time I'm going to be nice to him. I'm really working on my eye contact and my smile.

LINDA: That's good. Your smile looks very natural and friendly.

GLORIA: Does it?

LINDA: Yes. Your whole appearance is attractive, too. [She was very attractive, and I wanted to let her know that I viewed her this way.] Is there anyone you are interested in?

GLORIA: One lawyer who periodically comes to our office. Part of me wants to pursue him, and another part says that I should be more grown-up and less giggly. I don't think that I ever learned how to flirt. And there are so many people in my office that whatever I do is being observed by a whole audience. And then there is all the conversation after someone leaves the front desk.

LINDA: Tell me more about your "giggly part" that prevents you from flirting.

GLORIA: I always thought I was more sophisticated and intelligent than that. Most of the girls in my office giggle a lot. They cannot utter a sentence without giggling. It gets on my nerves. Even when I was little, I was never terribly outgoing. I like the affection and attention, but I don't feel comfortable soliciting it.

LINDA: So you've always been more reserved or cautious.

GLORIA: I used to be able to call men. I don't have enough exposure to men. You have to know them at least minimally to be able to call them. Before, I had a reason to call them because of the newspaper.

LINDA: What prevents you from being gutsy and calling men?

GLORIA: I don't know. Maybe my self-image is distorted.

LINDA: Tell me about your self-image.

GLORIA: I know it's distorted. It has to do with my eating.

LINDA: Tell me more.

GLORIA: My eating is because I don't have a romantic interest. When I don't feel love, I get depressed. I used to feel like I was a big rear end walking around with a little head on it. I couldn't wait to get home at night to pig out. I would make a pizza and eat the whole thing. Then I would want to throw up. But then this girlfriend of mine died from bulimia, and I haven't been able to vomit since. Matter of fact, it's like I have gone the exact opposite. There are times I cannot eat. But now, I get these terrible stomach cramps. I think I might have developed an ulcer. It's so bad that I went to the hospital to have tests run, and I'm waiting for the results.

LINDA: Anything else you want to tell me?

GLORIA: I threw up a lot in college, mostly when I would drink too much. I then learned how to do it when I overate. I could do it really easily. But not now. I can't do it. I think of my friend Nancy. I remember one Sunday, I had just eaten a whole meal of greasy fish, and I was standing in the bathroom with the toilet open looking at the mirror about ready to put my finger down my throat, and I thought, Oh my God, I can't do this anymore. I just knew somebody who died of this. I don't want someone to come into my apartment and find me dead. So I just said to myself, you ate it—so you can live with it.

LINDA: Nancy probably saved you.

GLORIA: She probably did.

LINDA: How do you feel about your weight now?

GLORIA: For the last two semesters, I took night classes to keep myself out of my refrigerator. It still obsesses me.

LINDA: Anything else you want to tell me about your eating?

GLORIA: Mom said I was a tall and skinny baby, and I remained that way. I was always taller than everyone. After college, I began to hang around with a co-worker who was obsessed with being thin. She hated the word *fat*. She was a big influence on me. I had just gotten out of a bad relationship with this guy, and I was having trouble meeting someone new. I began to tell myself that if I could lose ten pounds, then I could meet someone. I was this huge rear end walking around. I went to one of the weight loss centers. Then once I lost the ten, I thought maybe I could lose another ten, and this kept on going. In three and a half months, I lost twenty-nine pounds. I also quit menstruating. I looked like a skeleton. I went from the 140s to 119.

LINDA: What turned you around?

GLORIA: I finally realized I had a problem. I was twenty-eight, but I was like a teenage anorexic. I decided to make some major changes. I joined an exercise spa to up my metabolism so that I could eat like a pig. I was really into food. I was obsessed with eating. Food was my solace. If I did not have a date, then I would console myself with something good. I replaced many of the relationships with food. I lost a lot of relationships with my dieting because I could not go anywhere there was food or drink. Instead, I would go into my apartment and do flower arranging so that I didn't have to be around food or people. I severed so many relationships. I finally realized that at the age of twenty-eight, I had an eating disorder. I'm thirty-two, and I still feel like I have an eating disorder and an addictive personality.

LINDA: Would you like to tell me anything else that you feel is significant? [In order to encourage clients to talk and to establish the therapeutic environment, I am willing to listen to their whole story at the first session.]

GLORIA: I have tried to convince myself that my weight doesn't matter as long as I'm healthy. Two years ago, I gave away my bathroom scales, and that was a big thing. I used to get on them several times a day.

LINDA: Giving away the scales was really good.

GLORIA: Yes, I felt like I had accomplished something.

LINDA: Let me summarize. You don't vomit anymore, but you still "pig out" occasionally. But you still feel obsessed with food.

GLORIA: Right.

At first sessions, I am willing to listen to symptoms so that I get a good idea of the function that they play in the client's life, but I try to keep this to a minimum. As soon as I can, I present a notebook entitled "My Picture Album," which has each of the needs on a separate page in a clear plastic cover. I talk about the needs, and I relate them to my own life. I have a picture of my family that I slide into the clear plastic cover to demonstrate how we move pictures into our internal album.

LINDA: Where do you get your loving/belonging need met?

GLORIA: My parents are pretty good to me, but I know I need other relationships. I really don't have a bunch of close friends. I think the one friendship I have at work is destructive.

LINDA: How about any one else at work?

GLORIA: I work with married women who drive Mercedeses or

BMWs, because their husbands make good money, and I drive a Honda. They even pointed it out at lunch the other day. I feel pressure to buy a more expensive car, even though I don't want to do that.

LINDA: Do you feel like they are imposing their values on you?

GLORIA: Yes. And I don't like it. I don't want to be like them anyway. I have always been the type to carry my own weight and not count on someone supporting me.

LINDA: Sounds to me like you don't get much of your love and belonging need met at work.

GLORIA: You can say that again.

LINDA: Let's take a look at your other needs. How about power? Do people listen to you, give you approval, and put you in charge of doing things?

GLORIA: That's pretty low, too. Not much at work at all.

LINDA: How about fun?

GLORIA: Most of the things I do are by myself, like reading.

LINDA: Would you like to be more social in your fun?

GLORIA: Yes.

LINDA: How about freedom?

GLORIA: Probably too much freedom. It is too easy to go into my house in the evening and isolate myself and do whatever I want. But I do what I want with my time and my money. I would say that one is fine.

LINDA: In order to get a good feel for where you are, I am going to ask you to fill out this form evaluating your psychological needs. Would you be willing to do it?

GLORIA: Yes.

LINDA: In order to get a direction for the work we are going to be doing, I want you to think about where you want to go with your life. I have another form I want to just hand to you, and you can begin to work on it to help you. It's called "What Do I Want in My Picture Album?" [I use these two forms with most of my clients to help them see where they are and develop a picture of where they want to go.] Would you be willing to work on it too?

GLORIA: Sure.

Name: Gloria   Date_____

Evaluation of my psychological needs using reality therapy

A= Very Satisfied (no frustration signal)
B= Mostly satisfied
C= OK
D= Mostly dissatisfied
E= Very dissatisfied (large frustration)

Need	Question	Person/Group	Rating	Overall
Love / Belonging	Do I have relationships which meets my needs for affection, attention, sharing, cooperation, etc.?	~~Spouse~~	A B C D E	
		~~Children~~	A B C D E	
		Mother	Ⓐ B C D E	
		Father	Ⓐ B C D E	
		~~Sister~~	A B Ⓒ D E	
		Brother	A B Ⓒ D E	
		Friends	A B C Ⓓ E	
		_____	A B C D E	Overall, I would rank my love / belonging needs as
	List organizations, clubs, or groups in which I feel affection, inclusion, and belonging.	_____	A B C D E	A B C Ⓓ E
		School	Ⓐ B C D E	
		Work	A B Ⓒ D E	
Power	Who listens to me, agrees with me, and follows my ideas? Who recognizes my abilities? Who compliments me on my accomplishments?	Boss	A B Ⓒ D E	
		Co-worker	A B C Ⓓ E	
		~~Spouse~~	A B C D E	
		~~Children~~	A B C D E	
		Parents	Ⓐ B C D E	Overall, I would rank my power needs as
		Friends	A B C Ⓒ E	
		_____	A B C D E	A B Ⓒ D E
	Do I accept my worth as a human being?		A B C Ⓓ E	
	Do I appreciate my good qualities & competencies?		A Ⓑ C D E	
	Do I acknowledge my achievements?		A B Ⓒ D E	
	Do I make a daily effort to compliment myself?		A B Ⓒ D E	
Fun	Do I laugh enough?		A B C D E	
	Do I engage in learning in order to enjoy myself?		A B C D E	Overall, I would rank my fun needs as
	List fun activities I do with others: travel	And Frequency: 6x yr.		A B C D Ⓔ
	List fun activities I do alone: sewing / reading	And Frequency: 2x wk / 5x wk		
Freedom	Do I do what I want without feeling controlled?		A B Ⓒ D E	
	Do I feel free to express myself without being criticized?		A B Ⓓ E	Overall, I would rank my freedom needs as
	Do I spend my time the way I want?		A B Ⓒ D E	
	Do I spend my money the way I want?		A Ⓑ C D E	A B Ⓒ D E
	Do I feel like I run my own life (or do I let others down)?		A B Ⓒ D E	

Linda Geronilla, Ph.D.

LINDA: When would you like to talk again?
GLORIA: How about next week?
LINDA: Fine.

After I had written this case study, I asked Gloria if she

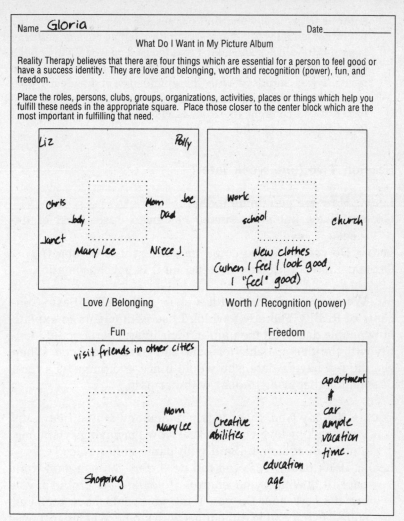

Name Gloria _____ Date _____

What Do I Want in My Picture Album

Reality Therapy believes that there are four things which are essential for a person to feel good or have a success identity. They are love and belonging, worth and recognition (power), fun, and freedom.

Place the roles, persons, clubs, groups, organizations, activities, places or things which help you fulfill these needs in the appropriate square. Place those closer to the center block which are the most important in fulfilling that need.

Liz Polly	work
Chris Mom Joe	school church
Jody Dad	
Janet	New clothes
Mary Lee Niece J.	(when I feel I look good, I "feel" good)
Love / Belonging	**Worth / Recognition (power)**

Fun	**Freedom**
visit friends in other cities	apartment #
Mom	car
Mary Lee	Creative ample
	abilities vacation
	time.
Shopping	education
	age

would like to read it and make comments. Following is what she wrote about the first session:

I went into the first session feeling frustrated because I felt out of control of my life. I may have hoped that Linda would have the answers to my needs and that our sessions would consist of my telling her what I wanted and she, in turn, telling me a no-fail way of getting it—all nice and neat. I was focused on what I didn't have rather than what I *did* have. When we examined the four basic needs, I was surprised with the abundance of freedom I possessed. The worksheets made me uncomfortable in that they forced me to confront those areas where deficits existed, and I found that to be painful.

Session Two (one week later)

LINDA: How are you doing today?

GLORIA: Okay, but my stomach has been upset most of the week.

LINDA: Do you think you could be causing it to be upset?

GLORIA: I have a friend who tells me it is psychosomatic.

We spent some time with a chart called "The Basic Concepts of Reality Therapy," which I use with clients to explain how people deal with the pain in their lives. Gloria could identify with the give-up behavior—she had given up on men. When she did not have a date, she would binge and purge as a form of symptom behavior to deal with her pain.

GLORIA: Oh my God, there it is in black and white! I gave up. I was making love with a pizza! Now I'm having symptoms, and I feel addicted. [Said with panic in her voice.]

LINDA: Don't panic. Yes, you did do it. But you can gain it all back. It is within your control. If you are the problem, you are the cure, too. Do you think you could have replaced some of your eating difficulties with stomach aching? [I was thinking that this was probably one of the best cases I had ever seen of symptom substitution.]

We talked about stomachaching as a way to keep her weight down. She had seen a physician and was awaiting test results, but admitted she was prepared to acknowledge that the cause of her stomach aches was not physical. I shared with her that I had been a headacher in the past.

GLORIA: Part of me would be relieved to find out that I was okay physically, but part of me would prefer that there be something wrong. Sounds crazy, doesn't it? I don't feel in control. My mother called me today to see if I was okay. She says I inherited my father's stomach. He is a mess. He lets it control him. He can't be in certain situations, like family reunions or crowds. I don't want to live that way. A friend of mine believes it is all psychosomatic. It all started with a trip I was supposed to take to London several months ago. I woke up that morning a mess—vomiting and diarrhea. I have been having symptoms ever since. It's probably the stress of working full-time and taking nine hours of classes. I took the nine hours so I would not stay home and pig out. I did fine until winter break, when I fell apart.

I diverted the conversation to talk about the forms she had filled out. She was aware that because she had few friends, she was clinging to her parents for love and belonging. She said it was important to change this.

LINDA: I want you to think about what you do want and where you want to direct your time and energy. You might want to think about ways to meet and connect with people, like clubs or social groups. For example, I like a ski club. Going on your trip was a good way to meet people.
GLORIA: Yes, I was really proud of myself when I signed up.
LINDA: The fact that you signed up shows you are already thinking about it.
GLORIA: My mother is upset that I lost the thousand dollars. I'm trying not to think about it.
LINDA: I think it is a good idea to ignore what your mother has to say. It's what *you* feel that is important. We could spend the rest of our lives trying to please other people and still not be happy ourselves.

I then spent some time sharing examples of how my family tries to control me. Gloria enjoyed this.

Looking at the other three needs, she decided that she could add more pictures to all of them, but the one of highest priority was love/belonging.

In order to teach the procedures for change, I give my clients a sheet called "Motivation Using Reality Therapy." I asked Gloria if she would be willing to fill it out. I usually start the sheet in the session and have the client finish it as homework. Gloria and I talked about the basic procedures listed on the sheet, and then I asked her to take it home and finish it.

Session Three (two weeks later)

GLORIA: Here's my homework. I worked real hard on it. [The last meant as a joke.]

LINDA: [Laughing.] So you don't want to be an old maid.

GLORIA: Don't you think that I already qualify for one?

LINDA: No. You have to be fifty to be an old maid. [Both laughing now.]

GLORIA: I now think that I know where I am headed.

LINDA: That's good.

GLORIA: You were right about my stomach. Doctor says I'm okay. I'm still having trouble believing that I do it to myself. I believe it, but sometimes I don't.

LINDA: How did the past two weeks go?

She described a weekend visit to a friend that had ended unsatisfactorily in some ways. The behavior and dress of her friend's husband were an embarrassment to Gloria, especially in public. She decided to tell this to her friend, not knowing how this would affect the friendship, but she felt good for having mentioned it.

LINDA: It's good that you could begin to express yourself. Sounds like you were embarrassed to be with him.

GLORIA: I don't appreciate people who do things to draw atten-

Motivation Using Reality Therapy Linda Geronilla, Ph.D. If it's to be—it's up to me.		Determine that the thing can and shall be done, and then . . . find the way. —Abraham Lincoln
What do I want? List my goals in precise terms.	What am I doing (or not doing) now to meet my goals?	Is it helping?
Find right person, get married	think about it	?
Make more friends (male & female)	Nothing	No
Feeling like I belong somewhere	Nothing	No
Finish master's degree for future career options	Taking classes	Yes

What are my plans to do better? (simple, specific, realistic and a "do" plan)	Am I committed to follow my plan daily?	What excuses do I usually make? List them.	What are the consequences of not doing my plan?
Be open and friendly to men- have eye contact	Yes	What if they don't respond to me?, what if they think I'm weird?	Old-maid-city for sure
Make overtures toward people	No	They're too busy	Limited # of friends
Start attending a church & join some clubs	Yes		Feel lonely
Continue 6-9 hr/ semester	Yes	None	Limit job options

When you are debating what to do—ask yourself:
1. What do I want? Restate your goals.
2. Is this going to help me reach my goals? Yes or no.

tion to themselves by being different. Bizarre. I can't tolerate it. I have a friend who has eight earring holes.

LINDA: What goes through your mind when you see people who are different?

GLORIA: What assholes they are! Can't they get their attention in other ways?

LINDA: So they do it to get attention, but why do you take it in and allow yourself to get physically sick over them?

GLORIA: It must be through the association that I am with them. Therefore, people must be looking at me and thinking I'm weird, too.

LINDA: I want you to think about how much control you have over the situation. How much control do you have over Tom? How much does your friend have over him?

GLORIA: None. He tries to control her. He tells her not to wear a bra, and she doesn't. She sags, and her nipples hang through. I think it doesn't look becoming on her.

LINDA: Does the fact that you got physically sick concern you? Would you like to get to the point where you don't get sick over what someone else does?

GLORIA: Yes. I'd also like to get to the point where I could tell him how strange he looks and how embarrassed I am.

LINDA: There are tactful ways to say things, and there are rude ways to say things. But what I want you to begin thinking about is how much control you have over yourself and your physiology, and we'll talk more about that later. [I wanted to initiate the idea that she did have control without going into a lecture at that moment. I knew it would come up again in other ways, and I think it's good to collect several instances and then show the connection between them.]

GLORIA: I want to talk about work.

LINDA: Okay.

GLORIA: I have to figure out how to get more space at work.

LINDA: How are you going to do that?

GLORIA: Cry.

LINDA: Is that what you really want to do?

GLORIA: No, but it has worked in the past.

LINDA: It might have gotten you what you wanted, but did you ever think about the kind of person you want to be and how you want others to see you? If you cry, then they will say you are a crybaby. Ask yourself, do they promote crybabies?

GLORIA: Good point.

LINDA: So what do you want to be? Get a picture in your head and describe that person to me. Let's go through the four wheels of the behavioral car.

GLORIA: I want to be open and approachable. I want to say "hello" to everyone I meet. I want to be patient and helpful, but know when to draw the line. I don't want to be taken advantage of. Professional and businesslike. Someone people would like to both work around and socialize with. Just a pleasant person.

LINDA: Describe how that person thinks.

GLORIA: That person believes that people are basically good. All people are on the same level. People that you deal with are appreciative of what you do for them. If people would take the time to get to know me, they would be appreciative of me.

LINDA: How would that person feel in the inside?

GLORIA: Fulfilled and happy all the time. Nothing gnawing away.

LINDA: How would that person's body feel?

GLORIA: Like calm water on a lake. No ripples. Smooth.

LINDA: Sounds like you have a good picture of the person you would like to be.

GLORIA: Yes, I'm beginning to see what you mean. I can become the person I want to be if I try.

We reviewed what Gloria was doing, going home to be alone mostly, and devised a plan to make a change. She would contact a male friend, Jody, who was "like a dear brother," and invite him over.

Gloria's comments on this session:

My level of frustration was still high. My medical tests were clear, and that meant I was "choosing" to have these awful symptoms. I was also having trouble communicating my feelings to others (for example, about Tom's mode of dress), and this was further frustrating me. I think Linda diverted my energies here toward doing something socially constructive, rather than allowing me to dwell on my helplessness. It was well-timed, because I would have just gotten more and more depressed.

Session Four (two weeks later)

LINDA: Did you see Jody?

GLORIA: Yes, I invited him over for dinner. We had a good time. I also went out to lunch with an old classmate at the Tidewater. By the way, my stomach is better. Only once did it get upset. [Note that she said "it" got upset, not that she upset herself—obviously I had more work to do.]

LINDA: How was the lunch with your classmate?

GLORIA: Good, except for my stomach. I think it was half the coleslaw and half the waiter. He did not treat us well. I bet he thought that we were two silly women who were low tippers. I tip well.

LINDA: What did you do that may have given him that impression?

GLORIA: Me do something? Don't you think it was his problem?

LINDA: Maybe. But just for a moment I want you to think through the whole situation and think about what you might have done to give him the impression that you were a couple of women who were low tippers.

GLORIA: We talked the whole time he was explaining the menu, and we ordered their cheapest lunch special.

LINDA: If you were the waiter, how would you have felt if someone talked through your whole speech?

GLORIA: Probably the same way.

LINDA: What could you do next time to change his impression?

GLORIA: I would stop talking, give him my full attention, and make more eye contact with him when he is talking. In general, I could have been more assertive.

LINDA: Sounds good to me.

GLORIA: Let's talk about work.

LINDA: What about it?

GLORIA: My boss has been nicer to me. I went in and told him that my problems were psychological and not physical. He told me that I could "try to get as much space as I needed" when things start to get to me at work. Like go for a walk or take a break in the cafeteria.

LINDA: Sounds like he has been nicer to you. Is he still as incompetent as he was?

GLORIA: Yes. The guy has "legitimate power" because he is the head of our division, but he sure does not have "expert power" in that he knows more than we do. Also, he is such a wimp. I hate the fact that he calls the whole staff together for some meetings when he really only needs to reprimand one person. He is afraid of hurting Bessy's feelings, so instead he wastes all our time for these group meetings. Worst part is that Bessy sits there all wide-eyed and looking innocent. I'm sure she does not think that he is talking about her.

LINDA: Do you want to talk about owning your own behavior?

GLORIA: Owning it? What do you mean?

LINDA: Things and/or people don't cause you to be upset. You cause them.

GLORIA: That's a lot of responsibility.

LINDA: Yes, that is a biggie! Do you want to be upset?

GLORIA: No.

LINDA: Would you like to feel better about your boss?

GLORIA: Yes.

LINDA: Let's look at one of the instances in which you upset yourself when he does something incompetent. What are some of the things you say to yourself to keep you upset?

GLORIA: When I am listening to his speech, I say things like, "He is taking up all my time. If only he weren't such a wimp!"

LINDA: What are you feeling?

GLORIA: I'm mad at her for her misbehavior and at him for being incompetent.

LINDA: What are you doing?

GLORIA: I am sitting there in a very closed position with my arms folded across my chest, while he is walking back and forth and looking at me instead of at her.

LINDA: How is your body when he is giving this speech?

GLORIA: Uptight, and my stomach is slightly upset.

LINDA: What would you like to do to change the way you feel?

GLORIA: I'd prefer to handle the whole situation myself. I'd tell Bessy off.

LINDA: Do you want to take over everything he is incompetent in doing?

GLORIA: No. He is being paid a big salary. He should do it.

LINDA: What else could you do to get yourself less excited?

GLORIA: I could imagine myself in his shoes and not wanting people to be angry with me.

LINDA: So it would be helpful if you could think about how other people feel instead of yourself?

GLORIA: Yes.

LINDA: Anything else you could think of to make your stomach less tight?

GLORIA: I could expect him to be less competent. And when he does something good, I could compliment him.

LINDA: Would that make your relationship better?

GLORIA: Yes.

LINDA: Would you like to try some of those things this week and see if your stomach is less upset?

GLORIA: Sure.

Session Five (two weeks later)

Gloria had gone to her boss's house because she was contemplating buying it. Her mother had urged her to "make an investment." Although she decided against the purchase, the encounter went well.

She was planning on spending the weekend with her mother, claiming at first that she had nothing else to do. Then she admitted that Brian, a young lawyer in the office, had invited her to a party in his resort home. She was reluctant to accept the invitation. Her reasons were that others in the office might say that she was "fast" and that Brian was younger than she, so his friends would be younger, and she did not want to be considered "old." We talked about caring less about what other people thought.

GLORIA: I think to myself that I don't care what other people think. But I do care!

LINDA: Do you like that image?

GLORIA: No.

LINDA: What would you like to do?

GLORIA: I'd like to go up to see Brian.

LINDA: Sounds like you did a good job of talking yourself out of going, even before you went.

GLORIA: I sure did. [With disgust.]

LINDA: Would you like to change that?

GLORIA: Yes, I really would. I'd like to go up there and really enjoy myself. I'd like his friends to say to Brian that they really enjoyed meeting me and they would want to invite me to their parties. I'd like to be comfortable.

LINDA: What are the things that you need to do in order to have this happen?

GLORIA: Drugs. [Laughing.] Or anti-anxiety medication.

LINDA: I want you to picture walking in the door. What would you look like? What would you do? Run through the scene in your head, and tell me about it.

GLORIA: I'd have a suntan on my legs. I'd go in and speak to everybody as I went in the door. I'd go over to Brian and touch his hand. I always get confused at this point. I really admire people who connect with people and make a good impression. I feel like I'm really lacking in that skill, because I get so nervous and overwhelmed.

LINDA: What are some good lines that you can use to connect with people?

GLORIA: I don't know.

LINDA: Can I make a few suggestions?

GLORIA: Yes, please do.

LINDA: Whenever I have to do the cocktail-type party, I ask the people I do not know how they happen to know the host or hostess of the party. They usually say they live next door, or they went to the same school, or they work together. Then I say something like "Tell me more about how you really got to know him/her." Or I might say, "What have you been doing to keep yourself busy?" People love to talk about themselves, and you wouldn't believe how they go on and on.

GLORIA: Good suggestions.

Gloria usually remembered the first names of people she met, and when they did not remember her, she was embarrassed. We role played how this could be an asset. I wanted her to see remembering people's names as a strength, but as we role played, I realized how lacking she was in social skills.

We spent time looking at her repertoire of behaviors in approaching men. Gloria had one male friend with whom she would have liked to have gotten more involved, but she had never indicated her feelings to him because he was dating a girl who lived out of state. She did not want to interfere or look pushy. She asked me for ideas about how to approach the situation. I made some suggestions of what she might say.

LINDA: I would love to spend more time with you, but I don't want to take up time that you would prefer to be with Barb. I enjoy you as a friend, and if that is what you want from the relationship, then I'll learn to be happy with it. I don't want to lose you as a friend. You're special to me. If things don't work out between you and Barb, I just want to let you know that I'd be interested.

GLORIA: That's good. I thought about saying something like, "There is no sense looking around since Barb has dibs on the perfect man" to let him know that I thought of him in that manner.

LINDA: That's good. Do you think he will take it as a compliment?

GLORIA: Yes, now that we talked about it, I think he would be flattered by it. But before I thought that he would think I was "fast" and get scared and run off.

We spent time talking about how values have changed in the last twenty years and how relationships are more fifty-fifty. Women are more assertive in pursuing men.

LINDA: What would you like to do about it?

GLORIA: Joe works too much, and he appreciates the fact that I drag him out to have fun occasionally. I could call him and drag him out one day next week.

LINDA: Good idea.

Session Six (one week later)

GLORIA: I know what you are going to ask. And the answer is that I didn't do any of the things I was supposed to. I had to go out of town most of the week because of my work. Brian is going to have another party this weekend, but I had already planned to spend it with a married couple I haven't seen in a long time.

LINDA: I understand that you would like to visit with your friends since you haven't been with them recently, but I want you to begin thinking about how you are spending your time in relation to what you want. I always talk about the fact that we have three major resources: time, energy, and money. I want you to think about how you are spending your time and whether it gets you what you say you want to accomplish.

GLORIA: I know. I know. I was with a cousin last week. He picked up my bare left hand, and I said "No luck." And he said, "I don't think you are trying real hard." And I said, "You're right." I've got to get some exposure. Coming out of your house is trying. Being with people is trying. I'm not trying, and I have got to.

LINDA: You've got to or you want to?

GLORIA: If I'm going to get where I want to be, I've got to. I want to be part of a pair. I've got to expose myself to people.

LINDA: So is spending time with the married couple going to get you where you want to go?

GLORIA: No, but I haven't seen them in a year.

LINDA: I understand that you have a conflict between your wants. You say you want to see them, and you also say you want to get exposure to unmarried men. Is there a way you can get both of your pictures met?

GLORIA: I guess I should at least call Brian and see him for a couple of minutes.

LINDA: When will you call?

GLORIA: As soon as I get to my friends, or else I might forget.

LINDA: Good idea. If the opportunity lends itself that you can get away from your married friends, would you be willing to go over to Brian's?

GLORIA: I don't know. I'm really out of practice. I hate it. Going to my friends' is like going to a cocoon. They eat and vegetate all weekend. I went to a home interior party last week, and I thought going to that was a big deal. Boy, how I have deteriorated! It was a big deal: before it was easier to stay home than get in my car and go. I'd like to be more social. There are a lot of social opportunities in the next several weeks that I should take advantage of.

LINDA: Do you want to take advantage of them?

GLORIA: Yes.

LINDA: How can you make sure you get to them all?

GLORIA: I don't know.

LINDA: Do you have a pocket calendar?

GLORIA: Yes.

LINDA: Do you write down your social events in it?

GLORIA: No, not usually.

LINDA: I don't know about you, but I tend to forget things unless I mark them down. I'm more likely to do it if I mark it down. It is easy to sit and vegetate. But the more things I can schedule, the more things I am likely to do. I remember when I used to force myself to go out for an hour a day.

GLORIA: *You* were the antisocial type? (shocked)

LINDA: I wouldn't say I was totally antisocial, but I just wasn't the extrovert that I am today. I was never your cheerleading type in high school. It was in college that I decided that I wasn't going to meet "Mr. Right" in my room in the dorm. That's when I made up my mind to go out for at least an hour a day. It was a lot easier to stay in my room than go out. I found a schedule of social events and marked them down.

GLORIA: I was okay in college. I always had a lot of friends. Why is this hitting me after thirty? I guess I don't have the exposure to people that I used to.

LINDA: Exposure and proximity are important factors. But are we going to let them get in the way and be an excuse?

GLORIA: No. That is a good idea. I'll start to mark them down.

Gloria reported a couple of "stomach upsets" that week, the first on her way to a cousin's funeral. She took a "few swigs of Maalox" and kept going.

GLORIA: I didn't let it stop me. The other time was at work. It is really stressful to work out of town. The drive. The traffic. I do not like the other person there, and my work piles up here. But at least I knew I was doing it to myself. It was a lot less than before. That's progress.

LINDA: That is progress.

GLORIA: I need to tell my boss that I don't like going out of town.

LINDA: Can you do that?

GLORIA: I think the key to my problem is that I need to talk to him more. I'd like to develop enough rapport so that I could talk to him every day. I need to get the communication line open. Otherwise, it's like going to the principal's office, and I freeze up. The only reason now that I talk to him is when I have a problem. And it blows everything out of proportion. I need a more casual relationship with him. He will stop at my desk and ask me what happened at a meeting and who was there. I need to do the same.

LINDA: How could you make an effort to connect with him?

GLORIA: I should make a point to have a conversation with him every day.

LINDA: What could you talk about?

GLORIA: I could say something funny like, "I thought I'd come in here and hide for a minute."

LINDA: That's good. You're getting good at cute one-liners.

GLORIA: It really helps to think about them ahead of time.

LINDA: Let's summarize your plans.

GLORIA: I'm to write down my social plans, and I'm to call Brian and maybe go over if I can get away from my friends.

In this session, I kept confronting Gloria's "give-up" behaviors. I helped her to specify and prioritize more of her wants and to work through her wants by means of some specific plans.

Session Seven (two weeks later)

GLORIA: Don't be mad at me, but I didn't do some of my plans. But even though I didn't do everything I was supposed to, I feel my social interest coming back. I had invited a male friend over for dinner this week, and he couldn't come at the last minute. Because I didn't want to eat the casserole and watch this video I rented by myself, I asked myself, "Who else could I invite?" This was an accomplishment. Before, I would have just shut the door and pulled the blinds. That is good.

LINDA: That is good. Wasn't that your assignment from the session before? [I am implying that she succeeded after all.]

GLORIA: Right. I am just a couple of weeks behind. You would have been proud of me. I initiated the dinner with Joe. I called him up and said, "Let's have supper, because I miss your face." It was great, and it wasn't that tough. I felt bad because I didn't do all those things we were talking about, but I feel good about my social interest coming back. Amazing.

LINDA: Let's ask a question. Has the rest of the world changed?

GLORIA: No. I changed. You know, I resented the fact that I didn't have a whole list of people to invite over to eat the dinner that I cooked.

LINDA: Want to do something about that?

GLORIA: Yes. I think I can. I'm on the road to it.

We had an extensive discussion of several of the social opportunities I was familiar with, ranging from skiing to a singles social group. Gloria was going to find out if the Chamber of Commerce had a list of social organizations.

GLORIA: I didn't get over to his house, but I did call Brian. We are going to see each other in two weeks. We'll do something. I'm going to see Joe next week. I was thinking back about how much better I am now. When I was dieting, that was when my social life started going down the tube. Ev-

erything I did with people involved eating and drinking. I
couldn't be around people because it would tempt me too
much. I associated socializing with overeating. That may be
why I lost my social interest. But being home alone was
even worse. I couldn't wait to get home and get that pizza
box open. I came home and made love to a pizza instead
of someone else. Yuck! I am trying to eat better now. I have
a fear of food. I love it, but I fear it. It's an odd relationship.
I enjoy cooking and eating. One of the things I love to do
when I get nervous is bake a cake. It's bad. I like to do it.
LINDA: I think you have to have a healthy respect for everything.
I think food is a lot like water. Water is good for cleansing
our body and nourishing us, but it can also flood us out and
drown us. There are two sides to everything. I want food to
nourish you and not destroy you. I believe in moderation
and variety in all things. I am not worried when you sit
down and eat one waffle, or cookie, or whatever. I want you
to enjoy it. If you are eating multiples and in excess, and
you are not using food to nourish you but rather as a way
to escape the pain of life or to fulfill your needs, then I am
worried.

We spent time at this session talking about what she was
eating. Gloria wanted some suggestions on how to get more
nutrients and less sugar, salt, and fat. I felt comfortable doing
this because I am a registered dietitian, as well as a psychologist
and counselor. People often have incorrect information about
food, and I spend time correcting this faulty information.

LINDA: I'd like to go back and talk about your response to me
about not doing your assignment. The one where you said,
"Don't be mad at me."
GLORIA: At first I said it was awful and terrible that I didn't do
my plan and I'd be disappointing you. But then I thought,
"Linda doesn't care. It's my problem."
LINDA: That's right. It's your problem. I am not going to yell or
scream or punish you if you don't do your plans. I will
simply let you suffer the consequences. What would the

consequences be if you hadn't made contact with anyone during the last week?

GLORIA: I'd be lonely and on my way to being an old maid.

LINDA: Right. I think there is one person's picture album you need to be the most concerned about. Whose?

GLORIA: Mine.

LINDA: Right. You still need to be considerate of other people and not interfere with their needs, but you need to focus on pleasing yourself.

GLORIA: You're right.

We talked again about needs, wants, and picture albums. Gloria was beginning to see how much she had changed. She even said, "I've changed so much." She left planning to become involved in a festival coming up.

Session Eight (one week later)

GLORIA: There's no directory of social organizations. I did call Joe. We went to the festival together, and I had a good time. My stomach acted up once this week. We had a big blow-up at work, and I want to talk about it.

A private office had become available, and everyone wanted it. Gloria did not expect it, but her friend, Liz, had become very upset when it was given to someone else. Liz "took it out on me." Even though Gloria did not think her boss had handled the incident well, she was mostly upset that Liz, in her anger, had cooled off in her friendship with Gloria.

GLORIA: You know I've really gotten to feel good about myself. I've been just full of myself lately, and she makes cutting remarks to me, just to take the wind out of my sails. I say things to myself like, Gloria, you have the prettiest eyes, and your hair looks so nice today. And people just can't handle it. It's nice to feel good about myself.

LINDA: I'm glad you feel good about yourself.

GLORIA: But people can't handle it.

LINDA: I know. They are jealous.

GLORIA: Yes.

LINDA: Do you always say these good things to yourself?

GLORIA: No, only occasionally.

LINDA: Would you like to feel that good all the time?

GLORIA: Sure.

LINDA: Who would you say is the most encouraging person you know?

GLORIA: My cousin.

LINDA: What would she say to you?

GLORIA: She would say how nice I looked and dressed. And how nice I was to be around.

LINDA: Would you like to be your own best friend?

GLORIA: Yes.

LINDA: Would you be willing to tell yourself the same encouraging things?

GLORIA: Yes.

LINDA: Especially when Liz attacks you.

GLORIA: Liz is so negative. She thinks everyone is out to get her. Ever since her last husband . . .

LINDA: I'd prefer not to get into that, if you don't mind. [Once I feel the rapport has been established, I'll try to cut off conversations about situations that are out of the client's control.] Are you going to have to deal with people like her the rest of your life, no matter where you work?

GLORIA: Yes, but especially her. Our desks are face-to-face. She says she is my friend, but sometimes people who are in a poor frame of mind put other people down to make themselves feel better. I don't deserve to be talked to the way she talks to me. She gets on the phone, and she is Miss Sunshine and all friendly and bubbly. She hangs up the phone, and she is Miss Bitch City. I want to say, "Listen, I don't want you taking your problems out on me." But do I have this right?

LINDA: I think you do. I think everyone should be courteous to everyone and respect them. How do you feel when people take their problems out on you?

GLORIA: I don't appreciate it. I avoid confrontation with her, because I think that all this poor lady has is work and I feel sorry for her. That's why I take what I do. But that's not my fault. It's her fault.

LINDA: You let it happen. Do you want to continue avoiding people like her, or do you want to learn how to deal with them?

GLORIA: Yes. But what do I do?

LINDA: Whenever she is in the heat of the passion and her physiology wheel is spinning, avoid her. But when she finally gets rational, then voice your opinion, but know that you may never change her attitude. Don't spin your tires and waste energy. I want you to decide how much time and energy you want to put into Liz. Is she someone you want for a friend?

GLORIA: I don't know about being friends. But this is someone I would like to assert myself with for my own peace of mind. I know I am afraid of her to a point. She can be cruel and inhumane. I do need to deal with it.

LINDA: Let's talk about assertive behavior.

Gloria had evaluated her behavior as not working but still needed to learn new assertive behaviors. We spent the rest of the session talking about assertive behavior. We broke it down into the four wheels and how those were communicated to people. I also encouraged her to read a book on assertiveness.

GLORIA: I forgot to tell you. I'm going to Myrtle Beach for a week.

LINDA: That's good planning. Have fun.

GLORIA: Let's see. I'm to read the book and have a good time on vacation. And be my own best friend.

Gloria wrote a letter about this session:

Liz was really a problem for me. My history of dealing with moody people like Liz was not a good one. Up until this session, I never considered *not* having a relationship with her. When Linda brought it up, it made me pause. If you are going to be your own best friend, the negative baggage has to go, and sometimes people are included in that baggage.

Session Nine (two weeks later)

Gloria had been on vacation, and two things had helped her to feel good about herself—reading a book on assertiveness and meeting a man she expected to phone her. But she had decided that if he did not call, she would not call him. There were still problems at work.

GLORIA: I have been liking myself and being my own best friend, until I had my anxiety attack.

LINDA: Tell me how you liked yourself. What have you been doing and thinking? Be specific.

GLORIA: If someone came into a room, I would smile at them and talk to them.

LINDA: Good.

GLORIA: It went well until I thought I was going to throw up at lunch. I should never have gone out to eat with the senator.

LINDA: Isn't this the one you like?

GLORIA: Yes, but he is so powerful. He scares me.

LINDA: Did you know that you make him "powerful" through your thinking?

GLORIA: He is powerful.

LINDA: Would you like to enjoy him and relax with him?

GLORIA: I'd like not to repeat what I did the other day.

LINDA: Tell me what happened.

GLORIA: All three of us got our food and sat down. I took one bite of my hot dog and a drink of my soda, and I immediately felt as if I was going to pass out.

LINDA: What were you thinking about?

GLORIA: I felt like everyone in the place was looking at the three of us. Everyone wanted the senator's attention. I'll never go to lunch with them again. I excused myself. Once I got downstairs by myself, I was fine. I feel handicapped.

LINDA: Is this something you want? Do you want to go to lunch with the senator and be relaxed?

GLORIA: Yes, I never want to experience that again. I don't want to limit my life because of these attacks. How embarrassing! Here's what I thought about. If some guy calls me up and asks me out, am I going to do this on a date with him? What a great first impression! I'd either throw up on the table or get diarrhea. I don't want to do that. This could be the man of my dreams. [Laughing.]

LINDA: If you really want to work on this, you have to tell me step-by-step the things that you said to yourself and did. What did you say to yourself to cause your heart to race?

GLORIA: I'll probably drop my hot dog. I'll get something stuck between my teeth and not get it out. I should have packed my lunch.

LINDA: Even before anything happened, you were predicting the worst disaster—doom and gloom. When you think about chaos, how do you feel?

GLORIA: My heart was pounding, my intestinal system stopped, and I went flush. I threw my system into turmoil by thinking that way.

LINDA: Does thinking that way help you?

GLORIA: No.

LINDA: Would you like to give it up?

GLORIA: Yes.

LINDA: What could you think about instead?

GLORIA: Thoughts in the opposite direction.

LINDA: Like?

GLORIA: Imagining myself taking tiny bites of a gourmet hot dog and daintily wiping my lips with a napkin and being a delightful luncheon companion. I would be so delightful that everyone in the place would want my phone number so that they could invite me out to eat. [Laughing.]

LINDA: Fabulous. Could you practice that a lot?

GLORIA: Sure. Part of the problem is that I don't eat out very much. Most of us brown bag our lunch. I probably should eat out at least once a week to overcome it.

LINDA: Sounds good to me. You are going to practice eating out. You can also visualize it when you don't go out.

GLORIA: I like it. I'll do it.

LINDA: Who can you go out to lunch with this week?
GLORIA: Janet.
LINDA: Good.

Session Ten (one week later)

Gloria was trying to eat out. Despite an unpleasant experience meeting a former boyfriend in a restaurant and finding she could not eat what she ordered, she was continuing to go out to eat. Out with Janet, she tried charming the waiter and felt good about it. I suggested that next time, instead of Janet, she invite someone with whom she was less acquainted. Gradually she would work her way up to eating out with the senator.

Problems getting along with Liz continued. We discussed how Gloria might approach Liz to try to be more comfortable with her. Then we talked about why people make cutting remarks—to help themselves feel superior or powerful. I told her I felt sorry for people who need to do this. She was going to try to remember that when it happened—that it was the other person's problem, not hers.

LINDA: How could you control the conversation so that Liz takes it the right way and doesn't get madder?
GLORIA: I could say, "You seem rather unhappy this week." I don't know what else to say. Any suggestions?
LINDA: I really appreciate our friendship, and I'd like to keep it that way, but I feel bad when people bark at me, especially when I had nothing to do with it. I realize that I am responsible for my own happiness. I am learning how to handle my reactions. If you are in a bad mood and just going to be negative, I'd prefer that you didn't talk to me. I'll be glad to talk whenever you can be positive and encouraging.
GLORIA: I'll do it tomorrow. She can be a dear person or a witch.
LINDA: We've had ten sessions so far, and I'm going to ask you to do an assignment for me. I'd like you to write a few sentences about how you have changed.

This is what Gloria wrote and mailed to me:

I'm trying to use humor to let things go. I tend to dwell on things people say to me (hurtful things) because I have lots of time to think. If I can make a joke that is funny to me concerning the remark, then I can have myself a good laugh and let it go.

I feel like I am starting to become my own best friend. I use remarks to myself (and aloud) that I have pretty eyes or nice teeth, and it is my way of convincing myself that I am okay. They are useful in helping to convince the real me, the me who lies beneath the superficial, that inner person, the true person, that it is okay, too.

Session Eleven (one month later)

We had agreed to meet again in two weeks, but as it turned out we were unable to get together for an entire month. Unfortunately, things did not go well for Gloria, nor did she handle them well. A number of obstacles impeded the completion of her plans. She had a stomach attack that kept her home from work. After listening to several instances, I asked her to make a value judgment about what she had learned.

GLORIA: In one way, I've come a long way. In another way, I feel like I have just opened up all these issues that I now have to deal with. I have gone through stages of depression in learning to deal with things, but then I have so many good days in which I feel so much better that it all balances out. It is tough taking responsibility.

Gloria decided that she needed to become more assertive and focus on her needs instead of listening to others. I agreed that she needed to expand her repertoire of behaviors. We agreed that it might be helpful to sign up for an assertiveness class. Also, she agreed to get a book on social behavior and to continue her luncheon engagements.

Session Twelve (ten days later)

I wanted to start this session on a more positive note, so I brought in a cartoon. I love to use cartoons to make points—they are truly worth a thousand words. Although I brought the cartoon in with one purpose in mind, I was able to use it to confront Gloria with her irresponsible behavior.

LINDA: I brought this cartoon for you.

GLORIA: I like that. . . . I really like that.

LINDA: What do you get from the cartoon?

GLORIA: Instead of running around and banging your head against the wall, just use your ingenuity and pull out the chain saw and buzz your way through. I like that.

LINDA: There are a number of different ways to get what you want, and a number of ways to get through the crap.

GLORIA: I didn't make it through the crap since our last session. I hardly did any of the things we talked about for plans. But I've been doing a lot of fantasizing. There is one radical attorney who represents most of the human rights cases. I'd like to get to know him and pick his mind and find out why

he turned out so nice compared to other attorneys. Then I say, "You can't do that." I would like to invite him for coffee. But I don't know if I can do it.

LINDA: I don't know if I can do it! I don't think it is a question of can, but rather if you choose to do it.

GLORIA: It is so against my normal behavior that I would really have to concentrate on doing it.

LINDA: Do you want to be like the typical rat or the rat in this cartoon?

GLORIA: I do. I do. I do. I'm tired of running in circles. Life is too short. And I can really convince myself when I am not near the situation where I am supposed to be doing it.

LINDA: Thinking it is one thing, but doing it is another.

GLORIA: Right. Thinking has it all rationalized out, and it makes perfect sense. I have a right to learn more about other people I think are interesting and to ask them to share their time with me. But the doing part makes me drop my head and go the other direction.

LINDA: I think your problem is when you say, "I can't."

GLORIA: I have got to do a contract with myself and keep it.

LINDA: So when are you going to do it?

GLORIA: I don't know.

LINDA: It's your life.

GLORIA: I know.

LINDA: How did the rat get through?

GLORIA: This maze is my office and work. It gets in the way of my personal life. I don't have my personal life as my top priority. I let too many other things get in the way. I either have to change it or quit whining about it. One or the other. I will do better next time. I don't want to be some old spinster with her mother living with her. But it's the direction I'm headed in.

LINDA: Yes. So you have a picture of what you don't want. What do you want? Describe it.

GLORIA: I want to be a part of a two-party unit. A good solid male/female relationship. I want to be some man's best friend. There is something between me and getting that across to men. I want to get up and scream, "I'm damn fascinating!" How do you get from where I am to where I want to be?

LINDA: One step at a time. Do you want to take the steps?

GLORIA: I don't know.

LINDA: How many holes did the rat have to cut to get out?

GLORIA: Lots. There is pain in everything.

LINDA: There is a cost in everything. There are no free lunches. Is it worth it? What is worse, a little discomfort and work now or being a spinster?

GLORIA: There are a lot of ways I could distract myself or entertain myself, but I don't want to be by myself any more. I have to quit using excuses. I have to make myself known so they know how wonderful I am. Not convinced? [Laughing.]

LINDA: You or me? For several weeks you have been talking about it.

GLORIA: Good lip service.

LINDA: I don't know how much more miserable you are going to have to get before you get serious with this!

GLORIA: I have got to put my social life above all else.

LINDA: How are you going to do that?

GLORIA: I should do one social thing each day.

LINDA: Will you, or is this lip service again?

GLORIA: I have to make a plan.

LINDA: No. Do you want to?

GLORIA: I'm going to invite Joe over to eat.

LINDA: Good. What do you want to do for the rest of the week?

GLORIA: I don't know, but I'll promise you that I will do something every day.

LINDA: Good. I have faith that you can and will do it.

Gloria had these comments about Session Twelve:

I reacted to this session with anger and hurt. I went home and rummaged through the cabinets and refrigerator and then collapsed face down on the sofa. I knew I deserved to be confronted, but that didn't keep it from hurting. My reaction only lasted a short time and was replaced with a determination to change.

Session Thirteen (two weeks later)

I started by asking Gloria what she had been doing—I was tired of hearing about feelings, thinking, or physiology. She had started an assertiveness class and was busy socializing.

GLORIA: You confronted me last time, and I went home and ate. I upset myself because I wasn't doing the things I needed to do. I have been giving a lot of lip service. I really needed to think about if it was worth working for.

We talked about the two sides, the pleasure and the pain, of almost everything. I told Gloria that I did not see her as she saw herself. Coincidentally, we had been at a party together at which she had been socializing well. I encouraged her to try to relax and be herself and not to worry about critical people because she did not need them. She really was making excellent progress, I thought.

GLORIA: I had class on the weekend but I interacted at every break and meal break. Monday I went out to eat with Joe. Tuesday I went to Nautilus and talked to guys there. Wednesday I went out for drinks with two guys from work. I initiated it. Thursday I made two calls and went to exercise. Saturday I took a friend to celebrate her birthday. Sunday I went out to friends' to see their new baby.
LINDA: How did you feel about everything you did?
GLORIA: Good. Real good.
LINDA: I think you did a fabulous job.
GLORIA: I figured I should after the last session.
LINDA: Are you doing it for me or for you? If you are doing it for me, you missed the point.

I wanted Gloria to see her old self as passive and her current self as assertive. I wanted her to move forward. A holiday was coming, and she would be seeing her family, whom she perceived as very controlling. Her father used his symptoms to get away from family members who were very controlling.

Gloria left with a plan to continue making at least one social contact a day. More importantly, her new picture of herself was coming into focus.

Session Fourteen (two weeks later)

GLORIA: I've really enjoyed my assertiveness class. I have been using my new assertive body posture [sitting up very straight with head held high] and making lots of eye contact. I'm excited. There are eighteen women in the class, and I'd like to make friends with a couple of them. There is only one class left. I'm trying to think of ways to make social contact with them. There is one lady in particular who told me that she enjoyed my remarks in class.
LINDA: So what could you do about that?
GLORIA: I thought about inviting them out for coffee after the session.
LINDA: That's good. What happens if they don't have the time then?
GLORIA: I could ask them if they want to meet for lunch occasionally.
LINDA: That's good. Let's talk about what we just did.
GLORIA: I think I know. First we talked about what I want, and then I looked at what I am doing. Then I evaluated my behavior, and we made a plan.
LINDA: Right. We also made a backup plan. There are many ways to get what we want.
GLORIA: Right.

We spent some time talking about her assertiveness class. She had made a number of good observations and had been trying to practice the skills.

GLORIA: I have been trying to practice my assertive voice, and I discovered that I sound just like a female lawyer. Female lawyers are loud. My mother would always say to me,

"You're too loud" and now I have this whiny, thin voice. I have to work on it.

LINDA: Tell me more about how your picture of yourself has changed.

GLORIA: The assertive person acts confident and self-assured. Has good voice quality and good eye contact. People are responding better to me. Some people don't know how to handle it. I was even assertive with my boss about my appointment today. It worked out real well. I'm kicking butts and making waves. [Laughing.] It's great.

LINDA: Boy, how you have changed! [When it came to male/female relationships, however, she claimed to feel lost.]

LINDA: What do you think about the idea of taking everything you learned about assertiveness and using it? What can you say to yourself, for instance at a party when you would like to talk to a man?

GLORIA: I am as interesting as anyone in this room. He would be fascinated to have a conversation with me. [Laughing.] I really like it.

LINDA: Okay. That takes care of the thinking wheel, but how about the doing? How can you make sure you are in a room full of single males?

GLORIA: Nautilus, exercise club. With the holidays coming, there are lots of parties, and I'm going to seize every opportunity. [Faraway look on her face.]

LINDA: What are you thinking about?

GLORIA: I was thinking about what I should assign myself to do for the next week.

LINDA: That's good, what you just said.

GLORIA: I'll go to Nautilus twice and invite some friends for the weekend. I'm going to have a party so that I won't be lonely during the holidays.

We went into the specifics of planning a party.

LINDA: I think you have made such progress.

Session Fifteen (two weeks later)

We talked in great detail about the party Gloria was planning. We then discussed satisfying her needs at work, where she felt she was still putting too much energy into trying to please others. I brought in another cartoon to share. It showed Santa sitting on a couch facing a therapist who was saying, "Your only problem is that you are a people pleaser." Gloria agreed that this was her problem at work.

Gloria went on to tell me that she was becoming more assertive with her family, her mother especially. We were both pleased. I complimented her on her progress in working to develop a healthy relationship with her mother. She had asked her mother to stop putting her father down in Gloria's presence, and her mother was no longer doing it. She was also letting her mother know that she could not tell Gloria what to do and expect Gloria to do it.

Session Sixteen (two weeks later)

GLORIA: My party was great. I also had my discussion with Liz. I told her I'd be good to her as long as she was good to me, but I wouldn't talk to her when she put me down. For three days, I didn't talk to her. I was fine. Before, my throat and stomach would have been upset. I definitely got my point across that I don't want to be treated badly anymore. Like you said, "It's not good to let yourself be surrounded by people who beat you down." And that is what she was doing to me. [She went into great detail of how she handled it.] It felt so good. I've gotten rid of this garbage. I feel like I was constipated and now I've gone to the bathroom. I was a little nervous how she was going to act at my party, but she was okay.

LINDA: It's nice to see how well you are handling things and how vivacious you have become. Do you have a new picture of yourself?

GLORIA: A little bit. These were all people I knew and felt safe with. People said that it was good and that they want me to do it again. Jody asked me to help him with his party. I also got good feedback from people who were invited by my friends to come along. My picture is that I am a pretty good party thrower.

LINDA: Gloria the party thrower. How does that feel?

GLORIA: Good. Real good.

LINDA: How about your picture of you at work?

GLORIA: I picture myself "stepping forth and being more direct" instead of feeling everyone out. I feel like I'm the rat with the chain saw and I've buzzed my way through two walls, which are my boss and Liz. I'm so very, very aware that I am where I am because of lack of action. It aggravates me that I acted like such a victim. I'm sick of it.

We went into a conversation about the self-concept. This time we talked about the past picture, the present picture, and the future picture of what she wanted to become. We talked about how her image had changed. I asked her to get a picture of what she wanted for the future and how she planned to get it.

LINDA: How about the book you read on social behavior?

GLORIA: It was really helpful. I was aware of what everyone was saying to get conversations started. One of the lines I heard several times at the party was, "How do you know Gloria?" It was like an echo. Every time I heard that I thought, "Have they been seeing Linda, too?" [Laughing.]

LINDA: I'd like to know where you want to go with counseling?

GLORIA: I'm still high from the party and feeling good about the other things at work. I have myself so booked for the next few weeks that I don't have time to see you.

LINDA: Hooray! You are doing it. You are following through.

GLORIA: But it is all with safe people. I do wish you would keep kicking my butt and making me go forward. I would never have had this party if it weren't for you. No way. I don't know exactly what I want from you.

LINDA: Would you think about that for next time?

GLORIA: Yes. It was really hard for me to visualize the stuff in the beginning—the picture book, wants, needs, and so on. My mind is now engaged to think that way. I think I can be more specific now. I'll work on it.

I felt that Gloria was finally self-motivated and that I did not have to get specific when she said, "I'll work on it." I knew that she would.

Session Seventeen (three weeks later)

LINDA: [After some discussion.] All kinds of exciting things have happened.
GLORIA: I went to help at a church party for some disadvantaged children, and it wasn't even my church. My friend asked me to help, and then she backed out at the last minute. I did go, and it went great. It was a good experience because it was with people I didn't know. A year ago I wouldn't have gone. My self-esteem and self-concept have changed. But, still no man. [Said disappointedly.] A reporter asked me out the other day. He seems like a nice guy, but I'm not overly attracted to him. I'd like him as a friend. What happens if he puts the move on me, and I don't want him to?
LINDA: Want to spend time talking about that?
GLORIA: Yes. [Said desperately.] I'm afraid I won't be able to assert myself gracefully in a situation like that.

This was the last of the "big" issues we discussed. Because Gloria still did not know effective intimate behaviors, she avoided intimate contact. Teaching clients to expand their behaviors is extremely important. We discussed eye contact, social distance, and verbal and physical cues that lead people on to intimacy. We also talked about how dating norms have changed and about what to do when a man made a pass and she wanted to decline. I described a number of situations, and we talked about what she could do in each. She said it was very helpful to talk about it and that she was going to have to practice. We laughed most of the way through this discussion. Even though we were talking about such an intimate subject, it flowed so much easier than in the beginning.

LINDA: Let's talk about how you are doing since you started therapy.

GLORIA: Really well. I'm acting better, thinking better, feeling good, and my physiology isn't messed up. Occasionally I might feel like I'm getting sick, and I just say to myself, "You can't do this. You have to go to work." I just drink Maalox and keep going. Before I would have been paralyzed for a couple of days. I just don't let it get me down.

LINDA: Let's look at the chart that we looked at before.

GLORIA: Boy, I was a mess. I was addicted to food and a lot of symptom behaviors. But I still need to work on fulfilling and positive addictive behaviors.

LINDA: Can I tell you how I see you?

GLORIA: Please.

LINDA: You are doing a good job of identifying your needs. You looked at your behavior, evaluated it, and then decided upon a plan to change. Sometimes we get better, but we don't realize we are better. Remember the three images of our self-concept: past, present, and future. Just think about where you were and where you are now. Remember that we will always have future pictures or more wants because we are constantly in a state of change.

GLORIA: I see what you mean. So I shouldn't expect to stay in therapy until I get married.

LINDA: I think you are understanding the process of change. I hardly say anything in a session. You are doing it yourself. I don't think you really need my help.

GLORIA: I have come a long way. Can you wean me?

LINDA: Sure. When do you want to come again?

GLORIA: Three weeks.

Later that week, Gloria sent me a cartoon in the mail with a note that said, "When I saw this cartoon, I went crazy. I think it was the expression on the face of the girl anteater. It reminded

me of what we were talking about this week."

I thought it was great that Gloria was able to see the humor in something she was trying to deal with.

Session Eighteen (three weeks later)

Gloria brought me an owl mug was a present. (I collect owls.) I let her know how much I appreciated it.

LINDA: How have you been doing?
GLORIA: Great. I did write out what I told you. Can I read it to you?

WHAT DO I WANT?

I want to feel secure in myself. I want to be sure of who I am. I think I know. I think I know what I need.

I need to be needed. I need to be a part of a family unit. That may be a husband only, but I believe it means a husband and children. Looking at that from a distance, I think I could pull off being a wife and a mother and still be a person. I could be so and so's wife and so and so's mother, but not to the extent that I still wouldn't be Gloria.

I read a book—I think it may have been "Smart Women, Foolish Choices"[2]—and I stopped and thought about it a lot. I think I am attracted to men with whom I am not compatible. I tend to be drawn to the type with strong personalities—the powerful, verbally confident type. Unfortunately, I react to them in a way

[2]Connel Cowan, *Smart Women, Foolish Choices* (New York: Clarkson N. Potter, 1985).

that shows me as a shy, quiet, maybe even insecure person. I dated a man who was like that. I saw him from time to time, and he had that impression of me. One of the last times we went out, I showed my real self. I was confident—I had a devil-may-care attitude. He commented on how relaxed I seemed.

The point of all this is that I need to be looking for a man who is quiet, unassuming—someone who would not stifle my personality, perhaps. Does that make sense?

Because I have always been independent, I have thought it would be impossible for me *not* to work. I still have a problem with retiring to raise a family completely, because being in the workplace and moving and shaking is such a part of me. I like to organize people and set things up and see things through. I can't imagine getting that kind of fulfillment at home. Besides, I hate housework.

I even feel confident that I could leave familiar surroundings and my family and go somewhere and start a new life with or without a husband. I have always liked that about myself. Until I got stuck in my present job, I always loved the challenge of moving to a new place and meeting new people. I think I could do that again.

I feel good about me. I feel like I have something I can grasp now. I don't know how I got to the place I was when I was anorexic and bulimic. Somewhere I got the idea that thin was the answer to all my problems—it would fill my dance card and make me win friends and influence people. Funny thing was, my social life came to a halt when I started doing the dieting thing. I couldn't believe it. I plan on staying out.

I am trying to think about what it was I was feeling when I started in therapy. I was in serious pain—old pain and ongoing pain. That seems so far away. I look at my boss now and think, "How could I have let him affect me so?" I feel so "above" all that right now. I feel like if I got fired tomorrow it would just give me an excuse to do something else with my life that I have wanted to do. Is that wild?!!

I know now that I have a technique to accomplish what I want to do with my life. If I don't do it, it will be my own fault. I never wanted to take responsibility for my own happiness before, but now I feel better that I am responsible for it. It is too important to leave in the hands of others.

Gloria

LINDA: Wow! That is great.

GLORIA: I am going to see a guy in Washington in two weeks. I have had several dates in the last couple of weeks. I'm doing something every day. I'm no longer a couch potato who is starved for affection. Thanks for your help.

DR. GLASSER'S COMMENTS ON "STARVED FOR AFFECTION"

What Gloria had been choosing to do is called an "eating disorder." By the time she came for counseling, she had made the decision to stop both the binging and purging parts of this behavior because she was afraid that she would risk her life if she continued. But when she tried to eat normally, she was stomachaching so severely that she could hardly eat. Because of the pain and cramping, she suspected that she had an ulcer. At the time she came for help, she was waiting for the results of some medical tests to see if this was true.

"I was really into food. I was obsessed with eating. Food was my solace. If I did not have a date, then I would console myself with something good. I replaced many of the relationships with food. I lost a lot of relationships with my dieting because I could not go anywhere there was food or drink. Instead, I would go into my apartment and do flower arranging so that I did not have to be around food or people. I severed so many relationships. I finally realized that at the age of twenty-eight, I had an eating disorder. I'm thirty-two, and I still feel like I have an eating disorder and an addictive personality."

The common addictive behaviors that people like Gloria (with addictive personalities) choose are the addictive use of drugs (especially alcohol), pathological gambling, overexercising, and overeating. As it often does, overeating in Gloria's case included starving and purging. Through counseling, Gloria was able to learn to satisfy her needs, especially her needs for power and love, by interacting with people much more effectively than before. She was then able to give up the addictive behavior related to eating that had been a part of her life for so long.

What I believe defines people with an addictive personality is that, for reasons not yet known, they settle for what they have learned is a sure and easy way to get some pleasure. They repeat this behavior over and over, even when it becomes obvious to others, and sometimes even to themselves, that what they are choosing may cost them their lives. Gloria was able to stop the purging after her friend Nancy died, but she was not able to stop other aspects of the same basic disorder until she was involved in counseling.

Throughout this book, I have stressed the control theory axiom that we can control only our own lives. Many of the cases have pointed out how hard it is for people to learn this. It is, however, a lesson that addicts seem to learn too well. Gloria certainly wanted friends but because of her addiction she did not actively seek them until she entered counseling and found it was possible to make them. Many addicts, especially drug addicts and alcoholics, are much further into their addiction than Gloria; they do not even try to control others by being friendly and pleasing; they do not care very much whether others like them or not. They accept what most of us reject; the only effort worth making is to control themselves, which to them means to engage compulsively in their addictive behavior.

This does not mean that addicts like alcoholics are not violent when others cross them, especially when others tell them to stop drinking, but what they are asking of the others is to be left alone to pursue their addiction. As they do, they separate themselves more and more from those they need and settle for what they know will give them pleasure—their addiction. That their behavior affects others who love them or need them is rarely their concern.

Food addicts are different from all other addicts in that, unlike drug addicts or gamblers, they cannot give up their addiction completely: they must continue to eat. The best they can do, and many like Gloria try, is to restrict their eating. As they literally starve themselves, many of them discover that there is also great pleasure in starvation or purging. Suddenly and unexpectedly, they are so much in control of their own lives that they can successfully defy those who love them, whom they also see as trying to control them. They do this by saying, directly or indirectly, "Very thin is right" and "All you who want me to eat and be fat are wrong." For many of these eating-disordered people, who have never had any sense of importance, this heady power trip will cost them their lives. Fortunately, Gloria saw that danger and did not go that far, but she still needed counseling or she would have been stuck where she was with her choice to stomachache or withdraw.

To summarize, an addiction is a behavior we choose that we can do easily, that does not depend on others, and that consistently gives us immediate pleasure or, we believe, will soon give us pleasure. Driven by the belief that ecstasy is just around the corner, many drug addicts and alcoholics drink or use drugs long past the time that their use gives any pleasure at all. They continue because they have not yet (and many never will) given up the hope that they will feel as good again as they did in the past.

This whole book clearly shows that where others are concerned, there is a balance in life that many people fail to find. On the one hand, all of us need to accept that we are dependent on others if we wish to satisfy our needs, but if the others choose not to do as we want them to, we should not ruin our lives trying in vain to get them to do what they will not do. Phil, in Chapter 10, comes to mind as someone who needed help to see this.

On the other hand, we should not be so dependent upon ourselves and rejecting of others that we settle for an addictive behavior that feels good but precludes any chance to satisfy our needs through responsible relationships. Gloria is the only example in this book of someone doing this, but addiction, especially alcoholism, is among the most common of all personal problems.

The bulk of the counseling described in detail in this case study shows how Linda Geronilla helped Gloria to give up on keeping total control of her life and to move out from the "safe" world of addiction into the "chancy" world of social relations. Just as most recovering alcoholics need the safe haven of Alcoholics Anonymous, Gloria needed the support and guidance of an accepting counselor. One of the hallmarks of addiction is that most addicts need the help of a group, for example, Alcoholics Anonymous or Overeaters Anonymous or any other 12 step organization that deals with addictions, to give up the total control of their lives that is so self-destructive. Addicts can almost never do this by themselves, and it makes sense that they can't because it was "doing it by themselves" that got them into the trouble in the first place.

As I mentioned when I discussed the case of Everett in Chapter 4, one of the mistakes made by inexperienced counselors, more in the treatment of addicts than in the treatment of other problems, is to talk to the addict about stopping what he or she is doing. Dr. Geronilla did not make that mistake because she knew that we cannot stop any behavior that we believe is highly need-satisfying, as addicts believe their addictive behavior is, unless we can replace it with another that is reasonably need-satisfying. She talked to Gloria about what she could do, such as socializing and getting more power at work, that was much better than sitting home and arranging flowers while her stomach hurt.

Even without help, Gloria was able to give up some of her eating-disordered behaviors. She could not give them all up, however, until she had learned more satisfying behaviors. Fortunately, she had many work skills and she also was attractive, which gave Dr. Geronilla a lot to work with, but even after she gave up almost all of her "eating" behaviors, her stomachaching remained.

Stomachaching, like any other painful or miserable symptomatic behavior, accomplishes three things for the frustrated people who choose it. First, it restrains the anger, as I explained when I discussed Everett's depressing in Chapter 4. Gloria had a lot of anger, but she knew that letting it out at work or in her social life would have made things worse. To keep it in, she had to replace it with something else, and paining, in her case stomachaching, is a very common choice. Second, this behavior is a way to ask for help that is acceptable to all. No one rejects a person with a stomach ache. It becomes a way to ask for help that never implies that the person asking is incompetent. This is why painful or miserable symptoms are so popular: when we choose one or more of these, we do not lose power. To be seen by others as begging is unacceptably powerless to almost all of us. Finally, when we ache or choose any other symptom, we are able to get out of situations we fear. When Gloria was starting to move out into the social world that she feared she could not handle, she started to stomachache again. Because of her need for power, she could not say, "I'm afraid to do all this new socializing." But she could and did stomachache, and no one expects a person whose stomach is upset to do much of anything. As soon as she got more confidence, she was able to stop this, but as explained earlier in the case of Susan in Chapter 9, Gloria knows how to stomachache, and she should be alerted to get help if she starts to do it again.

Finally, we should all keep in mind one technique that Dr. Geronilla used. Many of those who seek counseling (in fact, many people everywhere) have trouble dealing with bosses. Gloria was advised to take the time to talk to her boss about her work on a regular basis. This helped them to develop a much more comfortable relationship, which meant there was much less tension when there was a problem. In any relationship, it is never good if the parties talk seriously only when there is a problem, yet this is too often the case. What Gloria did helped to prevent problems from occurring.

At this point as I review this case and the others in my mind, I feel it necessary to caution any readers trying to improve their counseling skills. As useful as it should be to read these cases, no one can teach another person exactly how to counsel. This is not a cookbook profession. However, we can learn much from each other if we share what we do, and it is my hope that this book will be shared and discussed. If any of you who counsel have questions as you try to use what you have learned here, feel free to write to the Institute for Reality Therapy (see address on page 308). We will be happy to answer your letter.

Contributors

All the authors listed below have been certified in reality therapy by the Institute for Reality Therapy. They have successfully completed a course of training over at least one and a half years, which consists of three weeks of intensive training and field work between those weeks. This is work supervised by practicum supervisors who have had special training with the Institute for Reality Therapy. Most of the authors have this status with the Institute. Some of the authors are also faculty instructors, which means that they are accredited by the Institute for Reality Therapy to teach two of the three intensive training weeks. Four authors are senior faculty, accredited to teach all three weeks.

Shelley Anne Brierley
Master in Counseling Psychology
Senior Faculty, Institute for Reality Therapy
President, Oasis Consulting, Ltd. (Consulting and Seminars)
Private Practice
White Rock, British Columbia, Canada

Mary A. Corry
Master in Education
Practicum Supervisor, Institute for Reality Therapy

Resource Teacher/Counselor, High School
Private Practice
Portsmouth, Rhode Island

Megan G. Fates
Master in Arts
Practicum Supervisor, Institute for Reality Therapy
School Psychologist
Private Practice
East Orleans, Massachusetts

Dr. Linda Shimko Geronilla
Master in Nutrition
Ph.D. in Counseling Psychology
Associates in Counseling and Training, Inc.
1215 Quarrier Street East
Charleston, West Virginia 25301

Suzy Hallock
Master in Education
Senior Faculty, Institute for Reality Therapy
School Counselor
Private Practice
Institute for Reality Therapy Liaison and Advisor to Institute
   for Reality Therapy, Ireland

Barbara Hammel
Master in Counseling
Faculty, Institute for Reality Therapy
School Social Worker, Long Branch, New Jersey
Adjunct Professor, East Stroudsburg University
Field Associate, Educator Training Center
Institute for Reality Therapy Faculty Representative to
   Iceland
Highlands, New Jersey

Georgellen Hofhine
Master in Counseling

Faculty, Institute for Reality Therapy
Life Redirection and Consulting-Management (Private
    Practice)
Thousand Oaks, California

Terri Leonard
Master in Education Psychology and Counseling
Reality Therapy Certified
School Counselor
St. John's, Newfoundland, Canada

Thomas J. Smith
Master in Psychology, Counseling and Guidance
Faculty, Institute for Reality Therapy
Affiliated Psychological Services of Colorado (Private
    Practice)
Reality Therapy Associates of Colorado (Consulting and
    Seminars)
Monument, Colorado

Tom Ashley Strohl
Master in Education
Practicum Supervisor
Private Practice, Esteve, Schwendeman, Strohl and Young
Allentown, Pennsylvania

Dr. Janet A. Thatcher
Master in Personnel Counseling
Ph.D. in Counseling Psychology
Faculty, Institute for Reality Therapy
Private Practice, Consulting
Cincinnati, Ohio

Dr. Robert E. Wubbolding
Doctor in Education
Senior Faculty, Institute for Reality Therapy
Chairman, Professional Development Committee, Institute for
    Reality Therapy

Center for Reality Therapy (Seminars and Training)
Center for Counseling and Management (Private Practice and
   Consulting)
Professor, Counseling Department, Xavier University
Cincinnati, Ohio

Dr. Roger D. Zeeman
Master in Educational Psychology
Ph.D. in School Psychology
Senior Faculty, Institute for Reality Therapy
Director of Pupil Services, Montgomery, New Jersey,
   Township Schools
Private Practice
Bridgewater, New Jersey

William Glasser, M.D.
President and Founder, Institute for Reality Therapy

For additional information, contact any of the above or:

Institute for Reality Therapy
7301 Medical Center Drive
Canoga Park, California 91307

Selected Reading List

Other books on reality therapy by contributors to *Control Theory in the Practice of Reality Therapy*:

Glasser, Naomi, *What Are You Doing?* 1980
Glasser, William, *Control Theory*, 1984
———, *Control Theory in the Classroom*, 1987
———, *The Identity Society*, 1972
———, *Mental Health or Mental Illness?* 1961
———, *Positive Addiction*, 1972
———, *Reality Therapy*, 1965
———, *Schools Without Failure*, 1969
———, *Stations of the Mind*, 1980
Wubbolding, Robert E., Ed. D., *Using Reality Therapy*, 1988

(All books listed above were published by Harper & Row, Publishers.)

Index